# Leading
# High-Performance
# Projects

Ralph L. Kliem, PMP

Copyright ©2004 by J. Ross Publishing, Inc.

ISBN 1-932159-10-X

Printed and bound in the U.S.A. Printed on acid-free paper
10  9  8  7  6  5  4  3  2  1

**Library of Congress Cataloging-in-Publication Data**

Kliem, Ralph L.
    Leading high-performance projects / Ralph L. Kliem.
        p. cm.
Includes bibliographical references.
    ISBN 1-932159-10-X
1. Project management. 2. Leadership. I. Title.
    HD69.P75K579 2004
    658.4′04—dc22                                              2003023948

Phone: (561) 869-3900
Fax: (561) 892-0700
Web: www.jrosspub.com

# DEDICATION

To my daughter, Tonia,
the leader of the family pack.

# TABLE OF CONTENTS

# PREFACE

Project management keeps gaining in popularity and the interest in relevant seminars and literature abounds. Silver bullets, from software to methodologies, hit the market with promises of success. Still, projects seem to have just about the same results: missed dates, budgets exceeded, and poor quality. The key question, of course, is why.

Ironically, what is needed, I believe, is not more seminars or silver bullets. Although project performance has improved to some degree, the real secret is not a new tool, technique, technology, or methodology, but something less tangible but all to obvious when missing — leadership.

As a project manager, it has been my experience over the years that the real ingredient for successful projects is project leadership, not more project management. As an officer in the U.S. Army, under the now-famous General Norman Schwarzkopf, I learned some key principles of management that have helped me throughout the years to lead and manage projects. From that point onward, I experienced bruises and injuries in the corporate world which also provided me with the insights that have proven valuable in my career as a project management professional and, more importantly, as a project leader.

Fortunately, I have had many more successes than failures. Through serious reflection, I have realized that many of the successes came under arduous circumstances without the benefit of silver bullets, but they provided the necessary leadership.

I am not boasting to be the world's greatest project leader. However, I do have the benefit of experience and years of study and, like other project managers, have and will likely "step on it" from time to time. In addition to being a project manager, as an information technology auditor I have had the opportunity to evaluate projects of all sizes and types in a Fortune 100 firm. One observation as an auditor is that many projects have plenty of "blanks" for silver bullets, but very little project leadership.

In the following pages, I share my insights. Look at them as "lessons learned" from a seasoned professional in project management. Hopefully, while leading your projects, you can take one or two insights from this book and apply them. You may also be able to use these insights to "piggyback" a few of your own. In the end, my goal is to help you become more of a project leader because, quite frankly, industry does not need more project managers. There are plenty of them. What industry needs is more project leaders.

# ABOUT THE AUTHOR

**Ralph L. Kliem, M.A., PMP**, has in-depth, varied experience in project management. He has over twenty years of combined experience working with Fortune 500 and medium-size firms in manufacturing, financial, and information (IT) environments in managerial and technical positions such as corporate auditor, project manager, seminar leader, writer, and methods analyst. In addition to being President of Practical Creative Solutions, Inc., a firm that specializes in project management consulting and training, he is a senior program manager for a Fortune 500 company.

Mr. Kliem is a former adjunct faculty member with Seattle Pacific University, an instructor with Bellevue Community College, founding editor-in-chief of the *Northwest Artificial Intelligence Forum (NAIF) Journal,* and former editor for the newsletter for the Puget Sound Chapter of the Project Management Institute. He has been a presenter before the Washington Software Association, NAIF, and the Information Systems Audit and Control Association (ISACA) and has been interviewed by trade publications and national radio.

The author or co-author of over a dozen books that have been translated into several languages and over 200 articles in leading business and trade publications, Mr. Kliem is a member of the Project Management Institute and a former member of the Institute of Internal Auditors and ISACA. He has taught seminars and workshops on project management throughout the United States and Canada.

*Free value-added materials available from*
*the Download Resource Center at www.jrosspub.com*

At J. Ross Publishing we are committed to providing today's professional with practical, hands-on tools that enhance the learning experience and give readers an opportunity to apply what they have learned. That is why we offer free ancillary materials available for download on this book and all participating Web Added Value™ publications. These online resources may include interactive versions of material that appears in the book or supplemental templates, worksheets, models, plans, case studies, proposals, spreadsheets and assessment tools, among other things. Whenever you see the WAV™ symbol in any of our publications, it means bonus materials accompany the book and are available from the Web Added Value Download Resource Center at www.jrosspub.com.

Downloads available for *Leading High-Performance Projects* consist of organizational engineering slides and tips for effective project communications, teaming, motivation, and managing change.

# DIFFERENT PERSPECTIVES OF LEADERSHIP

The subject of leadership has been studied for eons. Yet few people, scholars and practitioners alike, have come to any universally accepted definition. Here are some samples:

- "While management works in the system, leadership works on the system."[1]
- "...the genius of leadership lies in the manner in which leaders see and act on their own and their followers' values and motivations."[2]
- "Leadership is an affair of the heart, not of the head."[3]
- "Leadership is the process of persuasion or example by which an individual (or leadership team) induces a group to pursue objectives held by the leadership or shared by the leader and his or her followers."[4]
- "Leadership is what gives an organization its vision and its ability to translate that vision into reality."[5]
- "Leadership is an art, something to be learned over time, not simply by reading books."[6]
- "Leadership is the process of influencing the activities of an individual or a group in efforts toward goal achievement in a given situation."[7]
- "Leadership is the privilege to have the responsibility to direct the actions of others..."[8]

As these definitions demonstrate, however, there appears to be an overall trend towards emphasizing people relations as having as much importance — perhaps more — as production. The following review on leadership thinking and studies provides a similar revelation.

## TRAIT THEORY OF LEADERSHIP

For many years, experts on leadership focused their attention on what has become known as the trait theory of leadership. It rests on the idea that leaders possess certain physical or psychological characteristics that enable them to "stand above the pack." For example, a person as a leader might be tall, intelligent, or achievement oriented.

This approach often concentrated on historical figures like Napoleon and Caesar. Experts concluded that leaders were born, not made. While a few experts give some credence to trait theory, no definitive list of essential characteristics exists, leading to a declining interest in the topic. The few lists that do exist are value laden.

Nevertheless, the work of Edwin Ghiselli and Ralph Stogdill has provided some useful insights. They look at two categories of traits: personality and motivational. Personality traits include intelligence, initiative, self-assurance, and others; motivational traits include needs for financial reward, self-actualization, and power. They attempt to associate these traits with characteristics like supervisory ability, achievement, intelligence, honesty, and self-confidence and determine that leadership ability is associated with judgment and verbal ability. They conclude, however, that a person could not be associated with a specific set of traits.[9]

Interestingly, if one trait seems to stand out under contemporary leadership studies, it is that a leader's effectiveness depends on whether he or she is people oriented. Some common characteristics of leaders include being expressive, honest, trustworthy, warm, and cooperative. Leadership effectiveness tends to decline, however, with characteristics like being aloof, impersonal, and cautious.[10]

## MANAGEMENT VERSUS LEADERSHIP

As the debate in trait theory faded, a growing interest arose that helped to shed more insight on leadership, specifically the differences between leadership and management. For some time, of course, experts made no distinction between the two. They combined both leadership and management under the rubric of "classical management."

Under classical management, the topic of leadership was skewed towards three areas: standardization, specialization, and functionalization. What is known today as the "people side" of management was emphasized very little. The very qualities of a manager were assumed to be the very same ones for a leader: analytical, logical, organized, methodical, consistent, orderly, and task oriented.

The lack of distinction is based on the theories of classical management thinkers like Frederick Taylor, Henri Fayol, Chester Barnard, and Lyndall Urwich. Such thinkers emphasized planning, organizing, controlling, and commanding with little consideration of the psychological and behavioral factors behind such activities. Most came from a scientific management and classical management perspective; eventually the trait and classical management perspectives showed their inadequacies by ignoring behavioral aspects.

Today, experts generally agree that a marked difference exists between leadership and management. The characteristics are quite clear. In *On Becoming a Leader,* Warren Bennis provides an excellent list of distinctions between the two. Some major distinctions include administering versus innovating; maintaining versus developing; controlling versus trusting; and, perhaps most importantly, doing things right versus doing the right things.[11] Other top leadership experts agree, including Max De Pree, Stephen Covey, and Barry Posner.

## SITUATIONAL LEADERSHIP

The situational perspective is another approach for looking at leadership. Experts define it generally as the relationship between a leader's style and his or her environment to influence the performance of subordinates. The overriding assumption is that a leader can adopt an "appropriate" style under certain circumstances. One of the most common situational theories is Fiedler's contingency theory.[12]

In a nutshell, contingency theory looks at the relationship between the leader's style and his or her environment. Three situational dimensions are considered: leader-member relations associated with the confidence in the leader; task-structure, the degree of routine in tasks; and position power, formal influence in a position. He also defines two different leadership styles: task oriented (production) and person oriented (relationship).

Fiedler uses a continuum or index known as the Least Preferred Coworker (LPC) scale to determine his findings. He concludes that the style of a leader and his or her situation will determine effectiveness. Three options are available for negative situations: change the leader's style, change the environment, or move the leader to an environment more suitable to his or her style. Under certain circumstances, a task-oriented style might be more appropriate, and for others, the person-oriented style is more appropriate. In general, a task-oriented style is best when all three dimensions are very favorable, and the person-oriented style is better in a mixture of all three dimensions.

The Vroom-Jago, or Yetton, Model determines the extent to which subordinates participate in decision making under different circumstances and time requirements. In other words, once again, the appropriate leadership style depends on the circumstances. The model identifies five leadership styles that are appropriate, depending on the answers to a set of questions that address the quality of a decision and subordinate acceptance. The leadership styles relate to the degrees of being autocratic, consultative, and group oriented when making decisions. The model accounts for situational variables, such as significance of decisions, commitment, and expertise.

The model reveals that a participative decision generally works best; however, the important point is to match the appropriate style to certain conditions, e.g., different combinations of answers to the set of questions.

The Vertical Dyad Linkage Model, also known as the Leader Member Exchange Theory, is based on the assumption that a leader does not treat subordinates equally. Rather, he or she often has an "In" and "Out" group, treating each one differently. For In-group members, a more positive relationship exists, typified through informal interactions and trust, accompanied by better performance, more commitment, and greater satisfaction. Leadership exhibited towards the Out-group members, however, is more "negative," e.g., more aloof and formal. The implication is that the results of the In group are more spectacular than for the Out group.

Another look at situational leadership is Robert House's Path-Goal Theory.[13] According to House, a leader can increase effectiveness through goal satisfaction using an appropriate leadership style. He or she matches a subordinate's perceptions and behavior with a desired outcome by matching the appropriate style to situational factors (e.g., type of task), which results in a more satisfied and productive subordinate. The Path-Goal Theory is related to the Exchange Theory of Motivation, whereby the behavior of the individual is influenced by the likelihood of achieving a desired goal and the resulting award that will follow.

According to House, the four leadership styles are: directive, where the leader is not seeking participation; supportive, displaying friendliness and interest; participative, seeking suggestions; and achievement oriented, setting challenging goals. Situational factors include a subordinate's personality, perceived ability, and environmental characteristics.

House concludes that, under certain situations, the leader's behavior can impact a follower to effectuate a specific outcome. For example, an ambiguous job situation may involve a directive style to provide a clear path to reach a goal. In this case, and others, leadership style influences the motivation, satisfaction, and performance of subordinates by clarifying their path to achieve goals under a given set of circumstances.

Robert Tannenbaum and Warren Schmidt provide a leadership continuum of seven different styles.[14] The choice of style depends on the relationship between the authority of the leader and the latitude given to subordinates. The extremes range from an autocratic, boss-centered style that is very task and control oriented to a democratic, subordinate-centered style that is very relationship and people oriented. Tannenbaum and Schmidt did not embrace a particular style. Rather, they determine that the most effective leaders adopt the most appropriate style suitable to circumstances.

Perhaps the most widespread situational model is the one developed by Paul Hersey and Kenneth Blanchard.[15] The model consists of two dimensions that reflect the connection between task and relationship behavior. The element that ties the two dimensions together is the ability and willingness of the subordinate to perform a task; in other words, the maturity of the subordinate.

The two dimensions create a matrix divided into four quadrants: delegating, participating, selling, and telling. Delegating reflects low task and low relationship, allowing the subordinate to make decisions. Participating is high relationship and low task, allowing the subordinate to participate in a decision. Selling reflects high task and high relationship, where the leader makes a decision and sells it. Telling is high task and low relationship, where the leader decides and proclaims the decision.

The overall conclusion by Hersey and Blanchard is that no "best" leadership style exists. Instead, a leader, particularly an effective one, must adjust his or her style accordingly depending on in which quadrant, or circumstance, he or she finds himself or herself in connection with task and people relationships. Once again the key is to match one's maturity level and situation in question. This requires leaders to constantly know their subordinates, as well as develop their own ability and willingness to change styles, such as participating and telling.[15]

## BEHAVIORAL LEADERSHIP

One of the most well-known behavioral theories is Douglas McGregor's Theory X and Y.[16] While not a leadership theory per se, it provides an insight into leadership styles. A subscriber to Theory X reflects a manager's negative view of subordinates, believing subordinates dislike work, avoid responsibility, and lack ambition. A subscriber to Theory Y believes that subordinates seek work that is physically and mentally rewarding and want to control their destinies.

Naturally, a manager who subscribes to Theory X will apply the "stick" to motivate subordinates, while one who subscribes to the latter will apply the "carrot."

Rensis Likert conducted research at the University of Michigan to determine the style that best results in high-producing groups. He looked at two styles: employee centered and job centered. An employee-centered style stresses the human side, a style that emphasizes communication, trust, and goal setting. A job-centered style is more task oriented, with emphasis on meeting production standards and supervising closely.[17]

Likert notes that the employee-centered style results in high-producing groups. These groups have less absenteeism and turnover in addition to high productivity. Overall, these groups involved general, not close, supervision.

Likert also provides a continuum that identifies four leadership styles: Systems 1, 2, 3, and 4. System 1 is very task oriented, when management has a negative orientation, such as the use of threats and punishment. System 2 exists when management exhibits very modest confidence in subordinates, but decision making still rests at the top. System 3 exists when management exhibits a considerable trust and confidence in subordinates and allows for some specific decision making at the lower levels. System 4 occurs when management has complete trust and confidence in subordinates, allowing group decision making and building supportive relationships. The implication of Likert's work is that System 4 is the best approach.

Another well-known behavioral theory is Robert Blake and Anne McCanse's Managerial Grid. The basic idea is that five managerial styles exist that are created by considering two major dimensions or concerns for production and people. The concern for production focuses on performance, results, and profits. The concern for people focuses on relationships and motivational factors. The grid formed by the two dimensions creates five management styles: Impoverished, Authority Compliance, Middle of the Road, Country Club, and Team. An Impoverished manager displays little concern for production and people; he or she avoids getting involved, and does the minimum. An Authority Compliance, or task, manager emphasizes efficiency over people issues. His or her concern is to achieve results through control, even domination. A Middle of the Road manager focuses on balancing both concerns. The words "adequacy" and "reasonableness" pertain to this managerial style. A manager exhibiting the Country Club style places people over production. He or she emphasizes satisfying relationships among people; the words "pleasing" and "approval" are often associated with this managerial style. With the Team management style, a manager builds commitment to production by coordinating and integrating work to achieve results. The words "interdependence" and "respect" are often associated with this style.

Unlike other managerial styles indicating that the preferred style depends on the situation, Blake and McCanse believe the best managerial style is team management. Here the focus is on achieving results without sacrificing people as is the case with the Authority Compliance style or catering to people attributed to the Country Club style.[18]

Ohio State University conducted studies of leadership. The Ohio State studies considered two dimensions of leadership: initiating structure and consideration. Initiating structure dealt with formality towards organization, communication, and procedures; consideration dealt with people issues like trust, respect, and feelings. Using a questionnaire, the study found that the two dimensions were distinct but not mutually exclusive, that is, a "high" in one meant a "low" in the other. The study resulted in a quadrant that reflected the different relationships between the dimensions: low structure and low consideration, high structure and low consideration, high consideration and low structure, and high structure and high consideration.

## LEADER'S ACTIONS

Increasingly, a marked change has occurred in the study of leadership. Rather than look at traits, situations, and behavior, the shift has been on actions or priorities and results. This does not imply, of course, that there is no attention to other areas but the focus is action that achieves desired results. What follows is an overview of insights by some of the leading thinkers.

In their best-selling book, *The Leadership Challenge,* James Kouzes and Barry Posner[19] identify five basic practices that leaders apply to achieve results.

- Challenge what they refer to as the process
- Inspire a shared vision
- Enable others to act by encouraging collaborative endeavors and development
- Model the way
- Encourage the heart

While Kouzes and Posner stress these five practices, they also emphasize the importance of credibility. They imply that if a leader sacrifices credibility, the leader will have difficulty executing the practices above. Credibility of action, according to the authors, significantly determines whether or not people will follow.[20]

In *Leaders,* Warren Bennis and Burt Nanus[21] basically distinguish the difference between managers and leaders by the phrase: Managers do things right while leaders do the right things.

To do the right things, Bennis and Nanus[22] identify four competency areas:

- Attention through vision
- Meaning through communication
- Trust through positioning
- Deployment of self through positive self-regard

In *Leadership,* James MacGregor Burns distinguishes between two categories of leadership: transactional and transformational. A transactional leader is "when a person takes the initiative in making contact with others for the purpose of an exchange of valued things."[23] This idea is similar to Bennis and Nanus's doing things right. Burns refers to this idea as "values of means."[24] It is essentially what a manager does daily to sustain operations.

Transformational leadership is "when one or more persons engage with others in such a way that leaders and followers raise one another to higher levels of motivation and morality."[25] This idea is similar to doing the right things, motivating people to go beyond day-to-day activities. Leaders focus on, to use another term of Burns, "end-values."[26] In a sense, transactional leadership is of the head; transformational leadership is of the heart.

In *Managing for Excellence,* David Bradford and Allen Cohen identified four misperceptions of what a good leader does: knowing what goes on at all times, possessing the most technical knowledge, solving any problem that arises, and having sole responsibility for performance. They refer to these perceptions as a hero worship style.[27] This perception results in two types of managers: manager-as-master technician and manager-as-conductor.

The manager-as-master technician portrays the image of the "know-it-all" of work who can address every situation and know every answer. The manager-as-conductor manages through people but does so in a very task-oriented, command and control manner.[28]

Both types have harmful effects. These managers spread themselves "too thin," fail to use the talents and skills of subordinates, and demotivate.[29] As an alternative style, Bradford and Cohen propose the need for a new type of leader: manager-as-developer.

The manager-as-developer avoids being "all things to all people." Instead, he or she seeks to share responsibility and control with subordinates to develop them, while simultaneously pursuing a common vision. According to Bradford and Cohen,[30] these leaders actually augment performance, their own power, and control.

In *Primal Leadership,* David Goleman, Richard Boyatsis, and Annie McKee take a different perspective on leadership. Using Goleman's work on emotional intelligence (EI), they focus on the role of emotion in leading groups, referring to it as primal leadership. This shift is important because the emotional side of leadership has been ignored for a long time, focusing more on rationality. They observe that organizations tend to view emotions as disruptive to their otherwise orderly, rational institutions, and this causes them to overlook the powerful impact of those leaders who generate emotional resonance and enable people to contribute and grow.[31]

In the context of leadership, they define EI as how people handle themselves and relationships in different situations.[32] The authors highlight the effect of negative emotions by some leaders, which they refer to as negative displays of dissonant leadership.[33]

The opposite of dissonant leadership, which is synchronous with positive emotions, is resonant leadership. It involves leaders who are attuned to the feelings of subordinates, leaving them feeling enthusiastic, upbeat, and inspired.[34]

The authors contrast this perspective with the current overemphasis on the rationality of leadership, noting that intellect is not enough to designate some-one as a leader. Leadership, they observe, involves motivating and inspiring, for example, to generate resonance.[35]

After careful analysis, they identify four leadership competencies that, in turn, lead to six leadership styles: self-awareness, self-management, social awareness, and relationship management. Self-awareness involves aspects like self-confidence, self-management like self-control, social awareness like empa-thy, and relationship management like conflict management.[36]

In both his books, *Leadership Jazz* and *Leadership Is an Art,* Max De Pree takes the view that leadership involves the heart more than the head and is less about domination of subordinates and more about serving them. De Pree says that leadership is an art that can only be learned over time through experience and building on relationships.[37]

De Pree insists on the view described above — that leaders should function more as stewards of relationships, ensuring that followers realize their full potential by achieving results. He lists four tasks that enable leaders to do just that: leave behind assets and a legacy; provide and maintain momentum; be responsible for effectiveness; and develop, express, and defend civility and values.[38]

De Pree basically sees leadership consisting of multiple relationships that influence growth, participation, understanding, and diversity. He describes lead-ership as having a covenantal relationship, whereby a leader shares commitment to goals and processes and provides meaning. He contrasts covenantal relation-ships with the typical contractual relationship, similar to the transactional lead-ership described by Burns. A covenantal relationship involves people working together without focusing on meaning and growth potential.[39] De Pree recog-nizes that a covenantal relationship does not just happen. Leaders must also have and exhibit certain traits, such as integrity, vulnerability, humor, breadth, discernment, and courage.[40]

Although Peter Block (in *Stewardship*) focuses more at a high level in an organizational context, his main points directly relate to the behavior of managers in general, but also when dealing with subordinates at all levels.

Block observes that traditional organizations are based on maintaining control, consistency, and predictability. This emphasis has resulted in organizations, at all levels, taking a patriarchal approach towards managing people. This emphasis is exhibited in a hierarchical organizational structure, for example, and imposition of constraints. Such an environment encourages indifference and passive-aggressive behavior, resulting in people who come to work not fully engaged.[41]

What is needed is stewardship, which he describes as being willing to be held accountable for achieving results, but in a manner of providing a service rather than exercising control or forcing compliance.[42]

The result of stewardship is a greater distribution of ownership, responsibility, and accountability of the work to do. People, too, become empowered, which means that people find their unique contributions based on making their own decisions about choices.[43]

Leaders who take the stewardship route will not find that path. It requires them to establish a social contract that relies on partnering and empowerment that, in turn, means not acquiescing to the desire for protection and control.[44]

In *On Leadership,* John W. Gardner, like Max De Pree, takes a "softer" view of leadership. He sees leadership as having a servant-leader who strives to bring out the best in subordinates and identifies nine tasks to leadership: envisioning goals, affirming values, motivating, managing, achieving workable unity, explaining, serving as a symbol, representing the group, and renewing.[45]

These tasks, of course, go beyond the typical responsibilities of managers. They enable and empower subordinates and other stakeholders. Gardner says that a leader recognizes the needs of followers, addresses them, and builds their confidence to achieve desired results. They must also remove constraints that inhibit the motivations of followers to do so.[46]

He avoids stating that no one single style is effective, however, observing that leaders have no single style and may, on occasion, act authoritatively if circumstances warrant it.[47]

He does, however, tackle the attributes of leaders. These attributes include not just being physical but also qualitative, such as the capacity to motivate, the need for achievement, the capacity to obtain and sustain trust, and the ability to be adaptable and flexible.[48]

Like Peter Block, Harold J. Leavitt, author of *Corporate Pathfinders,* addresses the concept of leadership obliquely. He observes that management in organizations has emphasized compartmentalization in style, giving preference to rationality and action.[49] He notes that very little emphasis has been placed on the visionary aspects of managing which deal more with the emotional side of leadership. This situation has not been without great cost because managers who deal with human emotions are perceived negatively, thereby relying on rational means. Yet, this reliance of rationality often creates problems.[50]

## PROJECT LEADERSHIP

Interestingly, the studies and research on project leadership come to many of the same findings and conclusions as the general studies of leadership. While the "hard" side of project management, e.g., developing work breakdown structures and scheduling, are important, they also do not appear decisive in project leadership.

## TRAITS OF PROJECT MANAGERS

Although no pattern on the physical aspects of project leaders appears to exist, there are some patterns of actions that relate to the "soft" side of project management.

Warren Opfer, Timothy Kloppenborg, and Arthur Shirberg, although not discarding the need for technical and administrative skills, note that project leadership requires strength in interpersonal skills, negotiation, and conflict management.[51]

Greg Skulmoski, Francis Hartman, and Roch DeMaere conducted a study on traits of project managers according to the different roles played. The authors note two types of competencies of project managers: threshold and superior competencies. Threshold competencies require completing tasks at a minimum and acceptable level. Superior competencies are those above others from a performance perspective.

The authors found that many soft skills populated both competencies. It was the threshold competencies, however, that were quite instructive including creativity, open communication, proactivity, decisiveness, trust, judgment, delegation, results oriented, and achievement drive.[52]

Their conclusions? They found that project managers needed competencies in areas like open communication and trust as well as in decisiveness and delegation.[53]

Dean Sitiriou and Dennis Wittmer conducted a study of project managers based on previous studies from 1974 onward. In their study, they noted that respondents rated negotiation, personality, and persuasive ability as very important, followed by competence for surmounting the authority gap that project managers often face.[54]

In an interview in *PM Network,* Daniel Goleman, co-author of *Primal Leadership,* stated that emotional intelligence determines a leader's success or failure because the soft skills, e.g., self-awareness and empathy, are the determining ingredient. He noted in the interview that his research of leaders in approximately 500 organizations found that EI had a 2 to 1 success ratio, but for project managers it was much higher.[55]

Horst Bergmann, Kathleen Hurson, and Darlene Russ-Eft conducted a study of about 1,800 "incidents" of leadership among nonsupervisory employees, not project managers per se. They note that "grass roots leaders" harness and control their emotions, such as self-management, self-reflection, and positivity.[56]

Keane, a major consulting company, developed what is known as the Project Manager Competency Model (PMCM), which identifies clusters of project management skills and behavior. These are:

- *Achievement cluster* — consisting of concern for achievement, results orientation, initiative, and business acumen
- *Influence cluster* — consisting of organizational and interpersonal astuteness, skillful use of influence strategies, team building, development of others, client/user orientation, and self-control
- *Managerial identity cluster* — consisting of project manager identity, self-confidence, and flexibility
- *Problem-solving cluster* — consisting of diagnostic thinking, systematic thinking, conceptual thinking, and monitoring information gathering

Although there does not appear to be one overriding cluster, the article that describes the PMCM observed that the two attributes that appeared to have importance were the ability to negotiate and manage conflict.[57]

Albert Einsiedel observed that project managers must have five qualities to lead effectively: credibility, creative problem solving, tolerance for ambiguity, flexible management style, and communication skills.[58]

Barry Posner observed that project managers had the following attributes, behaviors, and techniques in descending order: communication, planning, team building, leadership, coping, and technological skills.[59]

Interestingly, Posner took a somewhat narrow view of leadership, observing that it consists of characteristics like setting the example, being energetic, and positive. A strong case, however, can be made that some other skills, such as communication, team building, and coping, can be subsumed under leadership as it has for other studies. If that is the case, then the technological and administrative type skills are outnumbered by a greater factor.

## SITUATIONAL PROJECT MANAGEMENT

Oddly enough, not much has been done to address project leadership from a situational perspective. However, Dennis Slevin and Jeffrey Pinto have provided some useful insight. Using research based on responses to two questions, they describe the results in the context of a grid consisting of a Y-axis reflecting input to decision and an X-axis for decision authority. The two questions asked: When do you get information input (decision input)? and Where should you place the decision authority for this problem (decision authority)?

The authors identify four leadership skills: Autocrat, Consultative Autocrat, Consensus Manager, and Shareholder Manager. The Autocrat, of course, obtains little or no information from subordinates and makes decisions unilaterally. The Consultative Autocrat obtains input from subordinates, but makes most of the decisions him- or herself. The Consensus Manager receives group input and allows the group to make decisions. The Shareholder Manager does not encourage and does not take responsibility for obtaining input and allows the group to assume ultimate authority for decision making.

Slevin and Pinto appear to prefer styles leaning towards a people orientation. However, they explicitly subscribe to the situational or contingency approach to leadership, observing that no style fits all situations. They also add that the successful manager should be flexible by matching one's leadership style to the circumstances facing them.[60]

R. Max Wideman of AEW Services and Aaron J. Shenhar of the Stevens Institute have observed that a relationship exists between project management style and project type. Based on the work of Dr. Shenhar, they observe that style makes a difference as the technological complexity increases. Both authors identify a typology created by project management scope and technological uncertainty. They also identify four types of project leaders: Explorer, Coordinator, Driver, and Administrator.

The Explorer is the visionary who thinks strategically. The Coordinator is the facilitator who seeks compromise and encourages team participation. The Driver has a penchant towards actions and tends to be pragmatic and focused. The Administrator seeks stability and is very analytical.

Of course, Wideman and Shenhar do not appear to embrace a particular style. Again, flexibility in adapting styles to the situation is important. Both agree once again that no particular leadership style can accommodate all circumstances. Flexibility, therefore, becomes key to success. If project managers are inflexible, the affect on a team can be demoralizing. They also note that a high correlation exists between the type of leader and product, as well as the phase of a project.[61] A mismatch among all three can have negative results.[62]

Ralph Kliem and Harris Anderson apply the principles of Organizational Engineering (OE) to determine the most appropriate style under certain situations. OE is a branch of knowledge that seeks to understand, measure, predict, and guide the behavior of groups. The basis of OE is a person's strategic style, which is the behavior pattern that a person consistently manifests over a period of time when responding to situations. A strategic style is determined through two dimensions: method and mode. Method is the preferred approach to decision making, structured or unpatterned; mode is the preferred response, thought or action. The combination of method and mode creates four strategic styles: Reactive Stimulator, Relational Innovator, Logical Processor, and Hypothetical Analyzer.

A Reactive Stimulator is someone who is fast, direct, energetic, and independent when dealing with situations. A Relational Innovator is someone who is flexible, spontaneous, relational, theoretical, innovative, and futuristic. A Hypothetical Analyzer is someone who is analytical, definitive, conceptual, divergent, and reserved. A Logical Processor is someone who is practical, logical, methodical, precise, steady, and predictable.

According to Kliem and Anderson, a person's strategic style has implications for how they approach leading a project. A Reactive Stimulator prefers doing, has a task-orientation style, uses informal power, and applies negative incentives. A Relational Innovator prefers managing, has a people-orientation style, uses informal power, and applies positive incentives. A Hypothetical Analyzer prefers managing, has a people-orientation style, uses formal power, and applies positive incentives. A Logical Processor prefers doing, has task-orientation style, uses formal power, and applies negative incentives.[63]

The authors stress the importance of matching a person's strategic style with the overall style of a team. Otherwise, he or she will find it difficult to communicate and coordinate with team members. This situation can create such tension that it slows progress or even stops it.[64]

## PROJECT LEADER ACTIONS

As with general leadership studies, there has been increasing interest in what actions project leaders take to complete projects successfully. However, this area has received little attention as well.

One of the earlier comprehensive works on what project leaders do is the work of Wendy Briner, Michael Geddes, and Colin Hastings, which appeared in their book, *Project Leadership.* They list several actions of a good leader to include building credibility, creating a supportive culture, providing purpose and direction, and seeking feedback.[65]

Dr. Edward Hoffman and Dr. Alexander Laufer conducted a study based on stories told to them by project leaders. They capture "critical incidents" of successful project leadership. According to the authors, this knowledge is often tacit, which makes it difficult to quantify. Stories are one way to make such knowledge explicit.

They identify twenty-four patterns of behavior, summarized in four rules: adopt a will to win, create a results-oriented focus, foster sensitivity to context, and collaborate through trust.

Adopting a will to win is basically being a "man on a mission" who is willing to take calculated risks and "weather the storm." Creating a result-oriented focus is knowing what to achieve, identifying the means to get it, and moving with deliberate speed. Fostering sensitivity to context is being adaptable on both formal and informal approaches as well as being the project's advocate. Collaborating through trust is developing and sustaining commitment from all stakeholders.[66]

In an article for *PM Network,* Owen Gadeken described his research on project managers in the defense industry. He suggested that project managers now and in the future perform four roles: Strategy Setter, Consensus Builder, Systems Integrator, and Change Agent.

A Strategy Setter establishes goals and demonstrates commitment to achieve them. A Consensus Builder generates a sense of community through consensual decision making. A Systems Integrator brings together all the elements of a project and forms a cohesive whole. A Change Agent recognizes the need for change and embraces new ways of doing business.[67]

## SOME UNIVERSAL AGREEMENT?

If scholars and practitioners seem to agree on anything, it is that leadership influences, rather than commands, people to achieve some goal. The focus on the psychological and sociological aspects of leadership, both from a leader and follower perspective, are gaining more recognition as key determinants to the success of any organization, whether for a senior executive council of a Fortune 500 firm or a development project in a small- to medium-size company.

## REFERENCES

1. Stephen R. Covey, A. Roger Merrill, and Rebecca R. Merrill, *First Things First,* Simon & Schuster, New York, 1994, p. 245.
2. James M. Burns, *Leadership,* Harper & Row, New York, 1979, p. 19.

3. James M. Kouzes and Barry Z. Posner, *The Leadership Challenge*, Jossey-Bass, San Francisco, 1987, p. 271.
4. John W. Gardner, *On Leadership*, The Free Press, New York, 1990, p. 1.
5. Warren Bennis and Burt Nanus, *Leaders*, Perennial Library, New York, 1985, p. 20.
6. Max De Pree, *Leadership Is an Art*, Dell, New York, 1989, p. 3.
7. Paul Hersey and Kenneth H. Blanchard, *Management of Organizational Behavior*, Prentice Hall, Englewood Cliffs, NJ, 1982, p. 94.
8. Wess Roberts, *Leadership Secrets of Attila the Hun*, Warner Books, New York, 1987, p. xiv.
9. James H. Donnelly, James L. Gibson, and John M. Ivancevich, *Fundamentals of Management*, Business Publications, Inc., Plano, TX 1981, pp. 291–294.
10. Lorne Hartman, A psychological analysis of leadership effectiveness, *Strategy & Leadership*, p. 31, October–December 1999.
11. Warren Bennis, *On Becoming a Leader*, Perseus Books, Reading, MA, 1989, p. 45.
12. James H. Donnelly, James L. Gibson, and John M. Ivancevich, *Fundamentals of Management*, Business Publications, Inc., Plano, TX 1981, pp. 301–305.
13. Ibid., pp. 305–306.
14. Ibid., p. 295.
15. Paul Hersey and Kenneth H. Blanchard, *Management of Organizational Behavior*, Prentice Hall, Englewood Cliffs, NJ, 1982, pp. 183–219.
16. James H. Donnelly, James L. Gibson, and John M. Ivancevich, *Fundamentals of Management*, Business Publications, Inc., Plano, TX 1981, pp. 218–219.
17. Paul Hersey and Kenneth H. Blanchard, *Management of Organizational Behavior*, Prentice Hall, Englewood Cliffs, NJ, 1993, pp. 300–301, 338–340.
18. Robert R. Blake and Anne A. McCanse, *Leadership Dilemmas — Grid Solutions*, Gulf, Houston, TX, 1991, pp. 25–35.
19. James M. Kouzes and Barry Z. Posner, *The Leadership Challenge*, Jossey-Bass, San Francisco, 1987, p. 14.
20. Ibid., p. vii.
21. Warren Bennis and Burt Nanus, *Leaders*, Perennial Library, New York, 1985, p. 21.
22. Ibid., p. 62.
23. James M. Burns, *Leadership*, Harper & Row, New York, 1979, p. 19.
24. Ibid., p. 426.
25. Ibid., p. 20.
26. Ibid., p. 426.
27. David L. Bradford and Allen R. Cohen, *Managing for Excellence*, John Wiley & Sons, New York, 1984, pp. 10–11.
28. Ibid., pp. 33–45.
29. Ibid., pp. 55–58.
30. Ibid., pp. 283–289.
31. David Goleman, Richard Boyatzis, and Annie McKee, *Primal Leadership*, Harvard Business School Press, Boston, 2002, p. xi.
32. Ibid., p. 6.
33. Ibid., p. 19.
34. Ibid., p. 20.

35. Ibid., p. 27.
36. Ibid., p. 256.
37. Max De Pree, *Leadership Is an Art,* Dell, New York, 1989, p. 3.
38. Ibid., pp. 13–21.
39. Ibid., pp. 58–60.
40. Max De Pree, *Leadership Jazz,* Dell, New York, 1992, pp. 220–225.
41. Peter Block, *Stewardship,* Berrett-Koehler, San Francisco, 1993, p. 21.
42. Ibid., p. xx.
43. Ibid., p. 36.
44. Ibid., p. 85.
45. John W. Gardner, *On Leadership,* The Free Press, New York, 1990, pp. 11–22.
46. Ibid., p. 184.
47. Ibid., p. 26.
48. Ibid., pp. 48–53.
49. Harold J. Leavitt, *Corporate Pathfinders,* Penguin Books, New York, 1997, p. 2.
50. Ibid., p. 7.
51. Warren A. Opfer, Timothy J. Kloppenborg, and Arthur Shirberg, Project leadership — setting the stage, in *Proceedings of PMI Research Conference 2002,* Project Management Institute, Newtown Square, PA, p. 417.
52. Greg Skulmoski, Francis Hartman, and Roch DeMaere, Superior and threshold competencies, *Project Management,* 6(1), 13, 2000.
53. Ibid., p. 14.
54. Dean Sitiriou and Dennis Wittmer, Influence methods of project managers: perceptions of team members and project managers, *Project Management Journal,* p. 19, September 2001.
55. Jeannette Cabanis-Brewin, The human task of a project leader, *PM Network,* pp. 38–41, November 1999.
56. Horst Bergmann, Kathleen Hurson, and Darlene Russ-Eft, Introducing a grass-roots model of leadership, *Strategy & Leadership,* pp. 15–20, October–December 1999.
57. Jim Edgemon, Right stuff: how to recognize it when selecting a project manager, *Application Development Trends,* pp. 37–42, May 1995.
58. Albert A. Einsiedel, Profile of effective project managers, in *Leadership Skills for Project Managers,* Jeffrey K. Pinto and Jeffrey W. Trailer, Eds., Project Management Institute, Newtown Square, PA, 1998, pp. 4–6.
59. Barry Posner, What it takes to be a good project manager, in *Leadership Skills for Project Managers,* Jeffrey K. Pinto and Jeffrey W. Trailer, Eds., Project Management Institute, Newtown Square, PA, 1998, p. 13.
60. Dennis Slevin and Jeffrey K. Pinto, Project leadership: understanding and consciously choosing your style, in *Leadership Skills for Project Managers,* Jeffrey K. Pinto and Jeffrey W. Trailer, Eds., Project Management Institute, Newtown Square, PA, 1998, pp. 29–43.
61. Max R. Wideman and Aaron J. Shenhar, Optimizing Project Success by Matching PM Style with Project Type, http://www.pmforum.org/library/papers/PM_Style&Scss.pdf, p. 12.
62. Ibid., p. 13.

63. Ralph L. Kliem and Harris B. Anderson, *The Organizational Engineering Approach to Project Management,* St. Lucie Press, Boca Raton, FL, 2003, pp. 119–130.
64. Ibid., p. 136.
65. Wendy Briner, Michael Geddes, and Colin Hastings, *Project Leadership,* Gower, Aldershot, Hampshire, U.K., 1990, pp. 18–30.
66. Edward J. Hoffman and Alexander Laufer, Emerging research into factors of project success and failure, PMI Research Conference 2002, July 15, Seattle, WA, pp. 1–30.
67. Owen C. Gadeken, Third wave project leadership, *PM Network,* pp. 43–46, February 1999.

# 2

# THE PATTERNS OF PROJECT LEADERSHIP

With all these theories and research on leadership in general and project management in particular, what can we conclude? From my personal experience and years of research, ten patterns of actions distinguish project leaders from project managers:

- Shift
- Visualize
- Integrate
- Understand
- Decide
- Motivate
- Team
- Trust
- Communicate
- Respond

Allow me to explain. I refer to the above as patterns of actions. They are patterns because they do not always occur in the same level of detail or sequence. At the same time, their significance is immense and can determine how effective project managers are in leading their projects to a successful conclusion.

They are actions because, unless applied, they are useless. The actions become nothing more than theoretical constructs or platitudes without substance. When applied, however, projects inevitably achieve great results.

Effective project managers are the people who enable others to achieve great results by applying the patterns of action. However, project managers must exercise judgment when applying these patterns. They must determine the level of detail and sequence of each pattern. It is this willingness and ability to make such a judgment that, I believe, separates project leaders from project managers.

## ACTION #1: SHIFT

Organizations need more project leaders and less project managers. Unfortunately, many organizations confuse the two. This confusion has resulted in the application of project management tools and techniques in a simplistic, linear manner. What project managers need to do is exercise a paradigm shift that emphasizes, to use a popularized phrase by Bennis and Nanus, doing the right the things rather than doing things right. This paradigm shift, in the true sense of Kuhn and Barker, requires taking a completely different perspective, a nonlinear and systemic one. Project management currently remains in the shackles of a paradigm that emphasizes doing things right, not necessarily the right things. It needs to become more like what Burns describes as more transformative, less transactional.

## ACTION #2: VISUALIZE

If there is one common action that all leaders perform it is developing a vision. The works of Kouzes, Posner, Bennis, and Nanus highlight its importance. However, vision is not developed by someone who sits in a back room. Rather, a vision is something that everyone understands and feels committed to. In addition, leaders work to define and execute all activities based on it.

Most visions, unfortunately, remain a distant abstraction in people's minds. They lack the necessary emotional buy-in and ownership. The results are projects that often become an exercise in efficiency, not effectiveness.

## ACTION #3: INTEGRATE

Too often, project managers take a linear view of projects. The mere act of building a schedule, for example, suggests linearity. In addition, many of them focus on the tangible elements and ignore the importance of those subtle elements that affect an entire project, such as sponsors. Gardner and Gadeken see the value of taking an integrated approach.

Effective project leaders consider both the tangible and intangible factors and integrate the two. Again, take the example of building a schedule. Not only is it influenced by time and sequence, but also by the motivation of team members and external forces, e.g., the market and international conditions. Project leaders see such interrelationships and assess their impacts, positive and negative.

Failure to take such an integrated view can have serious consequences. Project managers may overlook key risks. They may act in a way that has serious ramifications, not necessarily up front but later. In the end, they embrace shortsightedness and react, not respond, towards their environment.

## ACTION #4: UNDERSTAND

Project leaders have a good understanding and knowledge about their environment. Block, Keane Consulting, Wideman, Shenhar, Kliem, and Anderson all recognize the importance of context. They understand the environment of the project. They also understand the forces that will affect the project's outcome, both explicit and implicit factors. By understanding the context of their projects, they can develop appropriate strategies and tactics to achieve results, both from behavioral and mechanical perspectives.

From a people perspective, many projects fail because they are in tune solely with the explicit factors of context, e.g., policies and procedures to follow. However, they tend to ignore or overlook implicit factors, such as politics, values, and mores. The result is often that projects are "sideswiped" by issues that no one considered.

## ACTION #5: DECIDE

Some of the other theorists recognize the importance of decisiveness when filling a leadership role in an organization, from CEO to project manager. They include Skulmoski, Kliem, Anderson, and Gadeken.

Too often, however, project managers make decisions too prematurely or too late. When deciding too prematurely, they make decisions without consulting appropriate people. When deciding too late, they sometimes wait for approval from too many people or the wrong people. Either way, decisions can become biased or incomplete, further leading to greater problems later in the project life cycle and beyond. Of course, it is one thing to perform the mechanics of decision making, it is another thing to involve the right people in the right way to come up with the right decision at the right moment.

## ACTION #6: MOTIVATE

When filling in a leadership position, many project managers assume they must control everything. In addition, they think that means speaking softly (sometimes loudly) and carrying a big stick. While that approach may work in diplomacy, the general result is that it spells "trouble" for projects. A more effective approach is to motivate people positively, which is embraced by just about all leadership theories. Kouzes, Posner, Bennis, Nanus, Bradford, Cohen, and Pinto — just to name a few — all have uncovered this insight.

Yet, for some strange reason, many project managers exhibit a desire to dominate, to control negatively, to "slash and burn" their members and other stakeholders. This behavior can produce cataclysmic results, such as high turnover, shoddy workmanship, and overall poor performance.

## ACTION #7: TEAM

Most project managers accomplish the vision of their projects through two or more individuals. How these people work together has a great impact on a project's success or failure. To make that happen, project managers must capitalize on people's skills in a manner that builds commitment and accountability. Kouzes, Posner, and Katzenbach are just some of the authorities who recognize the importance of building teams. They also recognize that the team leader lays the groundwork for synergy, that is, produces much more than the sum of individual team members.

## ACTION #8: TRUST

Credibility is perhaps a project manager's most important asset. Sacrifice credibility and project managers soon lose trust with the very people he or she needs to work with to successfully complete a project. Authors like De Pree, Burns, Kouzes, and Posner all recognize the importance of the relationship between credibility and trust. Along with trust are ethics and integrity. Both are tied closely with trust; sacrificing one or both will jeopardize trust and, ultimately, credibility.

## ACTION #9: COMMUNICATE

According to some sources, project managers spend 70 to 90 percent of their time communicating. Bennis and Nanus as well as Briner, Geddes, and Hastings agree. They would also agree that communication is very important for project leaders.

Ironically, many project managers really do not communicate frequently and if they do, they do so poorly. Their messages may be incomplete or inaccurate. The way they come across is often negative. They may choose an inappropriate medium or they may fail to tailor messages to the audience.

Whatever the reason, poor communication can prove damaging. It can increase negative conflict, can cause needless rework, can lower morale, and can strain relationships with key stakeholders. These are only a few of the consequences. Good project leaders recognize the importance of effective communication and treat it seriously.

## ACTION #10: RESPOND

The message is clear: Project leaders must adapt to their circumstances or they will fail. This circumstance is especially evident when applying the appropriate leadership style under a given situation, e.g., during a particular phase. From Fiedler's contingency theory and Hersey and Blanchard's leadership model to Kliem and Anderson's organizational engineering, for example, the appropriate leadership style can make a difference.

Adaptability involves others factors as well. Project leaders must be adaptable to new circumstances due to market changes; they must adapt to changing membership among stakeholders; and they must adapt to new tools, techniques, and methodologies. They must also anticipate such changes and respond through effective change management.

Their response must be more than mechanical. They must adapt in such a way that encourages and helps stakeholders to adapt also. Otherwise, project managers will experience resistance to change both on a personal level and stakeholder level. Resistance will occur and a project will fail.

## CASE STUDY: BACKGROUND

A case study is perhaps the best way to demonstrate the patterns of action that successful project leaders exhibit on a project. The following case study does just that. Although it is about a project within a large global corporation, the insights apply to projects within institutions of all sizes and industries.

XYZ Corporation, of course, is a fictitious corporation. It consists of four business units and over two dozen subsidiaries in the automotive industry. As you might suspect, the supply chain is a quite complex and intricate web of foreign and domestic manufacturing units. Its workforce is over 200,000 and is very diverse, from gender to ethnicity.

Recently, the corporate staff recognized that its policies and procedures infrastructure needed significant overhaul. With over 400 policies and procedures, the infrastructure had many shortcomings, which made management of the global business quite difficult. The technology behind the supporting system was a myriad of software patches that reflected an antiquated architecture. The content of the policies and procedures themselves was dated and contradictory. The organization or structure of the policies and procedures was inconsistent, e.g., policies were written like procedures and vice versa. Everyone complained about it.

The executive council of the headquarters business unit, consisting of members from the different business units and headquarters executive staff, decided that the time for change was now, especially after a major reorganization. Consequently, they assigned a senior executive sponsor and project manager and provided some high-level direction on how to proceed. About the only guidance the council provided was a need to have a new infrastructure in place, two years hence, and be supported by all the major business units and subsidiaries.

# 3

# SHIFT

Read just about any statistical study on the performance of projects and you will see virtually the same reasons causing their failures and successes.

## COULD BE BETTER

Several years ago, the Standish Group International, Inc. conducted a survey of thousands of projects. It discovered that 16 percent of projects finished on time and within budget. Ironically, it found that the larger the project, the lower the success rate. It is ironic because large projects, as opposed to small ones, often implement more formal project management.[1]

The Standish Group cited five reasons for project success: user involvement, executive management support, clear statement of requirements, proper planning, and realistic expectations.[2]

Since that time, the Standish Group has conducted several studies and found similar results with only a slight improvement in project success, rising from a success rate of 16 percent in 1994 to 26 percent in 1998. Once again, it noted that the larger the project, the smaller the opportunity for success.[3]

However, this time the study revealed an additional insight: A major contributing factor for success was having a competent and experienced project manager. I think it is fairly safe to assume that only a project manager can assure that user involvement, executive management support, clear statement of requirements, proper planning, and realistic expectations will likely occur.

The results of this study and others imply that the more project management disciplines you have the better, in terms of achieving project success. Applying more project management does not mean any greater guarantee of success, however. It can provide the groundwork for success, but it does not necessarily translate into success. In fact, more project management can add to the likelihood of failure.

In England, a research study was conducted of "runaway projects." The typical response was reacting to circumstances, rather than responding, by adding more of something or increasing pressure. The top five responses were extending the schedule, better project management procedures, more people, more funds, and pressure on suppliers. The results did not reveal whether adding more actually improved the performance of runaway projects.[4]

The pervasive attitude continues that more project management disciplines will mean more chances for success. A survey by the PM Boulevard on assessing project planning activities found that many firms only occasionally or never track the time spent working on tasks, never compare completion data to tasks, sometimes or never update schedules, or never update the project baseline.[5] The key question still remains: Will more necessarily translate into success?

My experience as an internal auditor of major development projects for a Fortune 500 firm opened my eyes to this very question. I have seen projects replete with the disciplines of project management. Plenty of in-depth plans and reporting mechanisms were implemented. Extensive reporting mechanisms were in place. Everyone had the latest tools. Executive support existed. Requirements were well defined up front. Yet, some of these projects were outright failures and only a few of them would be considered a success by traditional standards, e.g., on time and within budget. In addition, I conducted assessments and audits of projects that occurred using a minimum amount of tools, techniques, and disciplines. These audits raised the fundamental question in my mind: Why were some projects a success and others a failure?

The evidence is quite clear that project performance has not been stellar. More projects fail than succeed, especially if the criteria include delivering a project on time and within budget. The reasons imply that more of certain disciplines, techniques, or information will translate into project success. The problem is, however, that the reasons explained for the poor results are really symptoms of a much bigger problem. Many projects have succeeded with less, much less, than projects with much more. I believe the major contributor towards project success is something that is very difficult to measure but plays a pivotal role: project leadership. Greater user involvement, executive support, and proper planning, for example, will have a greater likelihood of occurring if good project leadership is exhibited throughout a project by the project manager and by stakeholders.

Why is it so difficult for many people to see the major contribution of project leadership to project success? A simple explanation is, of course, that it is difficult to measure. However, going below the surface reveals something much deeper than that: The prevailing paradigm of project management embraced in the professional bodies and educational institutions.

## THE ROLE OF A PARADIGM

What is a paradigm? It is a perspective on the world or within a specific discipline. It tells us what is important and how the world works. It determines our beliefs and values. It colors all our perceptions of what is happening and how we respond to reality. It determines what problems we choose to address and how to address them. The fact is: Everyone is encapsulated by a prevailing paradigm.

A paradigm, therefore, is a framework or model that helps to interpret and deal with reality. It serves as a perceptual map, to use the words of Edward de Bono, or mental model, as described by Peter Senge. The two top exponents of the role and influence of paradigms, however, are Thomas Kuhn and Joel Barker.

Kuhn talked about the power of a paradigm from scientific and academic vantage points. He postulated that scientific endeavors were greatly influenced by it. This led to his famous definition of a paradigm as consisting, for example, of laws and theories that provide tradition behind research, principally scientific research.[6]

Joel Barker took the substance behind Kuhn and applied it to business and other environments. He defined a paradigm as a set of written and unwritten rules and regulations that defines boundaries of behavior.[7]

A paradigm, of course, is not something that is "bad" or "evil." It is a consequence of being human and requires a means to interpret and deal with our surrounding world. In other words, it provides order, a means to predict the future, comfort, explanations, and enhances communication.

A paradigm is, therefore, really a belief system to explain how "things" work. It provides a schema to interpret the past and present as well as what occurs in the future. It is so strong that it influences our choices.

It is those very pluses, however, that generate the minuses associated with a paradigm. A paradigm can lead to rigidity in thought (even dogmatism), screen out innovative ideas, filter facts, and, perhaps most importantly, restrict people's perception and responses to reality. All that translates into leading to what I refer to as "professional blinders" and "hardening of the synapses." Unlearning becomes as difficult as learning.

Of course, change happens and presents complications before a paradigm. After a while, however, the stranglehold of a prevailing paradigm loosens. A paradigm shift occurs, thus opening the road to a new one. Problems begin to surface that cannot be addressed adequately by the prevailing paradigm. Anomalies become increasingly prevalent. The entire paradigm can eventually, perhaps even suddenly, come into disrepute. Failure occurs when applying the existing rules. Discontent begins to arise with practitioners, who question the very fundamental precepts of the dominating institutions and prevailing beliefs and values. As Kuhn noted, recognition of an anomaly can lead to discoveries that can weaken the prevailing paradigm.

Challenging the prevailing paradigm, of course, is not easy because a prevailing paradigm does not embrace creativity that well. The tools and technologies for the new paradigm lack maturity. A comprehensive body of knowledge does not exist. Most importantly, the subscribers to the new paradigm often face ridicule, even ostracism. That is because the adherents of the prevailing paradigm find themselves potentially on the losing end. The supporters of the existing paradigm begin to feel threatened. This sense of feeling threatened grows the higher one moves up the "food chain" because the potential to lose more is greater.

Despite the protectors of the status quo, change continues to march forward. A metanoia, to use Senge's term, occurs; that is, a shift of mind happens. Followers of the old paradigm fall into the ranks of the new one, more out of the heart than the head. Old and new adherents alike see a gradual breakdown in the paradigm, which causes a schism to surface. At a more frequent level, anomalies arise that whittle away at the very foundation of the prevailing paradigm.

Of course, the new paradigm does not discard the entire prevailing paradigm. Quite the contrary. Instead, it absorbs much of what is good but does not apply in the same manner. What gives the new paradigm the advantage over the prevailing one is that the former solves problems that the other could not.

## PROJECT MANAGEMENT AT THE CROSSROADS

Project management is now in the midst of a paradigm shift. The prevailing paradigm is starting to crumble. Discussions are already arising at forums and conferences that challenge the very foundation and prevailing knowledge base of professional bodies in the discipline. Presentations and papers are increasingly charging that the prevailing paradigm is mechanistic, eclectic, analytical, descriptive, and deficient. In the *Proceedings of the PMI Research Conference 2002,* Lauri Koskela and Greg Howell stress that the shortcomings in the foundation of project management are becoming more and more apparent, creating a crisis that is gaining recognition.[8] Bruno Urli and Didier Urli also agree and compare project management to a toolbox of different instruments rather than a body of knowledge in the traditional sense.[9]

Yet, change is not easily forthcoming. Koskela and Howell further observe that the culprit behind the crisis is a lack of a theoretical foundation in project management. This circumstance has led to overlooking anomalies or misinterpreting their meaning and significance.[10]

To a large degree, the prevailing paradigm is dominated by its mathematical and scientific past. Urli and Urli note that what I refer to as the "mechanics" of project management have received the focus of attention. The areas have a strong management science and operations research flavor, represented by the topics covered, e.g., resource leveling and Gantt charts.[11]

In addition to finding its basis in tradition, the prevailing paradigm finds itself protected by an army of adherents to preserve its mathematical and rational roots. Pernille Eskerod and Katarina Ostergren note that the desire to treat project management as a scientific discipline and create a supporting theoretical basis has led to inflexibility. The reason is the desire to build the "right theory" based on standardization.[12]

I believe the application of project management as we know it today can worsen, not enhance, project performance by establishing a bureaucratic infrastructure that impedes rather than enhances project performance. Alberto Melgrati and Mario Damiani observe that the overemphasis of rationality on a project necessitates a more balanced perspective that considers other areas, including political and cultural considerations.[13]

Even the very purpose of a project has come under question. Connie Delisle and Janice Thomas observe that the traditional emphasis on efficiency, e.g., on time and within budget, is devoid of real meaning in terms of what success is to stakeholders as well as to a project.[14]

Peter Morris agrees, noting that being on time and within budget does not guarantee that the result will be something that meets needs or expectations.[15]

Eskerod and Ostergren agree that the current crack in the existing paradigm has shed a new light on the purpose of a project, indicating that it goes beyond time, cost, and performance.[16]

All of the above insights have far-reaching implications on managing and, more importantly, leading projects. Project performance has not improved dramatically over the years despite the proliferation of tools, techniques, and expertise. As observed earlier, the larger the project, the chances of project success decrease despite the implementation of project management disciplines.

What is needed, I believe, is a change in the prevailing paradigm of project management, i.e., one that is a more balanced view that relies less on mathematical and rational orientations and more on what I refer to the "subjective" factors that play a major role in effective leadership, as shown in Figure 3.1.

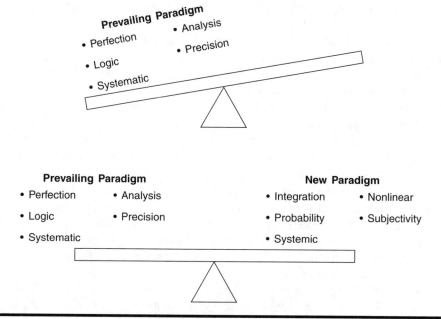

**Figure 3.1** Correcting the Imbalance.

Just about all the major factors that contribute to project failure and success link back not to more rationality and control, but to more communication and commitment, for example. Above all, projects are endeavors of human energy and ingenuity; not schedules, earned value analysis, and other tools and techniques.

Peter Morris observes that the major contributors to project failures relate to poor definition and control.[17] Such failures reflect more of a failure in leadership than the application of a tool or technique. With poor leadership, a sophisticated tool or technique only gives a bad leader the opportunity to do more damage. The person may be a better project manager, but he or she may not be a better project leader.

Project success, however defined, involves leading, not managing, people to accomplish goals. Christopher Bredillet agrees, noting that the emphasis on quantitative considerations constrains autonomy whereas qualitative ones provide the necessary freedom.[18]

The prevailing paradigm has led to a skewed perspective of what matters on a project. Kate Belzer says that knowing the "hard skills" of project management, e.g., tools, is an incomplete knowledge base. A good command of the

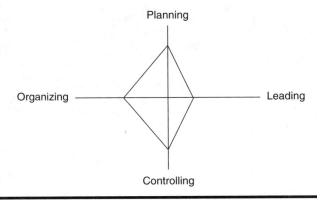

**Figure 3.2** Spider Chart Reflecting Emphasis Under Prevailing Paradigm.

"soft skills" is also necessary. This skill, which she refers to as the art of project management, helps to identify value, provide direction, and build teams to name a few. She also observes that a project has a larger chance of failure without the soft skills.[19]

There is, unfortunately, very little insight on the importance of leading rather than managing projects despite its salient influence on project outcome, as indicated in Figure 3.2. Peter Morris says that this lack of insight is quite apparent when discussing teamwork on projects, whereby little discussion has occurred on its impact on project success.[20]

The bottom line is that the field of project management needs a more balanced paradigm. It leans too far to the left side of the brain; that is, it emphasizes too much the capabilities of the left hemisphere of the human mind. As Warren Bennis, a leadership guru, would say: Doing things right. What is needed more is to ask whether project managers are doing the right things, that is, applying the right side of their brain.

Perhaps Tom Peters summed up the entire problem with the prevailing paradigm of project management when he said, in an interview for *PM Network,* that too much emphasis has been placed on traditional project management, e.g., PERT. According to Peters, this overemphasis has its pro's and con's, providing a skewed perspective on project management. What is often overlooked is the emotional, people side of project management. Not surprisingly, the role of such factors as enthusiasm and creativity are often overlooked in contributing to success of projects, creating a serious gap.[21] Leading, as displayed in Figure 3.3, restores the balance.

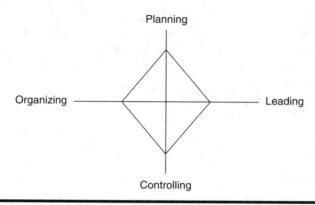

**Figure 3.3**   Spider Chart Reflecting Emphasis Under New Paradigm.

# CHARACTERISTICS AND CONSEQUENCES OF THE PREVAILING PARADIGM

The question arises: What are the characteristics of the prevailing paradigm that make it so difficult to manage and lead projects consistently to a successful conclusion? There are five key characteristics.

## Perfection

A salient characteristic of the prevailing paradigm is the overemphasis on precision before starting a project. In my experience, I have noticed that many project managers spend extensive time with other stakeholders to ensure that everything is "perfect." Not surprisingly, some people become extremely frustrated with the perfectionist approach because from an appearance perspective "nothing is getting done." Some project managers never go beyond the planning stage. They seek correctness in the plan without really knowing the criteria for determining what defines the perfection. Yet they constantly refine the plan, hoping that every detail is covered.

The reality is, of course, that a plan is a snapshot in time. Like all snapshots, it is incomplete. It is only a model and, like all models, only approximates what is or what is to be.

So why is there such a proclivity towards this sense of perfectionism under the prevailing paradigm? I believe it has its roots in early scientific thinking from a couple of centuries ago: The idea that mankind can master domination over the world through increased knowledge and understanding. With more knowledge and understanding will come predictability about the existing world and a subsequent confidence in our ability to predict, even manage, the future. The problem arises that too much abstraction takes over, becoming more important than actual implementation. The bookshelves of project managers are often filled with abstract plans and the subsequent results are not hard to understand. A plan developed without the involvement of the people who will implement it will not having meaning to them.[22]

## Analysis

Another characteristic of the prevailing paradigm is the desire to explode everything on a project into discrete components. In other words, a person takes an object as a whole and explodes it into minute details to improve knowledge and understanding and then reassembles it. This action is predicated on the notion that the human mind has a limited capacity to comprehend complex phenomena.

This approach is quite common in project management. Take a top-down perspective, identify all the major components, and explode each one into minute parts. Developing the work breakdown structure involves taking this approach and often works quite well. However, what frequently happens is that the desire to explode further and further into the constituent components results in a seemingly endless endeavor. Sometimes drilling down the work breakdown structure becomes so deep that splitting the atom seems to occur. Coupled with the desire for perfection, this approach towards building a work breakdown structure becomes endless.

Some great costs are often attributed to this analytical approach. The construction of the object, in our case the project, is built by artificial yet fixed boundaries, making it almost impossible for people to adapt to a dynamic environment. What I have witnessed is that the explosion becomes treated as something so sacred that many people cling to it even when it no longer makes sense. The work breakdown structure, for example, is adhered to with such rigidity that it becomes unrealistic to follow because of the difficulty or, more importantly, the reluctance to change.

Another great cost during the explosion, for example, is the loss of the relationships (often subtle in nature) among the components. The very result of an exploding work breakdown structure causes the loss of many relationships and often the imposition of artificial ones among those components when constructing a network diagram. The network diagram often becomes a poor reconstruction of the relationship among the elements because, by its very nature, it is an incomplete model.

There are, I believe, several reasons for the desire to emphasize analysis and again it is rooted in our scientific past. In the *Turning Point,* Fritjof Capra agrees by observing that there is a strong tendency to break phenomena into basic building blocks and try to understand their interactions. He calls this behavior reductionism and says that it has been a dominant characteristic of scientific thinking.[23] Our organizations have mimicked this reductionism from the top down to the project level.[24]

Breaking everything into constituent components is seen as a way to improve understandability about something and then rebuild it in a way to identify the relationships. It is all based on Cartesian thinking, which is very analytical, whereby everything must be broken into pieces and then rearranged in a logical order. The problem is often that some of the key relationships are not identified or are done so incorrectly, particularly for nonlinear systems, like a project. The result is a loss of synergy.

Perhaps more disturbing is that it leads towards a reductionist perspective. Every attempt is made to define the project in a simplistic, fundamental way. Often, the attention is paid to the arbitrarily identified components themselves and not the relationships. In other words, emphasis is placed on the properties of the components and not, or to a lesser degree, on the relationships among the components. Everything is then perceived as some machine governed by mathematical laws. This perception also permeates our thinking about people and we look at them as machines. There is, however, a fundamental difference between machines and organisms. The behavior of machines is determined by structure; not so for organisms, which are determined by process. The former are inflexible, based on precision. The latter are flexible, adaptable to changing circumstances.

Project management is replete with examples of the above insights. Often great emphasis is made to identify the components of a project and then try to artificially reconstruct the relationships based on a construct like time. Throughout the life cycle of a project, every effort is made to juggle the elements of the iron triangle of cost, schedule, and quality in a manner that is often not captured in the project plan. In a project, a constant war goes on to impose some analytical abstraction onto the project. This only augments complexity, not simplifies it, even though the goal of this effort is to seek predictability and objectivity. Still this analytical approach does not put us at ease, but only contributes more to our angst because the focus is on parts rather than the entire system comprising of the former. This approach is very Cartesian and has strong implications of determinism behind it, similar to that of a clock. It leads to viewing the world, or a project, as consisting of parts arranged in a way that encourages thinking in terms of causality.

## Logic

The prevailing paradigm emphasizes the logical side of project management based on a cause and effect perspective. The very act of planning and managing a project is an exercise of logic. Energies are expended to develop a well-constructed, sequentially oriented plan that fits neatly together. The assumption is that the project will flow according to the sequence and success will arise. For example, the team does A, then B, maybe C and D together in a cause and effect link throughout the course of a project.

The reality, of course, is just the opposite. The project often does not flow according to plan for many reasons. Perhaps the plan is incomplete or inaccurate, a testament to the foibles of planning. The real reason is that the plan is treated like some timeless image for a project that everything follows. It is, however, only a linear snapshot of what ought to happen at a given point in time. Such linear thinking requires that we view objects as distinct states.[25] The consequence of this perception is that the plan often becomes an anachronism or an encapsulated abstraction that lacks relevance.

Despite the plan, the result may be the same based on the fallacious assumption that the plan contributed to successful results from a logic perspective. The conclusion may, in fact, be based on a false premise. Hence, a plan may be misconstrued as being valid when in reality other factors that are not necessarily quantifiable may be contributing to its success.

Pure logic in and of itself can result in an unyielding, almost dictatorial perception of the world around us. The world becomes a battleground between what should be and what is, particularly if the logic is linear and absolutist in orientation. A tendency exists to force a solution, a characteristic of sequential thinking. This requires identifying and performing one action at a time, creating an inflexible response.

The other consequence is that anomalies become treated as problems rather than opportunities to progress. More often than not, deviations from the plan must be corrected. While not all changes are good, a tendency exists to either ignore or discount anomalies, deviations to plans, as something intolerable. This perspective leads to inflexibility that, in turn, leads to an irrelevant plan. The assumption behind the perspective, of course, is that order and control must prevail; otherwise, chaos takes over the project. Hence, any deviation from the plan is an aversion.

The importance of logic has much of its roots in the work of Descartes. He placed the mind as the focus of everything. "I think therefore I am" led to man being perceived as a rational creature. Newton, of course, took logic to the heights of acceptance through the use of mathematical abstractions for understanding and predicting reality. Knowledge and understanding, coupled with logic, will enable domination over the environment.[26]

## Precision

One of the more fascinating aspects of the prevailing paradigm is the notion that a plan must be precise to be meaningful. The assumption is that everything on a project is definable and there is only one right way to approach it. It is not uncommon for project managers and everyone else, therefore, to want to develop and implement the "most efficient and effective" approach based on complete, accurate, clear, and relevant content.

This attempt to build the most efficient and effective system is often an exercise in predictability in the hope of discovering how things really work. Human beings have a tendency to build complex maps of the universe in an effort to achieve predictability and gain the ability to manipulate variables to gain desired results.

The reality, of course, is that a plan is a model, an approximation of a system, called a project. There will never be enough data and information and what little are available are often incomplete and inaccurate. Yet, for example, planning sessions often become debates over what is the right path. There may not be just one right plan, but multiple right plans.

I believe this desire for precision is based on the need for predictability exhibited through the scientist's need for predictability. It manifests itself in activities and topics not often deemed scientific, e.g., motivation theory and organizational design.[27] The assumption is that through sufficient inquiry one can uncover the "truth" or "right way." Discover the right answer and the "truth will set you free" becomes the overriding belief. This desire for precision is largely exhibited through Newtonian mathematical constructs to predict physical behavior.[28]

The consequences for project outcomes are immense. They become actual reflections of estimation, even inaccuracy. Yet every effort is made to preserve the plan and evaluate any changes under rigorous change management policies and procedures. This very act of evaluation is testimony that the plan is often inaccurate.

The desire for precision assumes that a project and its environment are static; that is, both are unchanging. Yet projects and their environments are constantly changing. Under such circumstances, about the best a project manager can do is to choose a path that will improve the likelihood of achieving success.

However, developing plans and executing them is often more of an exercise in approximation than precision. There are never enough data and information to be precise, I believe, and there is really no way to be truly objective. Quantification is not the answer either because what is selected to measure is as much an expression of values as the variables themselves.

The desire for objectivity assumes that the measurers can extricate themselves from their environment. Realistically, no one can do that. They are mired in the bog of their environment.

When you really think about the contemporary environment for projects, it does not lend itself to precision simply because there is too little time, too much data, and plenty of complexity.

## Systematic

Under the prevailing paradigm, a view prevails that projects must be managed systematically. That is, project managers need to approach a project in a methodical, step-by-step manner. By being systematic, all that is required is to simply follow a framework or methodology, and success is assured. Not surprisingly, many organizations purchase and try to deploy a framework or methodology with the expectation that projects will complete on time, within budget, and satisfy customers.

Behaving systematically satisfies a human need to feel in control by being methodical and complete. Frameworks and methodologies often give this false sense of control by providing a means to be methodical and complete.

Despite vendor claims, the record of project success is dismal at best and methodologies and frameworks have yet to show a strong record of success themselves. My experience has been that methodologies and frameworks can be useful, but they do not guarantee success as often as portrayed and, in fact, can be counterproductive. Most encourage a mechanical, almost paint-by-numbers approach and assume that a project will succeed. Rather, the framework or methodology ends up creating a bureaucratic infrastructure for projects and actually impedes work. Managing a project then becomes a matter of compliance and an exercise in administrative trivia. Sadly, many companies invest millions to form organizations, such as a project management office that specializes in methodologies, just to support projects to be systematic in their approach.

## Consequences

There are immense consequences attributed to the prevailing paradigm with managing and leading a project.

### *More Is Better*

Project managers apply the tools, techniques, and principles en masse. Instead of applying the right tool, technique, or principle in the right amount at the right moment, everything is applied in an almost shotgun manner. This situation is particularly the case when project managers lack the experience in discerning the difference between doing the "right thing" as opposed to doing the "thing right." Eventually, it leads to the bureaucratization of projects.

## A Project Is Merely an Exercise of Mechanics

Project management appears to be nothing more than following a series of steps. If a project manager follows a sequence, such as one suggested by a framework or methodology, good results follow. Often, however, this fails because the steps explain what and how to apply project management, but they fail to address the motivational side of project management. In other words, the people factor, which does not lend itself to a mechanical step-by-step approach, is ignored.

This attempt to take a mechanical approach perhaps lies with our perception of the world as being something like a machine, whereby everything moves according to some overall regular pace. A machine, of course, is made up of parts. Each part has a specific, defined role that must work with another part in a timed manner. The wrong part and the wrong pace and everything breaks down. Through analysis, however, the bad part can be isolated and removed. This machine analogy has permeated project management.[29]

## A Desperate Attempt to Find a Secret Weapon to Save Projects

This one is tied closely to the last point. Management in general and project managers in particular are constantly looking for some tool, technique, or methodology to help turn a project around. Time and money are often spent in this pursuit only to find the investment never turned the project around because the fundamental problem was not having that secret weapon. Frequently, the new tool, technique, or methodology is then considered inadequate as the pursuit for a newer and better one begins. The real issue rests somewhere else.

## An Overemphasis on Command and Control

The prevailing paradigm, by placing an emphasis on standardization and mechanization, encourages project managers to assume a "take charge" approach. That often means constant oversight of the minutest details of a project, including over what people do and how they do it. This results in a dramatic decline in ownership and commitment on the part of other stakeholders and, quite often, accountability flows back to the project manager. This behavior reflects the perception of our organizations, that projects are machines. Of course, projects are not machines, but project managers often treat them as such.

## A Black and White View of Managing a Project

This characteristic is based on the notion that a right way and wrong way exists for projects. Subscribing to a black and white perspective, often based on some methodology or body of knowledge, leads to polarization among stakeholders and eventual negative conflict. Project managers then surround themselves with a core group of "think alikes" that can negatively influence decisions as well as jeopardize morale on project teams. It can lead to destructive competition among stakeholders. It can also mean having an unrealistic view of the world.

## A Microscopic View of a Project

There is a saying that no man is an island; the same applies to projects. Under the prevailing paradigm, however, many project managers treat their projects as isolated enclaves operating in a separate world. They begin to filter data and information, hearing what they want, not needing to hear what occurs in the external environment. They often manage people in a way that fails to consider the impact of the bigger picture, which includes the external environment, on the performance of their projects.

## Conservative View of the World

The prevailing view of command and control that often accompanies the existing paradigm translates into a reactive rather than responsive approach towards managing projects. Risks and variances, for example, are seen as threats rather than opportunities on which to capitalize. Project management then becomes reactive rather than responsive. New ideas and new approaches are seen as threatening because the prevailing paradigm has a low tolerance for error and indeterminacy. Consequently, project managers find themselves policing their projects.

This perception is the result of emphasizing the need for a system, like a project, to maintain stability to preserve its overall structure. Increasingly, however, it is recognized that systems may fall into disequilibrium only to move into a different state to recreate themselves and adapt to their environments.

## Only Quantification Matters

Often, project managers focus only on the numbers, such as ratios and indices. This is based on the assumption that only what can be measured matters. An added benefit arises, too, that equations, being succinct and applicable widely, can be used to deal with a wide range of phenomena. This perspective, however, is shortsighted. Numbers are only a gauge, a means to an end, not the ends themselves. A good Cost Performance Index, for example, may indicate efficiency but not necessarily effectiveness. Stakeholders, including the team, may still be dissatisfied with the results. This emphasis on quantification may override qualitative considerations, resulting in an unrealistic appraisal of projects. Numbers are really indicators and not the end in itself as is so often the case under the prevailing paradigm. Yet, as Margaret Wheatley observes, such quantification becomes the focus of attention, playing a central role in mathematical calculations for making decisions on structure and organizational design.[30]

To some extent, thank Newton for this overreliance on number crunching on one specific piece of life — time. All of these calculations became the center of attention, not data, from a Newtonian perspective. Time became the principal recipient of calculations, construed as independent from all phenomena.[31] As we all know, the calculation of time plays a key role in project management and continues to be viewed as some independent abstract entity that can be expressed numerically.[32]

This desire for numbers is applied to everything, including the social science arena. This desire has permeated the social sciences in an attempt to ascertain behavior numerically. This very desire for numbers has also led to a misreading of reality. Quite often, the numbers become the measure of everything on a project. To a certain extent, this reliance on numbers is a religious crusade of intolerance towards nonquantifiable factors.

## Unrealistic View of the World

By viewing the plan as a perfect model, what often happens is a war on reality. The need for order and control almost necessitates treating the plan as "the true path" to success. Inflexibility takes over and the plan becomes a world of its own. As the environment changes, so should the plan. Yet this frequently does not happen. An unrealistic schedule, for example, becomes something that is imposed on the team. Under such circumstances, either team members become frustrated and ignore the plan or they give up and "just follow orders." Either way, project managers find themselves making difficult choices that can demoralize a team.

From a project leadership perspective, it seems that the prevailing paradigm should be discarded completely. There have been too many big failures and the shortcoming are immense. In truth, there have been few successes. What is needed is a shift in the paradigm to reflect a more balanced approach towards project management.

Indeed, the crux of the problem — the management aspects of a project. What is needed is a more complete, balanced view of the field — the leadership aspects of a project. Too much emphasis has been placed on the mechanics and less on the so-called softer side of project management. Kam Jugdev, Janice Thomas, and Connie Delisle acknowledge this trend toward a paradigm shift. They say that the iron triangle of cost, time, and scope and the view that a project is a temporary endeavor is yielding to a much broader, holistic perspective about project management. This perspective includes addressing needs and meeting expectations in a way that requires both hard and soft skills.[33]

## CHARACTERISTICS AND CONSEQUENCES OF THE NEW PARADIGM

What are the characteristics of the new paradigm?

### Integration

This one is of primary importance. Emphasis shifts from the components of projects to their relationships among each other. Relationships require a look at interactions and interdependence.

This means that projects are about more than just building schedules or plans. They are not about purchasing silver bullets or secret weapons to increase productivity and involve more than quantification. They are more than about acquiring a methodology.

This insight relates to James Bailey's description of neural networks and what he refers to as "intermaths." He opens our eyes to what really happens on projects. Many activities occur in parallel. Each node influences others and, in turn, is influenced by others. Many factors are sprawling, that is, entailing more than a few variables. A different behavior then emerges. He further observes that additional values come from the relationships.[34]

To realize this requires the adoption of a multidisciplinary view of project management. This shift from specialization is a move towards holism, with a focus on relationships rather than parts, requiring a very different approach. Instead of striving for analytical predictability, project managers accept reality as they see it and experiment to see what happens, with the expressed purpose of interacting with the environment rather than imposing a contrived abstraction. That means recognizing a project as a dynamic interplay of the process, performance, product, and — most importantly — people. In fact, as proposed in my book, the constant emphasis is on people as playing the pivotal role in improving process, performance, and product.

Integration requires, therefore, that project managers truly become leaders. They must focus on results by recognizing that everything on a project must fit together to achieve goals and objectives. Some form of "relational holism" is sought, whereby all the elements are tied by some sort of connectedness.[35]

This insight does not mean, however, that individuals become subservient to the whole. Rather, an intricate relationship is engendered by project managers between the need to function as a whole while simultaneously allowing each component the opportunity for self-assertion.[36]

To do that, project managers must take a macroscopic view of their projects. They "look at the big picture." Looking at the big picture requires, however, more than just looking at the components of projects. It requires looking at their entire context, e.g., the context of an environment. It requires considering the external and internal environments of projects and not treating them as isolated entities. Project managers begin to see projects as open systems influenced by external and internal forces that can dramatically impact process, performance, product, and people. They become truly divergent as well as convergent thinkers.

This new paradigm requires that project managers become multidisciplinary. They must begin to view projects as a diverse group of people with a wide range of expertise, perspectives, working styles, and talents. Emphasis shifts from considering narrow aspects of projects by ensuring that one element, e.g., perspective, does not predominate at the expense of the others. This new orientation helps to preclude dysfunctional behavior, such as divisive power plays and Groupthink.

It also means that project managers start to recognize the importance of structure and the configuration of the basic elements of projects. In other words, viewing projects less as a means to impose an unrealistic organization and more of developing flexible and adaptable structures and configurations suitable to a changing environment. This new perspective is in line with the general systems theory, whereby reality is seen as one of highly integrated relationships. These relationships make it difficult to "explode" or break into smaller, or basic, elements.

The new paradigm means viewing projects as an effort to create what I refer to as "focused synergy." That is, looking at all the elements of a project and managing their relationships in such a way to ensure a greater likelihood of achieving desired results as opposed to treating a project as a mere assembly of the pieces. How do you know when that focused synergy exists? In the final analysis, it is whether projects achieve their goals and objectives in a manner that adds value to the larger organization.

Finally, the new paradigm takes a systemic view of project management. In order for project managers to look at their projects requires that they synthesize all the different elements in the most effective way via systems thinking. By viewing projects as systems, project managers have a more holistic perspective to identify the key elements of a project and how they interact with one another on micro and macro levels. Being systemic avoids the danger of falling into myopia and analysis paralysis by allowing project managers to adapt their projects to a dynamic environment. It also gives project managers the ability to effect change by manipulating the relationships among the elements, not just the elements themselves. A project is then viewed not as a machine but as a network of dynamic relationships.

## Nonlinear

The new paradigm recognizes that projects are systems where the relationships can become quite complex among all the elements. Under such a perspective, there is a need to acknowledge that predictability is very difficult. There are, for example, too many local and nonlocal variables that affect outcomes. The typical straight line, linear approach towards managing projects is viewed as too simplified because it is impossible to predict what will happen next due to the sheer number of variables with varying degrees of impact. For that reason, plans, like new cars driven off a lot, lose their value almost immediately. As mentioned earlier, the reason is that plans often reflect a static, linear view of a project.

Under the new paradigm, project managers recognize that projects exist in a dynamic rather than static environment that provides many implicit and explicit influences on process, performance, product, and people. Projects, therefore, go beyond a linear — almost arithmetic — view. They are a dynamic interplay of many factors, both quantitative and qualitative, with considerable integration.

Many project managers schooled in the prevailing paradigm view chaos as something to be tamed, even eliminated. Project managers go through unrelenting efforts to develop complex formulations and structures in the short run to help them gain control, only to find that these fail in the long run.

Under the new paradigm, project managers view change as neither positive nor negative. Rather, they see chaos as likely representing an underlying order that needs to be harnessed in such a way to achieve the goals and objectives of projects. In other words, change may mean opportunity as well as risk.

Variances are seen less as something to eliminate and more as a challenge that requires further inquiry. Such a perspective enables greater flexibility and adaptability when managing projects.

A nonlinear perspective recognizes the importance of nonquantitative factors in addition to quantitative ones. It means accepting the fact that, for instance, a decision is more than just looking at an "S" curve or calculating earned value. It can also impact process, performance, product, and people in different ways and degrees. Hence, a project becomes a dynamic rather than static system.

The key for managing a project under a nonlinear perspective is to view a project as a system consisting of a complex interplay of many elements and relationships. Using a systemic approach, project managers can better ascertain the quantitative and qualitative impacts from a dynamic perspective. They can then identify key elements to manage and lead projects. By identifying key elements, often referred to as critical success factors, they can take responsive action. Rather than attempt to impose a one-size-fits-all approach towards their projects, they can identify what needs to change and then monitor the impact once modified.

Nonlinearity, ironically, requires viewing projects as a network of networks among elements and not in the typical analytical, top-down mechanical vantage point. That means foregoing the often simple deterministic, stimulus-response perspective and taking a non-Boolean, non-Euclidean approach. Perhaps, most importantly, it recognizes that projects are, by their very nature, unique.

The bottom line is that projects do not lend themselves to extensive linear analysis. The complexity is too great in many ways and circumstances will just not allow it. It is quite difficult, if not impossible, to determine what will happen next. We are too immersed in the world; hence, our interaction seems more ad hoc and less linear.[37]

## Probability

If you subscribe to the notion that all projects operate in a dynamic environment and are themselves dynamic, precision is seen as futile. It is virtually impossible to predict the future quantitatively. Yet, as every project manager schooled in the prevailing paradigm knows, considerable effort is made to plan and manage projects according to some quantitative criteria. That is because neat formulas often do not adapt very well to dramatic changes to situations.[38] This effort is futile; the most seasoned project manager will admit that no or very few projects proceed according to plan, regardless of the precision of the numbers. There are too many variables and influences to consider. Even if project managers pursue precision, they find it virtually impossible to know whether it is based on accurate data and whether any calculations have reliability and validity.

Under the new paradigm, project managers can only hope for approximation at best. They know that it is fundamentally impossible to predict precisely what will happen. They also realize that projects and their environments are too dynamic to try to determine the perfect approach and execute that approach with precision. The best they can do is predict the odds about what the future will be and adjust accordingly while focusing on the goals and objectives of their projects.

They know that individual events cannot be determined at a precise time; only that they can occur at an approximate time. Much depends on the interplay of many discrete and continuous variables that enable an event to happen. The best that they can do is to predict the odds of an event happening under a given circumstance because of the ambiguity existing in a project environment. Any environment is constantly changing and nonlinear, replete with implicit and explicit influences. Besides, there are never enough data and information and, if available, they are often inaccurate.

Taking a probabilistic view of a project requires recognizing, therefore, that determinism on projects is impossible. Attempting such precision based on a deterministic view only increases the odds of failure, not success. About the best that project managers can do is treat plans and their executions as approximations to accomplish goals and objectives. That means, of course, recognizing the impact of nonmathematical influences and having a tolerance for risk and error.

Two key approaches to deal with the world of probability from a project management perspective are to apply ranges for estimates and to look for patterns.

Ranges are, by nature, approximations. They are admissions that precision is impossible. I liken them to the "bracketing" that I applied while in the army as an artillery officer. The idea is to shoot one or more rounds over the heads of the enemy and then several in front of it. Then, you select a middle point between the two positions and fire for effect, making adjustments according to the buffer that you established. Under the prevailing paradigm, many project managers act as if they can hit the target with the first shot. They seek precision, ironically, when working with estimates until they feel they are accurate, creating what is humorously and paradoxically called an "accurate estimate." Realistically, estimating is more of an effort to narrow down ranges and increase the probability of success being precise. It is more a matter of applying fuzzy mathematics and logic than calculating a precise value to predict the future.

Patterns also play an important role under the new paradigm. This requires not focusing on individual factors or events but rather looking at overall behavior from an "average" perspective. Average in this context means looking at what behavior was exhibited in the past and over time. A specific element is, of itself, insignificant. A general quality is then exhibited above and beyond a specific event or action. What is required is to look at the range of behavior over time. With this perspective, project managers avoid jumping to conclusions and stereotyping situations and events. They can also take a more integrated and macroscopic view of their projects, not treating variances and anomalies as something "bad" and reacting to specific situations.

The recognition of patterns is, however, no guarantee of predictability, only probability. Two patterns that are similar may, due to some seemingly innocuous action, have profound, unpredictable effects. However, overall similar patterns will likely produce similar results.[39] Pattern is also subjective because the human mind has a strong ability to develop a perception or pattern or order.[40]

## Subjectivity

Perhaps the most controversial characteristic of the new paradigm is this one — objectivity is impossible on a project. Even quantification itself is a subjective act because it represents a belief or value system of what is and is not important to measure. Consider the constant tug of war that occurs under the prevailing paradigm over cost, schedule, scope, and quality. Which is more important? What is deemed important reflects more the values of a project manager.

Subjectivity, therefore, requires acceptance that an intimate relationship exists between participants and phenomena experienced on projects. A possibility exists that more than one perception of reality exists, posing profound implications for the choices while managing projects.

Hence, a project is less about achieving objectivity in measurement and more about leading people to achieve a common objective. As such, projects require thinking in ways that involve shades of gray rather than operating on a false pretense of facts and data. Selecting facts and data is, above all, an expression of subjectivity and can, and often does, reflect what is wanted rather than needed.

Subjectivity is often reflected in the actual act of measuring in itself. Observers cannot divorce themselves from their environments. The very act of attempting to know something interferes with what is being measured. Many status review meetings come up with the answer everyone wants to hear, but not necessarily what they need to hear.

In an unprecedented age of having too much data and information, subjectivity may play an even more important role, particularly in regards to having the ability to see projects differently rather than seeking to find the right answer;

sheer volume of data in today's environment makes thinking and viewing reality differently more important than computing power to process it all.[41]

By recognizing that projects are exercises in subjectivity rather than objectivity, project managers can become more tolerant of diversity that exists on many projects. This diversity, of course, goes beyond race, religion, and sex. It also includes differences in thinking and working styles.

Recognizing the prominence of subjectivity on a project requires having a greater level of tolerance for such differences. Since there is less emphasis on finding a "right, precise" way of doing business and recognizing that there is more than one perception of reality, managing projects becomes less of a Win-Lose scenario and more of a Win-Win scenario.

Also by recognizing the subjectivity and diversity involved with managing projects, project managers understand the need to take an integrated perspective of projects. From a people perspective, that means involving different stakeholders in a way that generates commitment and ownership rather than forcing compliance via command and control. The goal becomes having people involved and focused on the end results rather than bickering over the details of a given process or procedure that often occurs under the prevailing paradigm. Once that happens, to use a jaded and often euphemistic term in Fortune 500 firms, empowerment becomes possible. Even prescriptive and normative considerations play a prominent role in the management of projects; perhaps more so than descriptive ones.

By acknowledging the subjective nature of projects, project managers can more easily identify and address qualitative factors (e.g., morale, esprit de corps) and balance them with quantifiable ones. They can also concentrate on inculcating a focused, balanced synergy by capitalizing on people's strengths and compensating for their weaknesses. Projects then become ways of meaning and teaming while simultaneously providing flexibility and adaptability.

## NEW IMPLICATIONS

There are a number of implications for subscribing to the new paradigm of project management.

### Redefinition of a Project

According to the prevailing paradigm, a project is a temporary endeavor to create something, e.g., a service or product. A project is something short lived based on balancing an eclectic selection of a series of tools, techniques, and principles. This definition leads to treating projects as an endeavor akin to getting the "damn thing built" and throwing the end result over the fence. It leads to a near-term myopic perspective that can have negative consequences beyond the completion of a project.

Under the new paradigm, quite simply, a project is redefined into something much broader in context by becoming a focused, integrated human endeavor to achieve a specific, common purpose.

A project is a *human endeavor* because it is, in the purest sense, a result of people using their energies to produce something. Without people, no project exists. Tools, techniques, or methodologies become merely means to an end, not the goal as is often the case.

A project is focused in that all the human resources are employed in a manner that achieves desired results. All decisions and actions are taken in the context of furthering the purpose of a project. Without focus, a project can become (or not become) an exercise in efficiency but also ineffectiveness. When that happens, of course, projects begin to have a life of their own.

A project is *integrated* in that all decisions and activities are interdependent. A project does not have to be viewed as a balancing act of seemingly disconnected elements. Often, projects are seen as exercises of suboptimization, trade-off, and zero sum results. Someone or something wins and someone or something else loses. An integrated view necessitates taking a more holistic perspective that recognizes that decisions and actions have impacts. Managing a project becomes less of a juggling act and more of a deliberate, orchestrated approach.

Finally, a project achieves a *specific purpose*. From that perspective, all energies and efforts of a project are oriented towards achieving something that is shared among all stakeholders. Consequently, a project becomes an endeavor that not only achieves its own goal, but also furthers more expansive goals, such as those of a higher organization. A project cannot operate, in other words, as an island; its purpose should be aligned with a parent organization and stakeholders. Otherwise, a project will not only lack commitment from the "higher" ranks of the institution, but also the "lower" ranks, such as the team members.

## Results

The secret weapon or the perfect process no longer becomes the center of attention. Excellence comes from delivering a product or service that achieves a desired result. Unfortunately, having the best tool or most efficient process often becomes the end in itself, especially on technical projects. A tool or technique, for example, may generate code efficiently and ease the work of developers, but it may still generate something that fails to further the goal of a project. In other words, it results in "gold plating" a process as well as a product or service.

According to the new paradigm, decisions regarding the selection of tools, methods, and even people are oriented towards achieving desired results, not perfecting an activity unless, of course, it directly contributes towards achieving desired results.

## Interdependence

The new paradigm places less value on defining all the elements of a project in precise detail and more on how to define and improve their relationships to achieve desired results. The key to accomplishing that is to identify and improve relationships among the major elements of a project, whether resource, tool, technique, or methodology. Such items, therefore, are seen as enablers to improve relationships to achieve a common goal. Strengths become important as enablers and weaknesses as an opportunity to move forward.

James Bailey illustrates the concept clearly when discussing a flock of birds. In the past, the belief was that a flock of birds followed a leader. It has become increasingly clear, however, that each bird does not key off the leader but its neighbors, creating an overall behavior for the flock.[42]

Interdependence, from a project perspective of course, is more than a flock of birds moving in unison. It may be more a matter of mutual success and based on a symbiotic relationship.[43]

## Why

Under the prevailing paradigm, too much emphasis is placed on determining what must be done. This emphasis has led not only to implementing counter-productive tools, techniques, and methodologies, but also shackling the performance by instituting bureaucracy. The question should be, first of all: Why? Why a certain level of detail in planning? Why a decision to accept or reject a variance that has arisen? By asking why, the basis for a tool, technique, or methodology is questioned over whether it advances the goals of a project.

I once attended an effective listening class at a Fortune 500 training facility. The instructor, although very good, said that the most dangerous word to use in a business environment is "why" because asking such a question can make people defensive. I disagree. That question should be asked constantly, especially on projects. And everyone should ask it. Asking why, of course, is not a rebellion if the intent is to determine if something contributes towards achieving desired results. Only then will a project perform both efficiently and effectively.

The ability to ask why is very important from a motivational standpoint by giving meaning to people. The message from the holy mountain does little good in furthering ownership and commitment. Project managers can provide the necessary meaning by constantly asking the question for themselves and on behalf of others.

## Responsiveness

As discussed, project management has often been an attempt to force feed tools, techniques, and concepts on projects without really contributing to the goals of projects. Situated in a dynamic environment, projects can easily deviate from plans. In reaction, "more of the same" is implemented which, ironically, does not really change anything other than worsening a situation. More merely becomes symptomatic of reaction.

Under the new paradigm, more does not equate with better because a project and its environment are considered dynamic. The emphasis on responsiveness is achieved by determining why certain actions must happen. These actions are the ones that provide the most leverage to achieve desired results. By selecting the action that provides the most leverage, projects can function both efficiently and effectively.

Basically, a project functions as an adaptive structure, whereby as a system it adjusts to its environment based on feedback. A system then adjusts or optimizes itself to its environment.

This ability to adapt to its environment enables survivability. Clearly, then, systems that are so rigidly adapted to their environments are the ones most vulnerable to dramatic changes in the environment.[44] Systems that are most flexible in response to their environment have a higher probability of survival.

## Qualitative

The new paradigm recognizes that quantification is not the only driver of a project. In fact, it recognizes that quantification is reflective, if anything, of qualitative factors such as beliefs and values. The very decision on what to measure and the very selection of the measure itself is a qualitative decision and is affected by actions taken.

The criticality of the qualitative aspects is reflected in the importance of the people side of project management. Failure to successfully handle it can wreak havoc. As an information technology (IT) and operations auditor, the folly of relying on the quantitative aspects at the expense of people was often revealed to me. I have seen measures that reflected great efficiencies at the expense of effectiveness. What I discovered was that numbers only told part of a story. How the people performed on a project sometimes, and frequently, painted a different picture from what the numbers revealed. Frequently, the deciding factors on the performance of a project were items that were not directly measurable, such as the leadership abilities of project managers, constraints not readily quantifiable, and lack of political support from corporate headquarters.

## Dynamic

Under the new paradigm, projects are seen as dynamic entities. They are constantly going in and out of equilibrium due to interactions among their elements and their environment. At each point in the project life cycle, projects respond to changes differently. For example, membership among the stakeholders can constantly change, causing a shift in priorities. International events, seemingly remote to a team located in the basement of a large complex, may impact the team dramatically. Nonlocal factors can impact local environments and sometimes vice versa. The point here is that a project and its environment constantly changes and the new paradigm stresses acceptance of this reality.

Many project managers who subscribe to the prevailing paradigm view it as blasphemy. That is because a salient concept of management in general and project management in particular has an unrealistic emphasis on maintaining control. The idea is to impose a structure that requires an almost teleological, absolutist perspective. Subscribing to this perspective can result in a constant war of imposing rather than adapting project management principles and practices on projects. As discussed, such an approach can, and often does, prove counterproductive because it fails to enable project managers to be flexible and adaptable. The key is to apply the right approach at the right time at the right level, which is contingent on adapting to the dynamics of a project and its environment.

## People

Above all, the new paradigm stresses putting people at the center of a project. Without the willful participation of stakeholders, projects will inevitably fail or if they succeed, they do so at great cost. People are not seen as just another resource. They are the main resource, not time, money, or equipment. Under the prevailing paradigm, however, the people side so often receives lip service and the attention soon focuses on the "hard" side of project management. Yet, it is people who must participate not only in the formulation of plans, but also in the implementation of all the tools, techniques, and practices of project management. Without their agreement, project management becomes nothing more than an administrative exercise.

Under the prevailing paradigm, many of the causes of failures, e.g., unclear scope and poor scheduling, appear to relate to the hard side of project management. After careful assessment, however, such failures are manifestations of a failure in leadership. As long as the project managers subscribe to the prevailing paradigm, problems will continue to reappear because project managers are not addressing the real source of the problem — leadership.

James Bailey likens the current circumstance to one of a parent facing what he calls shades of gray. A need exists for the psyche of each sibling to work together with various groups and cultures in different, complex ways that require considerable adaptation.[45] The challenge for project managers is to move everyone in the same direction to focus on a common goal.

Out of the behavior of individuals comes a unique behavior in and of itself. The relationship between the person and his or her setting becomes important but not easy. It will not be easy because there will always be, at least potentially, different permutations of the relationships, thanks to the wide variety of people at different moments in time. The group behavior is different than the sum of all the individual behaviors added together. Looking at individual behavior does not lend itself to understanding and predicting group behavior.[46] This unique, group behavior impedes individuals to act rationally because they are constrained by the actions of others.[47] Out of this diversity come patterns of behavior. The struggle, therefore, is for project managers to manage the diverse relationships that exist on a project in such a way that furthers, not constrains, goal attainment.

## BALANCE

No longer do project managers have to exercise negative power indiscriminately and in a way that is counterproductive towards their projects and themselves. Margaret Wheatley says that the quality of the relationship is what makes the difference. If the "stick" is used, negative energy is evoked; if the "carrot" is used, then positive energy.[48]

Project leadership, of course, is not something that simply pops up on projects. It requires a paradigm shift. This paradigm shift is in line with what the contemporary scholars and practitioners have come to believe constitutes the patterns of leadership.

## CASE STUDY: SHIFT

XYZ Corporation was not averse to taking calculated risks to pursue new products in the market place. In terms of overall management philosophy about operations, however, it was solidly conservative. After more than five decades of history, tradition, and success, the operational side of the business contributed to this conservatism. The company rarely instituted change on a large scale and, when it did, success was marginal.

To a large extent, each of the business units operated fairly autonomously from headquarters and each was staffed with its own president and executive council. Past projects, sponsored by corporate, had previously attempted to manage large-scale business projects but with very little success. Projects invariably failed when headquarters tried to exercise a command and control approach. The project manager knew right away that the command and control approach would not work; a more collaborative approach might work.

Like many manufacturing and engineering firms, the firm emphasized perfection, analysis, logic, precision, and being systematic on projects. The "softer side" of projects was frequently overlooked. The project manager, to avoid past mistakes, shifted the orientation to a more integrative, nonlinear, and systemic one that was amenable to subjective factors. Doing otherwise would generate similar results of the large-scale projects that failed — progress would slow, roadblocks arise, and poor performance result, e.g., exceed budget, slide schedules, and cause rework.

The approach needed, therefore, was the participation by other team members from business units. The vehicle to achieve that was through participation when developing the project's vision and plan. The project manager knew that through greater involvement would come more ownership and commitment and less resistance to the implementation of a new policies and procedures infrastructure.

## REFERENCES

1. Rosemary Cafasso, Few IS projects come in on time, *Computerworld,* p. 20, December 12, 1994.
2. Ibid.
3. Jim Johnson, Turning chaos into success, *Software Magazine,* pp. 30–39, December 1999.
4. Robert L. Glass, Short-term and long-term remedies for runaway projects, *Communications of the ACM,* pp. 13–15, July 1998.
5. Survey looks at what projects lack, *PM Network,* p. 11, September 2000.
6. Thomas Kuhn, *The Structure of Scientific Revolutions,* University of Chicago Press, Chicago, 1970.
7. Joel Barker, *Paradigms,* HarperBusiness, New York, 1993, pp. 31–32.
8. Lauri Koskela and Greg Howell, The underlying theory of project management is obsolete, in *Proceedings of PMI Research Conference 2002,* Project Management Institute, Newtown Square, PA, p. 299.
9. Bruno Urli and Didier Urli, Project management in North America, stability of the concepts, *Project Management Journal,* p. 33, September 2000.

10. Lauri Koskela and Greg Howell, The underlying theory of project management is obsolete, in *Proceedings of PMI Research Conference 2002,* Project Management Institute, Newtown Square, PA, p. 300.
11. Bruno Urli and Didier Urli, Project management in North America, stability of the concepts, *Project Management Journal,* p. 37, September 2000.
12. Pernille Eskerod and Katarina Ostergren, Why do companies standardize project work? *Project Management,* 6(1), 36, 2000.
13. Alberto Melgrati and Mario Damiani, Rethinking the project management framework: new epistemology, new insights, in *Proceedings of PMI Research Conference 2002,* Project Management Institute, Newtown Square, PA, p. 378.
14. Connie L. Delisle and Janice L. Thomas, Success: getting traction in a turbulent business climate, in *Proceedings of the PMI Research Conference 2002,* Project Management Institute, Newtown Square, PA, p. 193.
15. Peter W.G. Morris, Why project management doesn't always make good business sense, *Project Management,* p. 12, January 1998.
16. Pernille Eskerod and Katarina Ostergren, Why do companies standardize project work? *Project Management,* 6(1), 34, 2000.
17. Peter W.G. Morris, Why project management doesn't always make good business sense, *Project Management,* p. 12, January 1998.
18. Christopher Bredillet, Mapping the dynamics of project management field: project management in action, in *Proceedings of the PMI Research Conference 2002,* Project Management Institute, Newtown Square, PA, p. 158.
19. Kate Belzer, http://www.pmforum.org/library/papers/BusinessSuccess.htm
20. Peter W.G. Morris, Why project management doesn't always make good business sense, *Project Management,* p. 14, January 1998.
21. Jeannette Cabanis, Passion beats planning, limiting scope is stupid, women rule…, *PM Network,* pp. 30–31, September 1998.
22. Ibid., p. 67.
23. Fritjof Capra, *The Turning Point,* Bantam Books, Toronto, 1988, p. 47.
24. Margaret J. Wheatley, *Leadership and the New Science,* Berrett-Koehler, San Francisco, 1994, p. 6.
25. Ibid., p. 21.
26. Ibid., p. 63.
27. Ibid., p. 140.
28. James Bailey, *After Thought,* Basic Books, New York, 1996, p. 27.
29. Ibid., p. 163.
30. Margaret J. Wheatley, *Leadership and the New Science,* Berrett-Koehler, San Francisco, 1994, p. 27.
31. James Bailey, *After Thought,* Basic Books, New York, 1996, p. 78.
32. Ibid., p. 46.
33. Kam Jugdev, Janice Thomas, and Connie Delisle, Rethinking project management: old truths and new insights, *Project Management,* 7(1), 36–43, 2001.
34. James Bailey, *After Thought,* Basic Books, New York, 1996, p. 133.
35. Ibid., p. 118.
36. Fritjof Capra, *The Turning Point,* Bantam Books, Toronto, 1988, p. 43.

37. James Bailey, *After Thought,* Basic Books, New York, 1996, pp. 173–174.
38. Ibid., p. 187.
39. Ibid., p. 146.
40. Fritjof Capra, *The Turning Point,* Bantam Books, Toronto, 1988, p. 95.
41. James Bailey, *After Thought,* Basic Books, New York, 1996, p. 203.
42. Ibid., p. 151.
43. Fritjof Capra, *The Turning Point,* Bantam Books, Toronto, 1988, p. 278.
44. Ibid., p. 149.
45. James Bailey, *After Thought,* Basic Books, New York, 1996, p. 174.
46. Ibid., p. 177.
47. Ibid., p. 180.
48. Margaret J. Wheatley, *Leadership and the New Science,* Berrett-Koehler, San Francisco, 1994, p. 39.

# 4

# VISUALIZE

There is a saying, apparently in *Alice in Wonderland,* that if you do not know where you are going, any path will get you there. It is amazing how many projects have no vision or concept of their destination, let alone their path. This lack of vision contributes to so many downstream problems and dismal results — poor quality, schedule slides, budget slides, high turnover — to name a few.

## NO BLURRED VISION

Several reasons explain why vision is so difficult to achieve on a project. The insights are as numerous as the consequences.

Dr. William Leban identifies four reasons why projects fail, each directly or indirectly associated with a poorly defined or missing vision:

- Improper definition and scope
- Improper systems usage of information
- Inefficient resource usage
- Poor communication of activities[1]

In *Information Strategy,* Nancy Settle-Murphy and Caroline Thornton identified four project "sinkholes":

- Competing and shifting priorities
- Lack of clarity articulating expectations
- No process for problem resolution and feedback
- Vague or conflicting project definition and scope[2]

## RIGHT START

Based on my experience, I feel all the above findings have merit. While I will not agree that a poor or nonexistent vision contributes to all of the problems on projects, I will say that it adds to many of them and the magnitude of their impacts. I also feel the above lists are incomplete. A poor or nonexistent vision can also cause a lack of focus on priorities, not determining priorities and thereby treating everything of equal performance, overlooking explicit and implicit elements or factors affecting projects, setting unrealistic goals and objectives, allowing scope creep, enabling biases to dominate thinking, causing negative conflict to surface, and, perhaps most importantly, sacrificing that Wow! experience that Tom Peters advocates the need to experience on projects.

However, I do not believe that the ultimate cause is a poorly defined or missing vision. Rather, it is a lack of leadership by the project manager to develop a shared vision that provides destination and meaning to stakeholders.

Many of the general leadership theorists emphasize the importance of leaders to provide a vision for an organization. Kouzes and Posner, Bennis and Nanus, and Gardner are prime examples of theorists and practitioners emphasizing this need. So, too, do project leadership theorists and practitioners like Briner, Geddes, Hastings, and Gadeken.

Without having a clear, definitive vision, the consequences are quite obvious. But what about having a vision? What are the consequences?

Many. To a large degree, they provide the opposite effects of an ill-defined or missing vision.

Perhaps most importantly, a vision augments the efficiency and effectiveness of stakeholders by providing meaning, generating commitment, obtaining buy-in, encouraging collaboration and communication, reducing conflict by clarifying priorities and values, sharing and understanding different perspectives, laying the groundwork for building processes and procedures, raising and framing issues and questions, offering a basis for communication, identifying of value most or all stakeholders, establishing rapport, laying the foundation for harmonious working relationships, and building greater trust and synergy.

The actual process and effort to develop vision also adds value. Values include challenging assumptions to determine their relevance and accuracy, identifying and addressing risks early, defining the purpose and scope of a project, involving key stakeholders, creating a common baseline for developing plans and controlling projects, raising and addressing business and technical issues, pinpointing potential opportunities for coordinating projects, and, perhaps most importantly, reducing the negative and augmenting the positive effects of decisions made early on a project.

## REASONS FOR FAILURE

With all the benefits of having a vision, why do many project managers fail to assume the leadership role in developing a shared vision up front?

One reason is that many project managers subscribe to the prevailing paradigm of analysis, precision, and perfection. They view defining a vision as something too wishy-washy or touchy-feely; as some nonquantifiable abstraction. Instead, they focus on the explicit, not implicit, side of project management.

Under the new paradigm of project management, the emphasis shifts to the implicit aspects of projects, recognizing that a project involves integrated, nonlinear thinking. This recognition acknowledges the existence of subjective factors in achieving results.

Interestingly, many project managers, if they do attempt to develop a vision, stress the quantitative factors. If anything is not measurable, it is omitted. Or they include many qualitative factors that are so high level that it is impossible to ascertain progress or successful completion. In the former case, a vision will likely fail to elicit passion, commitment, ownership, or engage people. In the latter case, they leave too much open to interpretation; provide the opportunity for disagreement (especially over semantics); allow for a lack of focus; and yield to unrealistic demands related to scope, quality, schedule, and cost.

A good vision requires a balance of the qualitative and the quantitative, reflecting these attributes:

- Allow visualization using both (left and right) hemispheres of the brain
- Be clear, that is, understandable
- Have an emotional meaning to stakeholders
- Offer tangible (e.g., measurable) and intangible (e.g., abstract) contents
- Provide the basis to align and focus all project energies and efforts

## SHARED VISION

Of course, a vision is not an immortal abstraction, impervious to change. It, too, may change as a project progresses through its life cycle, especially as stakeholders and the environment change. Hence, project leaders ensure that visions not only have the characteristics just discussed, but they must also be based on feedback regarding changes in the environment in which the project is being executed.

Perhaps the biggest challenge facing project managers when developing a vision for their projects is getting stakeholders passionate about it. With passion they will likely invest the necessary time, energy, and emotion in making the vision a reality.

The key is to share in a vision's development, that is, to elicit participation in its construction. The idea is to have each stakeholder formulate a vision that links to the project's. A shared vision will not make it just "their vision" but my "own vision." People then have a passion for the vision. As Covey notes in *First Things First,* a shared vision creates a passion and synergy that releases energy and talent, creating an order all its own. Trying to control, however, often creates just the opposite result.[3]

Of course, passion requires focus for achieving a vision. Although what Shakti describes is on a personal level, his comments also apply to projects in which vision, passion, and focus mix in a way that creates dramatic results. Shakti notes that imagination creates a picture and through "creative visualization" a person realizes that picture through focus until the picture becomes a reality.[4]

Unfortunately, many visions lack buy-in and commitment of key stakeholders on the same level of a personal vision. Instead, visions often reside in the minds of a few individuals and, consequently, have value only to a limited number of people. A few individuals proclaim it and assume that it generates the level of meaning and passion to others. Many visions, consequently, then sit on a shelf, sometimes even forgotten by the original authors. These projects end up having a "life of their own" and lack focus. When completed, the results frequently have no relationship between what was wanted or desired and what was actually delivered.

To develop and implement a vision for their projects, project managers should seek involvement and commitment regarding the vision of their projects. While most project managers would agree that a vision for projects is very important, few appreciate the need for involvement and commitment. Instead, many project managers accept a vision that someone else developed or they develop one alone. Either way, few stakeholders have any input into it.

Consequences can be severe without involvement and commitment. Stakeholders treat the vision as some type of remote abstraction, meaningful only to a select few. A small number of people may refer to it while planning and executing a project. That encourages a sense of rising expectations, leads to a lack of emotional commitment to its realization, leaves the opportunity for different interpretations that cause scope creep, mistakenly interprets silence as acceptance or concurrence, or leads to nonproductive arguments over semantics.

Obtaining consensus over a vision is not an easy task and perhaps that is the reason many project managers avoid it. There are many challenges including: verifying that a vision's contents are valid and reliable; interpreting contents differently due to varied backgrounds and perspectives; overemphasizing some aspects at the expense of others; disagreeing over what constitutes an achievable goal and objective; succumbing to pressures to accept a vision because it is quicker and cheaper; failing to distinguish wants from needs, resulting in "satisficing" through the life cycle of projects; and not defining and controlling scope.

For project managers, the project charter is the principal mechanism to identify the vision of a project. Its contents should identify the principal stakeholders, major milestones, goals and objectives, expected deliverables, major assumptions, risks, constraints, major responsibilities, and any other useful information.

Consensus, of course, is easier said than done. Stakeholders vary in perspectives, mental models, or frames; sometimes they have a self-interest orientation, e.g., WIIFM (what's in it for me); conduct rivalries for visibility and resources and may have competing projects; and operate according to hidden agendas. In addition, project managers must deal with history of poor project acceptance and performance due to "politics," splintered and unenthusiastic customers, and low morale; inclement economic conditions; poor availability and lack of sharing information; bad timing in general to put vision together, e.g., downturn in employment; and an atmosphere of distrust. If not enough, project managers must deal with the pervasive presence of informal networks that can help or hinder defining a project vision. If a vision is not clear or meaningful it can also lead to disunity and weakness in response.

## ETERNAL VISION

To develop and implement an effective, lasting vision, project managers should remember these points.

First of all, project managers must recognize that a vision is value based whether developed alone or with a group. It reflects what stakeholders consider important at a particular point in time. Often, a vision may have conflicting values that should be addressed during its development and resolved during the project's life cycle. For example, a vision may stress quality while simultaneously seeking to produce results as cheaply as possible. Project managers will often continually find themselves dealing with such circumstances.

Conflicting values in a vision really represent the multiple perspectives of stakeholders who participate in its development. People from a financial organization will stress costs, for example, while those from a technical organization might stress technique. All perspectives are correct and incorrect simultaneously because each one sees their own "piece" of reality. A project manager must be mentally prepared to deal with value-based conflicts and differences.

They must also lay the groundwork for building and sustaining openness and trust when developing a vision. Most stakeholders come with their own motives to participate. These motives are accompanied by emotions like fear, impatience, and intolerance. Project managers must work with all to achieve results. They must exercise good listening, conflict management, and empathic skills. In addition, they must encourage the sharing of information and concerns to overcome or break down the "walls of differences." Failure in this regard will only hinder progress, leading to a lack of consensus that translates into less buy-in and commitment.

Project managers must also recognize that a vision involves many variables to consider. Project managers must be particularly mindful of their influence on the overall quality of a vision and the commitment behind its execution. Variables include a willingness by stakeholders to develop a vision in the first place and their ability to implement it; their perspectives about a project; their overriding beliefs, values, mores, norms; circumstances concerning its implementation, e.g., economic climate; timing of the project; and strategic considerations.

A collaborative approach is clearly important. Since stakeholders will have different reasons to support a project and will likely take different perspectives, project managers should encourage stakeholders to work together. Project managers must identify mutual interests like goals and objectives while simultaneously dealing with emotional ones, requiring good conflict management and negotiation skills. They should also stress this need for stakeholders to exercise the same on the project. Because visions are value based, it becomes even more imperative that everyone exercises these skills. Project managers, by virtue of their position, must exercise them more adroitly since they are the "glue" holding everyone together.

Focusing on requirements for a vision offers many obvious benefits. It can raise the discussions to a higher level by depersonalizing them and generating opportunities to achieve genuine consensus over its contents. Some of the major contents of a vision should include goals and objectives, roles, responsibilities, scope, assumptions, constraints, risks, deliverables, and budget and schedule requirements. By focusing on these elements, there is less chance for negative conflict and greater opportunity for reaching consensus. However, it is easier to deal with any negative conflict early and forthrightly, rather than later when it is impacting progress at a critical point.

Seeking a Win-Win vision naturally follows the last point. Project managers should seek a vision that all parties feel comfortable with. They should feel that the vision serves individual interests as much as possible. It is imperative, therefore, that project managers exercise good principles of negotiation and collaboration so stakeholders, especially key stakeholders, do not feel they have capitulated, compromised, or been dominated into submission, which only results in a lack of buy-in and commitment.

Taking a wide-angle perspective is important for everyone. With a wide-angle perspective, e.g., seeing the big picture, project managers can avoid taking sides or getting involved in petty squabbles. Other stakeholders can "rise above the occasion" and seek mutual interests.

Involving the right stakeholders is very important when developing and executing a vision. Stakeholders are, of course, people or organizations that have an interest in a project. If the right stakeholders are not involved, resistance will assuredly arise, especially if something is very disagreeable with the vision.

By virtue of their position, project managers are the ones who can serve as a bridge to bring all the right stakeholders together to develop a vision. These stakeholders may be internal, such as a project champion or sponsor, or external, such as a customer representative or member of another project dependent on a deliverable from another project. Stakeholders can also be formal, informal, or both. Formal stakeholders are easily identifiable on any organizational chart. Informal stakeholders are those less easily identifiable. These are usually people who "get things done" or brokers who can provide information or insights that are not readily available and frequently do not appear on a formal organizational chart.

Managing relationships among stakeholders is absolutely crucial when developing and executing a vision. Indeed, like cost, schedule, and quality, relationships are often referred to as the fourth constraint of project management. The more complex a project, the greater the constraint in managing them. A high correlation exists between the complexity of a project and the complexity of relationships; project managers must strengthen this correlation in a way that leads to successful results.

When developing the vision, project managers can best manage relationships by assuming partnership and stewardship perspectives. With a partnership perspective, they can identify opportunities to further mutual interests among all stakeholders. With a stewardship perspective, they can lead by persuasion rather than manage through control. To effectively take on both perspectives, however, project managers must encourage interdependence, not independence, among stakeholders so the vision will generate synergy.

Understanding the Tuchman Model for teaming can help give project managers and other stakeholders some understanding about managing relationship patience when developing a vision. According to the model, teaming progresses through four successive phases to various degrees: Forming, Storming, Norming, and Performing. The Forming phase occurs when people assemble for the first time, representing more of a committee rather than a team.

The Storming phase occurs when people start to "battle" over turf and details. The Norming phase occurs when members are ready to achieve goals cooperatively. The Performing phase occurs when everyone focuses on goals and is receptive to new ideas. Of course, project managers want all phases to go smoothly. However, that is not possible. Instead, they should concentrate on ensuring that the Forming and Storming phases have progressed as smoothly as possible. It is at these two phases, especially when developing a vision, that project managers should exercise good skills in negotiating, conflict management, effective listening, and collaboration. Failure to apply these skills successfully can result in a vision that lacks buy-in or commitment.

Understanding the context of a project can help. It ties directly to the recognition that building a vision involves many variables. But identifying variables is only one step. The other one is understanding emotions. Project managers must listen for explicit and implicit variables to ascertain their meaning and significance to a project. Explicit variables are, of course, factors like strategy and resource availability. Implicit variables are less obvious, such as political relationships and informal networks. Project managers must not only be able to identify both, but must also determine their significance. Failure to appreciate these variables can add complications later in the project life cycle. Hence, it is wise to heed the advice of Stephen Covey: seek first to understand, then be understood.[5]

Being realistic about the vision can also help. Too often, visions can raise expectations unrealistically only to be dashed later when a project ends. The best way to avoid rising expectations is to recognize what is and is not achievable realistically. If a vision is unrealistic, any effort on a project, however heroic, will likely be perceived a failure.

Scoping, therefore, is very important. An excellent way to ensure that expectations remain under control is to consider Covey's notion of the Circle of Influence and Circle of Concern. The Circle of Concern consists of items on which stakeholders lack any direct influence; the items are so remote that no matter what happens, it is impossible to affect anything. The Circle of Influence, however, consists of items that they can affect, such as the strategic direction of a project. Good scoping via stakeholder participation can help define both circles. Stakeholders then determine what aspects of a project they can influence either directly or indirectly and what aspects of a project they can truly control. This perspective gives stakeholders a sense of being proactive, or responsive, to project requirements. They will be better able to function more effectively, identify obstacles, and determine useful strategies to deal with them.

Seeking buy-in is absolutely essential to realize a vision. This buy-in must go beyond the mere tokenism of nodding heads, but also does not mean complete agreement. What it does mean is having concurrence or consensus. The difference is that agreement encourages blatant acquiescence but not necessarily acceptance, while the latter recognition exists despite reservations and, therefore, proceeds accordingly. Mere compliance does not engender lasting adherence since once the threat of punishment for noncompliance is lifted, people deviate from the vision. With consensus, stakeholders feel that, albeit not perfect, they have consented to support it and the commitment will last longer and require less oversight. Vision becomes essentially the policeman and not a clique of stakeholders trying to control all activities.

Finally, keeping the vision in the forefront of everyone's mind is necessary. Even with extensive buy-in and commitment, the "fog of managing a project" can cause people to lose sight of a vision. Project managers must encourage stakeholders to revisit it constantly during a project. They should also encourage decision making and reinforce commitment by focusing all project activities around it. This approach prevents scope creep and avoids the tendency to concentrate on activities of a lesser priority. Project managers must also continuously communicate the vision, such as placing it on a project wall or on a web site.

## PROJECT VISION MAKING

Keeping these prerequisites in mind, how can project managers develop an effective vision? One of the best approaches that I have applied is to hold a facilitated workshop with all key stakeholders.

I refer to the workshop as the project vision workshop, or PVW. The PVW has several goals. The first and foremost goal is to obtain consensus over the overall vision of the project. Other goals include:

- Build esprit de corps and morale
- Deal with expectations and assumptions up front
- Engender a sense of purpose and direction
- Enhance communications and rapport
- Generate enthusiasm and support
- Identify priorities
- Obtain a realistic appraisal of the circumstances
- Provide the groundwork to build an effective plan
- Seek buy-in and commitment
- Share and clarify information, ideas, concerns, and challenges

These goals, of course, are easier to list than to realize. Nevertheless, you can follow three simple steps to help you to define a vision and to encourage everyone to accept it. I have very successfully applied this general approach on small, medium, and large technical and business management projects. The three steps are:

- Step #1: Prepare
  - ☐ Identify the key stakeholders to attend
  - ☐ Determine the contents of the vision
  - ☐ Plan the mechanics
- Step # 2: Execute
  - ☐ Apply good "people skills"
  - ☐ Keep the focus on the big picture
- Step #3: Act
  - ☐ Bring closure by seeking buy-in and commitment

## Prepare

To some degree, a PVW is a project in itself. Like all projects, the key to success is planning. By planning, project managers can avoid the disasters that often affect other workshops that I have attended: having the wrong people attend or missing key ones; selecting an inappropriate time and place; lacking supplies, equipment, and information; disregarding obvious significant issues; taking way too much time; and, perhaps most frustrating, generating no results. In this section of the chapter, I will focus less on the mechanics of setting up a workshop and more on the people issues and how project managers can deal with them.

### Identify the Key Stakeholders to Attend

A stakeholder is a person or organization who will be affected by the outcome of a project, either directly or indirectly. A direct impact can range anywhere from people building a product to an organization applying a product in a work environment. An indirect impact might be someone from a portfolio management group within an organization.

To identify the stakeholders, consider the many roles on a project. They include project executives, sponsors, and champions; customers; suppliers; contractors; potential core team members; functional managers; subject matter experts; and, of course, the project manager and other project managers affected by a project.

Perhaps the easiest way to identify stakeholders is to look at organizational charts. These charts will reveal who will have an interest. Another source is to look at the organizational charters. These will provide some idea of their mission, goals, and objectives. This approach is particularly useful for cross-functional projects, where resources may eventually be pulled from different organizations.

It is very important not to stick to stakeholders from a formal hierarchy. Some stakeholders who may be "low on the totem pole" can have tremendous influence, politically or technically. The informal network is often ignored at the peril of many project managers who often lack formal command and control over people. In *Harvard Business Review,* Rob Cross and Laurence Prusak note that most institutions consider informal networks negatively, thereby inhibiting progress. Consequently, executive and managers try to ignore or bypass them.[6] Project managers who ignore this insight will experience considerable frustration.

Cross and Prusak identify, using social network analysis, four types of people who play important roles in informal networks. A Central Connector is a person with whom others communicate the most. A Boundary Spanner is an "emissary" who connects with others throughout an organization. An Information Broker is a person who realizes that information is power and uses it accordingly. A Peripheral Specialist is the subject matter expert.[7]

Whatever the categories of "movers and shakers" in an informal network, the principal point is that project managers cannot ignore them. The challenge is how to identify them. There are some ways to do this without conducting academic studies. Project managers can first talk with potential formal stakeholders and ask for recommendations of whom else to invite. They can also use their own experience on other projects.

As a side note, one of the most important actions that project managers can take is to develop a formal or informal dossier on each stakeholder. This dossier might contain information like history of working relationships with other stakeholders, type and degree of relationships, historical performance on projects of a similar nature, and potential reasons for support or opposition to a project.

It is very important to identify the extent to which stakeholders might or might not support a project. A good approach is to develop a grid like the one described by Fred Borgiani. It involves creating a matrix that consists of a vertical axis representing the level of support needed and the level of support expected.[8] The matrix might reflect a combination of active and passive supporters and nonsupporters. Armed with this matrix, project managers can understand the reasons behind the support or opposition and anticipate any challenges that might arise.

### Determine the Contents of the Vision

The basic contents of a vision, or project charter, are relatively easy to identify. They are goals and objectives, scope, the overall strategy, assumptions, deliverables, roles and responsibilities, constraints, risks, and just about anything else deemed important. The difficulty is dealing with people side issues.

Identifying goals and objectives makes common sense, but the very act can pose considerable challenges. Some challenges include understanding the difference between goals and objectives, embracing conflicting goals and objectives, ill-defining goals and objectives, adopting unrealistic goals and objectives, and keeping focus on goals and objectives while developing the vision. Sometimes goals and objectives adopted are unrealistic or ill defined, raising questions over whether or not they have been achieved.

Of all the challenges facing goals and objectives listed above, two of them can seriously impact developing and executing a vision. Project managers should be mindful of them during the PVW.

The first one often overlooked is the interdependence of goals. Frequently, people treat them as being separate. Interdependence of goals may be positive or negative. For example, the pursuit of one goal may impede the achievement of another, e.g., reduce schedule flow time and keep costs to a minimum.

The other one is the lack of specificity, at least not enough to be useful. In *The Logic of Failure,* Dorner writes that exploding an unclear goal into discrete elements could have unintended effects. The result is that no criteria will then exist to determine actual progress.[9]

Scope definition is closely tied with goals and objectives. Unfortunately, sometimes some very important "oversights" occur. Because goals and objectives are not clearly defined, for example, the adopted scope could expand since its boundaries are vague, leading to misinterpretation. This enlargement of scope is known as scope creep. If poorly defined, scope will also lead to unrealistic plans by adding work.

Overall strategy is the general approach to achieve goals and objectives. The challenge facing project managers when determining strategy is that a lack of relationship exists between goals and objectives and the adopted strategy. Some people will confuse strategy with goals and objectives, bringing discussions to a halt. If strategy is merely dictated by a few stakeholders, commitment by others will be lacking. In addition, stakeholders often confuse strategy with techniques or tools. If this happens, stakeholders can fall into the trap of concentrating on the details at the expense of looking at the big picture. Consensus, consequently, becomes more difficult to achieve.

Another important danger is developing a strategy out of context, e.g., not considering the business conditions. This situation is known as deconditioning, that is, removing the decision from the context that affects it. The result is the adoption of an unrealistic strategy. Dorner observes that it could hinder adaptability to context because measurement and action may no longer apply to changing circumstances. This need for adaptability, however, often conflicts with the human desire to develop and apply abstract generalizations that may not fit well with current circumstances.[10]

Project managers need to address assumptions, explicit and implicit. Even explicit assumptions, like who provides certain resources, can easily get overlooked. Implicit assumptions, like who provides political support for the project, are more difficult to identify. Failure to identify them can result in erroneous decisions when developing and seeking acceptance of a vision. Later in the project life cycle, the "I thought you thought" scenario can arise, leading to serious complications, e.g., rework.

Deliverables are the main products that result from the efforts and energies expended on a project. Deliverable identification is closely tied to goals and objectives, scope, and assumptions. In the workshop, the danger with deliverables is a lack of definition at a sufficient level of detail to tie to expectations. When expectations about a deliverable are not addressed, everyone operates according to assumptions. Failure to sufficiently address expectations and assumptions surrounding deliverables can result in delivering an unwanted product.

Roles and responsibilities must be defined at a high level at least. These roles and responsibilities depend on the goals, objectives, scope, and deliverables. The challenge will likely not be delineating the roles and responsibilities per se, but identifying them at a sufficient, useful level of detail. Another challenge is determining roles and responsibilities that overlap among stakeholders. "Turf wars" can erupt or resentment over those who do not provide their fair share. Such issues must be addressed up front to avoid squabbling and little or no performance of key roles and responsibilities.

Constraints should be addressed, too. Constraints inhibit project performance, often related to cost, schedule, quality, and people. They affect the goals, objectives, scope, and assumptions for projects. The biggest challenge with constraints is that the goals, objectives, and scope frequently bear only a partial relationship with the constraints. For instance, the scope might be too large for the budget or the schedule is too tight for a project. Constraints often reflect "trade-offs" that can cause suboptimization of goals and objectives.

Risks pose a particularly interesting problem when developing a vision. Often risks reflect the degree of acceptance of risk held by the stakeholders. The other complication is who will assume responsibility to deal with certain risks. This issue becomes especially difficult when a risk has cross-functional impacts. When cross-functional impacts are involved, project managers must seriously consider challenges for obtaining consent to a vision.

The key point is to recognize that not everything is easily identifiable and challenges must be overcome. Most challenges can be addressed by planning the mechanics of the workshop.

### Plan the Mechanics

There are two aspects to consider when planning for a workshop. The first one is setting up the workshop; the other is its conduct.

Setting up a workshop includes the standard things that should be done for other workshops: ensure the facilities are comfortable, make sufficient supplies available, have it at a location that reduces opportunities for distraction, have it for an appropriate length of time, consider travel and lodging arrangements, address food and refreshments, and much more. While important, they are not enough.

Planning for the conduct of the workshop is just as important and is often overlooked. Though an agenda might be sent to everyone, there is much more including:

- Access to relevant data
- Approaches for capturing and disseminating comments and decisions
- Definitions of roles and responsibilities, such as a scribe and facilitators
- Follow-up actions after developing the vision
- Order of presentation of the vision's components
- Pace of topics covered in the agenda
- Rules and approaches for managing conflict
- Techniques for capturing buy-in and consensus
- Techniques for making decisions

An excellent approach to take prior to a workshop is to contact each stakeholder that will be attending. The purpose is to ascertain if any ideas, concerns, topics, or issues should be addressed prior to the workshop. More importantly, they might have similar items to address while conducting the workshop. By acting in advance, this will help to avoid challenges that may arise during the actual conduct of a workshop.

## Execute

The difficult part of the PVW is the actual execution. Project managers must deal with the realities of getting stakeholders to develop and commit to a vision. It is the "moment of truth" and lays the groundwork for what to expect in regards to buy-in and commitment during the life cycle of a project.

### Apply Good People Skills

During a workshop, project managers will face many challenges; many that are related to the interactions of people. Some challenges that will confront project managers are: differences in mental models; disagreements over the definition and specific contents of elements in the vision, e.g., goals and strategy; stake-holders' reluctance to share information and work together; an unwillingness to cooperate or follow rules while developing the vision; and commitment to decisions.

Project managers, therefore, must have some level of knowledge and exper-tise in dealing with different stakeholders, to include effective listening, col-laborative problem-solving, negotiating, and conflict management skills.

Effective listening requires that they seek first to understand and then be understood. There are two parts to being an effective listener. The first is to listen actively; to actively engage in what the stakeholders say. This engagement does not mean emotional involvement; rather, it means empathizing to under-stand not only what they say but also their perspectives. This approach will allow you to ask meaningful questions to glean important information and additional points for clarification. This information will enable you to identify opportunities to determine ways to develop a vision on which stakeholders concur. In addition, it will help determine the true meaning behind the reactions of stakeholders.

The second part is to show an interest in listening. The techniques involved are well known. They include maintaining eye contact; giving acknowledgment that you understand, e.g., response; and concentrating on the talker and what is said.

Negotiating is important. Although project managers will be facilitating, they must also agree with the vision. If a company can afford it, it could bring in a professional facilitator for the PVW, which is rare. If it cannot afford it, project managers must play that key role.

This thought brings up a key point. Project managers will be "walking a thin line." They must actively involve themselves in a workshop, but not lose objectivity at the same time. They must participate in a manner to ensure that they do not inherit an unrealistic vision or one that lacks qualities that cause more problems than not having any vision at all. At the same time, they must avoid falling prey to the tendency to join the turf wars, which may cause them to lose their objectivity and key support.

When negotiating, the best approach I have found is the one advocated by Roger Fisher and William Ury in their landmark book, *Getting to Yes*.

The authors note that people step into several traps when negotiating and these pertain to project managers. These include arguing over positions, being too nice, and being too negative. To avoid such dangers, they suggest the following:

- Focus on interests, not positions
- Insist on using objective criteria

■   Invent options for mutual gain
■   Separate people from the problem[11]

A good example is the discussion of goals. Stakeholders may start by arguing over who has a right to determine the goals. The project manager should naturally avoid letting this circumstance arise by managing the discussion in a way to separate the stakeholder from the issue and posture the discussion to focus on mutual interests rather than end in a Win-Lose scenario. If some problem exists over goals, project managers may identify different ways to rephrase them and then orient the discussions towards resolution of interests. If it appears that an impasse might occur, project managers can proceed to define another goal and later return to the one in dispute. This approach will provide a "cooling off" period and time to develop alternative ways to define a goal.

To increase the opportunity for effective negotiating among all participants, remember to engender a positive environment, increase the opportunities for mutual understanding and sharing of thoughts, encourage "give and take" during discussions, and foster good communication. Project managers should, above all, take the responsibility to ensure that all of this happens successfully.

Developing a vision requires that people work together. Obviously, this is easier said than done because many opportunities exist for collaboration to break down. These include people subscribing to different mental models, misinterpreting comments, and differences over priorities and resource allocation.

The keys to effective collaboration are to avoid putting stakeholders in a Win-Lose situation by:

■   Defining the issue, not the solution
■   Developing different solutions via brainstorming
■   Seeking consensus
■   Selecting the best solution

Defining an issue is 80 percent of the work. If a stalemate arises over strategy, for example, determine the causes for it by first determining the fundamental contributors to a stalemate. Try to depersonalize the issue as much as possible by not talking about positions and emphasizing more of the facts and data. Then, get their participation in developing several alternatives and criteria to select the best alternative. After selecting the alternative, project managers should question stakeholders whether a selected alternative is agreeable to all and revise, if necessary. Above all, avoid giving the impression that a solution represents a victory of one stakeholder at the expense of another.

Conflict management is closely associated with effective collaboration, except that it often follows after collaboration breaks down. There are, of course, many factors that can contribute to conflict, e.g., different personalities, general atmosphere, unclear or inflexible policies and procedures, mental models, and preferences for approaching a project. If not handled well, these factors can cause an impasse over important issues or lack of acceptance of a vision.

The primary objective of conflict management is to maintain positive relationships to ensure goal attainment. To effectively manage conflict requires that project managers follow these steps:

- Develop alternatives to address the issue
- Focus on the issue, not the personalities
- Use objective criteria to select the best alternative
- Verify consensus for the alternative selected

From my experience, I have often found that conflicts can be handled quite well when certain techniques are employed to define the issue. For example, often the use of words gets muddied over semantics and is accompanied with great emotion. Use of metaphors, visual images, e.g., maps and charts, and even role playing can help in resolving such conflicts. A diagram, such as a flow chart or even a picture, can help clarify an issue and lead to an acceptable solution.

Sometimes, however, emotions can run so high that any logical approach might seem impossible to employ. Under such circumstances, project managers can "table" an issue and move to another and return to it later. They can solicit outside help, preferably someone without a stake on the outcome, to mediate a solution. Regardless, all stakeholders should heed three simple suggestions when managing conflict, especially when embroiled in the middle of it: treat people with respect; listen until you experience the other side; and state your views, needs, and feelings.[12] By doing these three things, communication with one another will be better, which will increase the likelihood of developing a mutually beneficial solution.

### Keep the Focus on the Big Picture

During a PVW, it is so easy for everyone to lose focus on the overall goal — develop a shared vision. That is because there are so many opportunities to squabble. The one person who can help to prevent the squabbling from taking over is the project manager, because he or she is responsible for getting all the players to work together to support a vision. But, how does he or she make this happen?

A project manager has several options. The best approach is to gear all discussions from the context of how an idea, for example, can contribute to the overall purpose of a project. This approach is easier to employ if the goals and objectives have been defined. If the goals and objectives have not been defined, a project manager can reference a higher organization's goals and objectives. Another approach is to discuss the impact of an idea within the scope of influence and scope of control defined by a project. Another approach is to encourage people to consider an idea or issue from different perspectives and then address it from those vantage points. Project managers can also hire outside experts to address issues because they appear objective and lack a vested interest in the outcome of an issue. Also useful are internal experts, such as those from a portfolio management office or a project management office.

## Act

After completing a vision, however, commitment must follow it. The best way to achieve that is to treat the vision statement development as a stewardship agreement (as Covey discusses), meaning that it is not imposed on, but genuinely adopted by, all the stakeholders at the PVW.

### Bring Closure by Seeking Buy-In

An effective way to achieve that is to emphasize that stakeholders shared in the vision through joint decision making. Project managers should also emphasize that a vision will serve as a road map to guide the project to completion by serving as the authoritative source to make decisions. To solidify the consensus, project managers should take three actions.

First, they should ask all stakeholders at the PVW to sign the vision, or charter. If any stakeholder objects, then address the objection right away or determine if it needs to be directed to some higher level of management, if necessary, to be resolved.

Second, they should give each stakeholder a copy. The purpose is to give the stakeholders time to review it and, if necessary, call for a subsequent PVW to resolve any differences.

Finally, after achieving consensus, project managers should give considerable visibility to the vision. This visibility will increase the likelihood of adherence to it. An effective approach is to post the vision on a web site so that everyone can access it. Another way is to reference it during planning and subsequent activities.

## START WITH THE PROJECT MANAGER

All in all, project managers must develop an atmosphere of trust so that effective dialog can result in a vision that all stakeholders can follow. They can engender trust by following a consistent approach throughout the PVW. Actions include: looking like they are not playing favorites; being honest in both feelings and contents; remaining realistic without falling into the abyss of negativism; and being tolerant and open to different perspectives, opinions, and ideas. Project managers must stand above the fray to develop a vision that is meaningful to everyone and sustainable throughout the life of a project.

## CASE STUDY: VISUALIZE

Involvement by key stakeholders is absolutely essential for the success of any project. The project manager, along with the project sponsor, identified the key stakeholders and sought their active participation in developing the vision. While considering the team members, they wanted individuals who had decision-making authority because important decisions would have to be made immediately during the workshop.

The project manager then moved quickly to build a common vision. A workshop was scheduled with the expressed purpose of developing a charter that everyone would follow.

In addition to the vision, the project manager knew the workshop provided an additional benefit — overcome the first two tumultuous phases of team formation identified under the Tuchman Model. How these two phases were handled set the tone for the rest of the project. Through a workshop, stakeholders had the opportunity to reconcile their differing positions and interests while pursuing a common goal. The project manager knew that a common vision was the easiest and most lasting way to place differences aside or at least assuage them to the point of getting everyone to work together.

During the workshop, agreement was sought on goals and objectives, description of end results, assumptions, milestone dates, business and technical requirements, and scope. At the conclusion, the project manager had everyone sign the document and it was distributed to demonstrate commitment towards achieving a common vision.

The project manager also established what was known as a war room. The war room displayed the vision, the contents of the charter, and other pertinent information, e.g., As-Is and To-Be descriptions of the policies and procedures infrastructure. Such exhibition of the vision served as a reminder of its importance to the daily execution of the project, thereby providing focus.

## REFERENCES

1. Natalie Chalfin, Four reasons why projects fail, *PM Network,* p. 7, June 1998.
2. Nancy Settle-Murphy and Caroline Thorton, Facilitating your way to project success, *Information Strategy,* p. 37, Spring 1999.
3. Stephen R. Covey, A. Roger Merrill, and Rebecca R. Merrill, *First Things First,* Simon & Schuster, New York, 1994, p. 219.
4. Shakti Gawain, Creative *Visualization,* Bantam Books, Toronto, 1985, pp. 2–3.
5. Stephen R. Covey, A. Roger Merrill, and Rebecca R. Merrill, *First Things First,* Simon & Schuster, New York, 1994, pp. 212–215.
6. Rob Cross and Laurence Prusak, The people who make organizations go – or stop, *Harvard Business Review,* p. 105, June 2002.
7. Ibid., pp. 105–112.
8. Fred Borgiani, Stakeholder support: the key to getting your ideas implemented, *PM Network,* pp. 46–48, February 1998.
9. Dietrich Dorner, *The Logic of Failure,* Perseus Books, Cambridge, MA, 1996, p. 61.
10. Ibid., p. 98
11. Roger Fisher and William Ury, *Getting to Yes,* Penguin Books, New York, 1988, pp. 17–98.
12. Robert Bolton, *People Skills,* Touchstone, New York, 1986, pp. 221–222.

# 5

# INTEGRATE

Far too often, project managers take a narrow perspective when managing their projects. This narrow perspective can lead to reacting rather than responding to events and having little foresight about the consequences of their decisions and actions. To some degree, this is due to the prevailing paradigm of project management that emphasizes a mechanical view of how projects operate. Seasoned project managers recognize that a narrow perspective is not only naïve, but can cause unintended complications later in the project life cycle and beyond. So they emphasize the need to develop and maintain a wide-angle view of a project by looking at relationships; emphasizing interrelation, interdependence, and integration. In other words, they mean systems thinking. Fritjof Capra says that systems thinking is really process thinking, whereby opposites and relationships interrelate and interact in a unified manner.[1]

## NEW PARADIGM = REALISM

The new paradigm of project management requires that project managers take a more realistic view of projects, thereby avoiding a paint-by-numbers approach. The emphasis shifts to viewing projects as dynamic systems, relying as much on relationships as well as tools and techniques.

Unfortunately, a systemic approach towards managing projects is rarely taken, resulting in many problems and complications.

*It limits perceptions and possibilities.* By thinking linearly under the prevailing paradigm, project managers find themselves locked into looking for or seeing the right answer rather than what I refer to as an appropriate solution. The difference is that the former may be based on logical correctness but does not satisfy a need, e.g., a technical solution that fails to satisfy the needs of the customer. The latter might be a workable solution not based on logical correctness but provides a realistic, satisfactory answer. A systemic, not systematic, view, therefore, allows project managers to do the right things, not necessarily to do things right.

*It causes project managers to react rather than respond.* A systemic perspective does not enable project managers to anticipate the "upstream and downstream" impacts of decisions and actions and have some foresight about what can happen next, positive or negative. Taking a typical sequential, linear view often results in making short-term decisions and taking short-term actions to address only a small part of a wider problem. Difficulties can arise later in the project life cycle, and will be more difficult and costlier to address. In *The Logic of Failure,* Dietrich Dorner observes that increases in the desire to apply linear measures to nonlinear circumstances result in an inability to anticipate and understand what he refers to as "side effects and repercussions" of behavior.[2] An example is a "patch" to a technical issue that may later cause problems during the sustaining and operations of a product.

*It can lead to inflexibility in thought and action.* Since the prevailing paradigm encourages finding the right logic rather than a suitable answer, mental arrogance, e.g., possessing the only right answer or taking only the right action, can take over. The resulting solution may be incomplete, addressing only one or more symptoms and not the cause. An example is adding more people to a project to recover a sliding schedule.

*It leads to focusing on fixing parts rather than dealing with relationships.* This situation is very similar to the Newtonian perspective of looking at the universe as a machine. If a problem exists, replace the part. The problem with this approach is that this requires ensuring the availability of parts and asserting that the cause is localized. Often, however, the challenge lies with relationships among the parts, not the individual parts. Many project managers fail to focus on relationships simply because they view a project as an assembly of parts. If a project fails to progress, then the frequently quoted answer is to replace a part rather than improve relationships. An example is a project manager preferring to remove a team member rather than altering the work relationships.

*It leads to what Dorner refers to as "Methodism," that is, following the rules of a methodology, procedure, etc. correctly rather than assessing effectiveness.* Essentially, the process becomes more important than the results. This approach emphasizes a focus on what must be done and how to do it efficiently. In addition, it leads to a hierarchical, command and control orientation when managing a project to ensure correctness. The result is often dysfunctional behavior and complications, such as negative conflict as well as suboptimization

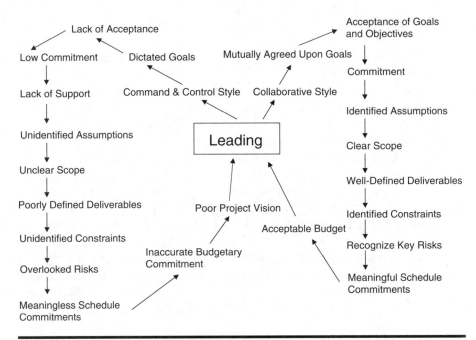

**Figure 5.1**    Systemic View of Different Leadership Styles.

of goals. An example is overemphasis on applying a methodology or technique at the expense of achieving results.

*It results in project managers subscribing to a skewed view of a project, e.g., looking at a project from a narrow technical or financial perspective.* In addition to subscribing to a fragmented view, it also means taking a stovepipe view, leading to many oversights, misinterpretations, and short-term solutions. An example is a project manager who focuses on managing the costs of a project without considering other factors, e.g., schedule, people, and quality.

*It can lead to a lack of acceptance of diversity regarding new or different ideas.* In other words, project managers refuse to consider different alternatives or insights that may improve project performance. An example is a project manager who believes in only one "right" way or methodology to conduct a project and who applies a command and control approach as opposed to a collaborative one. The consequences can be seen clearly from a systemic perspective as displayed in Figure 5.1. The command and control style often results in a stream of negative consequences, whereas a more collaborative style often has different consequences.

## BENEFITS

A systemic view of projects, however, provides many benefits to project managers.

*Focus first and foremost on the big picture by ascertaining how all elements of a project interact.* By understanding interactions, project managers can more easily determine the impact of their decisions and actions, negative and positive. Capra writes that a systems perspective really involves looking at objects as networks of relationships that are part of a much bigger system. Hence, relationships become more important than objects.[3] This unified perspective enables project managers to determine the most appropriate decision or action to further progress. For example, a project manager can determine the key elements and their relationships that need to change in order to achieve the best results.

*Provide a more balanced perspective between efficiency and effectiveness.* Project managers can see, for example, the impact of cost cutting of elements and their relationships, such as activities and resources, on overall effectiveness. Many project managers lack this visibility, falling into the trap due to their narrow perspectives.

*Be decisive and act in a manner that optimizes the overall performance.* For example, a project manager can identify opportunities for improvement and anticipate any possible negative impacts in advance. In other words, he or she can perform an impact analysis of their decisions.

*Step back and see how their decisions and actions impact an entire project and other stakeholders.* Project managers can handle organizational myopia more readily. They can also be more tolerant of who does not share the same perspectives. This ability to "elevate" perspectives offers another important benefit: consensus. Because people can see a project from other and larger perspectives and an appreciation of the impact of their actions on others, consensus is more achievable. Often, a lack of consensus occurs because of people's inability to understand the how and why behind other people's thinking and doing, resulting in needless negative conflict. A systemic view of a project enables easier consensus by recognizing diversity and encouraging understanding of issues and interests of all stakeholders in making decisions and taking action.

*See not only the impact of their decisions, but also ascertain a sense of the long-range impacts through understanding relationships.* That is what really makes systems thinking valuable. According to Peter Senge, systems thinking requires a holistic perspective that identifies interrelationships and patterns rather than what he calls "snapshots."[4] With this knowledge, project managers can

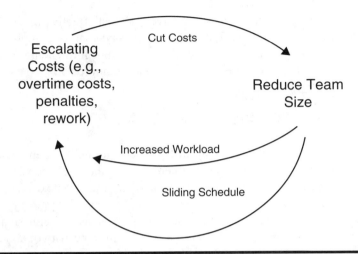

**Figure 5.2** Fixes that Fail.

develop more effective contingency plans, or set aside sufficient funds, e.g., management reserves, to deal with long-term consequences.

Figure 5.2 demonstrates the power of taking a systemic perspective to ascertain the impact of short-term fixes vis-à-vis long-term fixes. A common scenario is, for example, project managers having to deal with exceeding budgets. To cut costs, they reduce team size even though the scope does not change. The result is an increased workload that causes the schedule to slide, adding costs to the project, e.g., penalty payments and overtime costs.

*Focus on what to do and why, rather than how.* Mechanics of a process or a procedure, for example, become the most important consideration and not necessarily the steps. Project managers then have considerable flexibility to respond to different situations. For example, a project manager can consider different alternatives to achieve a specific objective rather than improve processes that may not necessarily contribute towards improving overall performance. In the end, he or she knows more of what is important and less of what is irrelevant. As Edward de Bono says, the reason that it is easier to notice an effect than it is to understand the causes for its existence.[5]

*Achieve synergy, the concept that system output is greater than the sum of its parts.* In other words, there is an increased value of the parts of a system because they are members in a system.

*Have a better means to adapt to the environment.* Because they identify interrelationships and relationships, project managers can modify processes, procedures, tools, and techniques in a manner to focus on goals and objectives.

This ability to bring about changes that have the most effective impact is called leveraging in systems thinking. Edward De Bono says that for complex systems, it is not really an issue of making results happen but influencing elements to get the desired effect. He calls this the "dynamic approach."[6]

## DIFFERENT CATEGORIES

A system can be classified in many different categories. Systems can be categorized according to size or scope. Dorner says that the world consists of many subsystems, and it is wise to think about them from the context of their interactions with one another.[7] A system may be part of much larger system; it is a microcosm. Or it might be large enough to encompass several smaller systems; it is a macrocosm. For example, a project may be part of much larger endeavor, such as a program with the former being a microcosm and the latter a macrocosm.

Another categorization is the distinction between a static versus dynamic system. A static system is one where little or no change occurs. A dynamic system is where change occurs quite regularly. For example, a project might be very stable or it might have to change its approach constantly.

Finally, a system may be categorized as closed or open. A closed system does not interact with its environment to adapt to changing conditions. An example is a project that fails to change its plans in response to a cutback in funding. An open system adapts to changing conditions. An example is a project that adjusts its plans to reflect a cutback in funding.

Of course, a system can fall into three categories at the same time. A system can be a microcosm that is open and adapts dynamically. An example is a project that changes its plans to reflect a change in scope.

## WHAT IS A SYSTEM?

A system is basically a perspective that looks at elements and their relationships under specific conditions. This perspective enables us to understand how something will affect a system under varying conditions.

Generally, a system can be divided into just about anything, e.g., objects, processes, functions, flows, constants, or variables. This explosion of a system into elements is called analysis. The need to put all the elements together to understand their interactions is known as synthesis.

A systems perspective requires both analysis and synthesis to truly understand how something works. Too often, the emphasis has been on analysis, not synthesis, reducing appreciation of the importance of seeing elements as part of an overall system. Russell Ackoff, one of the early proponents of systems theory, says that a system has two or more parts that cannot, ironically, be divided into independent parts. Otherwise, such a division will affect overall performance.[8]

Capra agrees, particularly in regards to systems that involve living organisms, and observes that systems theory acknowledges the interrelationship and interdependence of phenomena. This holistic view means that an integrated whole cannot be exploded into parts without having some negative impact, because a system can consist of subsystems.[9]

There is, of course, tremendous pressure to emphasize the analytical side, due largely to our educational and scientific heritage, and this has caused us considerable trouble and angst, despite the accompanying benefits. Yet, as Peter Senge notes, people learn to "fragment" problems and, indeed, the world. While this fragmentation may add simplicity, it can have serious impacts, e.g., not seeing the consequences of behavior. In an effort to increase understanding, great effort is made to reassemble the parts into some framework, but the effort proves impractical because something is lost in the reconstruction.[10]

Systems in general and systems thinking in particular, therefore, require a holistic perspective that looks beyond the mere assembly of parts. Only by thinking holistically can people determine the impact that a decision or action will have on an entire system.

How a system is constructed, however, is not objective. It is a very subjective effort even though it helps us to understand what is happening within and to a particular system.

The reason is that people cannot extricate themselves from their environment and its influences. They are continuously tied emotionally, psychologically, and physically in terms of time, space, and milieu. Hence, they view phenomena in a way that reflects the prevailing paradigm, mental model, or perceptual model to which they subscribe. The patterns that exist in our minds surface in the patterns around us and reflect our feelings and values.

## IMPLICATIONS

This inability to extricate themselves from their environment has tremendous implications on how people analyze and synthesize a system.

*It requires looking at something as a model.* Like all models, it is an incomplete view of reality. It is impossible to determine all the elements and relationships to form what a person perceives as a system. At best, it only approximates reality and becomes an educated guess at best.

*The selection of what is important and unimportant in a system is a value judgment.* To one person, an element may be important; to another, unimportant. At best, it is a tool that enables an understanding of reality. Change the original people who provide a description of a system and the chances increase that new people will describe and perceive it differently to some degree.

This behavior is due to the complexity of most systems and the desire to simplify; both involve subjectivity. Dorner says this desire to simplify is useful, but comes at a cost. He refers to the results of this desire to simplify as "supersignals." While supersignals reduce complexity, they can vary from person to person and result in "no objective measure of complexity."[11]

*There is one way to look at the world and it is subjective.* In today's world of specialization, people will likely describe a system differently, e.g., data, time, control, etc. Project managers need to be critically aware of this fact by trying to obtain a balanced perspective of a system. Dorner observes that each person's model may differ in correctness and completeness and this fact should not be overlooked. Unfortunately, people tend to forget about this insight, especially when confronted with uncertainty.[12]

*The boundary for a system will likely be unclear, particularly when involving social phenomena.* That is because the relationships can be extremely complex and may involve many intangibles. Identifying a boundary, too, is a judgment call.

*The relationships among the elements of a system are as important, perhaps even more so, than the elements themselves.* Relationships reflect interactions and integration among the elements based on specific conditions. Interactions and integration reflect a synthesis among all elements to satisfy goals of a system.

Due to the difficulty in developing an objective holistic perspective of a system, how can it be possible to develop anything meaningful? The answer is to involve people who subscribe to different views on how a system behaves. Ackoff agrees, noting that it is important to view problems from multiple perspectives. He calls this multiple perspective a "transdisciplinary point of view."[13]

It makes good sense, therefore, to involve people who hold different viewpoints to better understand phenomena. It is the only way, short of using instrumentation that can result in biasing insights because it will likely influence the phenomena being measured.

Project managers must not only identify the elements of their projects and their relationships, they should also encourage participative decision making and collaboration whenever possible to enable a better understanding of what is happening and what to do. Failure to do so can lead to assessing circumstances inaccurately and exercising poor judgment.

## GOAL-DIRECTED BEHAVIOR

A system is basically goal directed, that is, it exists to satisfy a specific set of needs, wants, or desires. Goals can be classified in several ways.

*Some goals are short term, meaning that the needs are immediate, whereas others are long term.* Of course, the difference between the two is a matter of judgment. From a project perspective, a short-term goal might mean satisfying a milestone date during the current phase. A long-term goal might mean meeting the final completion date.

*Some goals are explicit while others are implicit.* An explicit goal is obvious and clearly stated, such as finish a project by June 31. Other goals are implicit, meaning that they cannot be clearly articulated and measured. An example is a deliverable evaluated by a customer that involves an evaluative judgment, e.g., meets customer satisfaction.

*Goals can be internal or external.* An internal goal satisfies a need determined internally, such as a methodology implemented to streamline the technical performance of a project. An external goal is dictated outside the boundaries of a system. An example is when executive management requires that projects satisfy goals elaborated in a corporate vision statement as well as those identified in a project charter.

As mentioned earlier, a system consists of objects. An object is a distinct entity within a system. It may be a person, organization, or machine. The behavior of the objects influences the output of a system to varying degrees. On a project, an object might include different stakeholders or automated tools.

Each object has attributes, or qualities, that distinguish it from other objects. Some attributes are constants; they never change. Other attributes are variable; they change for various reasons. Variables often reflect certain parameters, reflecting ranges. These ranges are reflected in states that indicate different grades of conditions. An example on a project is a team member who possesses certain skills that may need improvement, depending on conditions.

Often objects within a system have varying degrees of freedom. These degrees of freedom represent the latitude granted to exercise decisions and actions within the constraints imposed or granted. An example is the level of delegated authority granted to a project manager to make certain types of decisions.

## RELATIONSHIPS KEY

Another important component of a system is the relationship among the objects. These relationships are usually identified by the links among objects in a system. This linkage reflects the transfer of something, such as data or signals, from one object to another. For example, one object produces an output that is used by another object or another system. A typical scenario on a project is that a deliverable produced in one phase is input to another in a subsequent phase.

A key concept about linkage of objects is the distinction between independence and interdependence. Independence is the degree of autonomy an object has from other objects within a system while pursuing its goals. Interdependence is the degree of interaction among objects to achieve a common goal. Both independence and interdependence are "two sides of the same coin," meaning that both exist to varying degrees vis-à-vis one another.

Integration reflects the relative degrees of independence and interdependence in the relationship. It is the combination of independence and interdependence that influences how effectively and efficiently a system achieves its goals. An example in project management is the extent to how much autonomy, e.g., independence, a team member has vis-à-vis how much he must work with others, e.g., interdependence, to achieve a common goal efficiently and effectively, e.g., integration.

Relationships can be categorized differently. One category is *explicit and implicit.* An explicit relationship is obvious, such as a person who provides specific data to another to produce a deliverable. An implicit relationship is not often discernible, such as informal approval of a politically powerful stakeholder. Often, the informal network serves as a perfect example of an implicit relationship.

Another category is *symmetrical and asymmetrical* relationships. A symmetrical relationship reflects a balance among all the objects or functions within a system, e.g., cost, schedule, and quality. An asymmetrical relationship reflects an imbalance, such as an overemphasis on cost at the expense of schedule and quality.

Relationships can be *causative or correlative.* A causative relationship is when the action and output of one object causes the behavior of another object. The former is referred to as being independent and the latter dependent. An example is a task that cannot begin until the predecessors have finished.

A correlative relationship exists when an object does something that influences a change in behavior of another object. There does not appear to be a direct relationship between the former and the latter due to some intervening object affecting the relationship. An example is reducing a budget to pressure the same outcome in the scope of a deliverable.

Relationships can be *hierarchical, relational, or integral.* A hierarchical relationship is when certain objects, such as people or functions, have a more important or decisive role in a system. An example is a project manager who insists on requiring his or her own approval for taking action.

A relational relationship exists when the objects are relatively equal to one another, almost in a neural network format. An example is a project manager who exercises a fairly democratic approach to decision making.

An integral relationship involves both hierarchical and relational aspects. An example is a project manager who employs participative decision making by consulting with team members, but exercises ultimate decision-making authority.

## CONSTRAINTS

Relationships are affected by constraints. A constraint is something that affects, often negatively, the quality of a relationship.

Controls and rules are two examples of constraints on relationships. A control restricts behavior to ensure adherence to a rule. An example is the required approval of an inspector before a deliverable can be available to someone else. Rules are a subset of controls that require compliance prior to taking action, e.g., complying with certain quality standards of a deliverable prior to release.

Resources can also be a constraint, both from qualitative and quantitative perspectives. They can be quantitative in that enough may not be available. They can be qualitative because they may lack the requisite abilities to accomplish specific tasks. Of course, constraints can be quantitative and qualitative. An example of a quantitative and qualitative constraint is people on a project. There might not be enough people with a specific skill and who may lack the ability and willingness to do the necessary work.

Not all constraints, like relationships, are apparent. An apparent constraint is cost and schedule. Many constraints in a system are implicit, which makes them very difficult to discern. On a project, a frequent example is whether or not a team member can perform specific tasks. Despite having a good knowledge of people's capabilities, it is very difficult to determine the degree to which they can actually perform tasks. Implicit factors might include a willingness and ability to perform a task. It is only through time and experience with an individual that project managers can really determine the degree to which people are a constraint. Often, project managers have no other choice but to accept a constraint in this regard.

This last example raises an important point about systems. According to systems theory, all systems possess "energy" to reach their goals. Unused energy is latent or potential energy; used energy is realized or kinetic energy. How this energy is tapped determines the degree to which a system performs efficiently and effectively. The measure of how well the energy is used is reflected in the quantity and quality of output. A good example is the use of the cost performance index and schedule performance index to measure efficient usage of realized energy on projects; defect rate is a good measure of the effectiveness of the realized energy of projects.

## INPUTS AND OUTPUTS

All systems consist of inputs and outputs, between and among their internal components and with their external environment. Inputs can take the form of data or signals that originate from other elements or the external environment. Outputs can take the form of data and inputs for use by other elements. The movement of data and signals from one element to another is known as flow. Often, data and signals flow to and from other people or functions; they may also go to a final destination in an external environment. Or, they may originate from an object in an external environment. The final destination is often called a sink; the point of origination is called a source. In some cases, an object may be both. An example is a project that provides information to and receives information from a project management office.

Cybernetics is the term used to study the flow of information among objects. The common term used for the actual flow of data and signals to adapt to the environment is called feedback.

A system has two basic kinds of feedback, positive and negative. Positive feedback is the basis for systemic growth. Negative feedback either helps to maintain equilibrium (or stability) or lose equilibrium (or dissipate). On a project, positive feedback might include outstanding schedule performance; negative feedback might be a high defect rate.

A system also often performs cyclically. One common cycle is a system with a behavior that occurs regularly, in a repeating manner; everything seems to operate in equilibrium, or self-sustaining mode. Everything within the system seems to "hum."

Sometimes, however, a system is out of equilibrium because a trigger, or event, upsets a cyclic behavior pattern. A trigger is frequently external, but can be internally generated, and may cause a system to move into disequilibrium, or out of balance, unless it can restore balance, known as homeostasis. When disequilibrium occurs, a system lacks sustainability to resist movement to a lower state of performance, known as entropy. An example of a project in equilibrium is one that follows a consistent pattern of performance, symptomatic of being on schedule and within budget on a regular, predicable basis. An example of a project out of equilibrium is one with a history of very good performance but suddenly deteriorates according to cost and schedule criteria.

The concept of equilibrium can be useful to the project manager. So can the concept of autopoiesis that ties back to the autonomy, or independence, of a system to determine its own response to an environment and adapt structures and configurations that allow it to respond to a changing environment. An example of autopoiesis is the ability of a project to determine the methodologies to change or forego a response to a changing external environment rather than being "forced" to adhere to an inflexible approach.

Maintaining equilibrium is a maintenance state for a system. It reflects the ability to maintain integrity. Sometimes, however, a trigger will cause a system to reach an excited state, resulting in movement towards disequilibrium.

The structure of a system is an important influence on its behavior when responding to conditions. It reflects the order of the elements; that is, how they are configured. The configuration of relationships within a system will determine its characteristics. This configuration is identified through the configuration of the physical components. The idea is that a change in the configuration of a system will result in a change in its behavior, e.g., reordering the processes, functions, and other elements to get the desired behavior. An example in project management is to change the reporting relationships among the stakeholders, e.g., move from a matrix to a task structure, to improve performance.

By changing structure, or configurations, therefore, one can alter the behavior pattern of a system to achieve results. Structure and behavior pattern are seen as closely related. Change the structure and the behavior pattern will change to achieve the desired results.

The idea of changing structure to alter behavior can be a very powerful tool for project managers. This ability to change structure goes beyond altering objects, e.g., tools. It is also applies to changing the relationships among tools, techniques, and team members. By changing the relationships among objects, project managers can dramatically influence the outcome of their projects.

They do not have to change every object or relationship, however. Rather, they can identify key internal and external ones and decide and act accordingly to achieve leverage. For example, project managers can alter working relationships among team members, resequence tasks, and change the reporting relationships with stakeholders. They can also adopt tools or techniques as catalysts to influence performance, e.g., changing teaming relationships to augment performance.

Implementing such changes is obtainable by recognizing that different categories of links or relationships among elements exist and taking advantage of them when necessary. Some links are causal; others correlative. Some links are additive, e.g., one element adding to the performance of another. Some links are balancing, e.g., an increase in performance of one result corresponds to a decrease in another.

Linkages can be mapped in several ways to reflect the topology of a system. Mathematical models are one way. Another way, which has increased in popularity, is through mapping. One popular approach is loop diagramming, popularized by Peter Senge. It is an effective way to illustrate the feedback loops existing in a system.

Loops are an effective way to illustrate the different behavior patterns that can occur in system. Loops are reflected in the form of curved arrows to show the "flow of influence." One category of loops reinforces each other, augmenting or decreasing behavior. The other fundamental category of loops is balancing, which stabilizes behavior. Both categories of loops have a profound influence on the behavior of a system. Senge identified several behavior patterns that he designated as system archetypes. These include balancing process with delay, limits to growth, shifting the burden, erosion of goals, escalation, tragedy of the common, fixes that fail, and others.[14]

## PROJECT AS SYSTEM

A systemic perspective of a project can be described quite easily using a systems diagram.

Most projects are not closed systems. They interact with their environment as an open system. Data and signals flow continuously in and out of a project and constantly affect the stakeholders' decisions and actions related to achieving specific goals and objectives.

A project also consists of many objects and relationships. Some objects include stakeholders such as customers, project managers, senior management, team members, steering committee, suppliers, vendors, contractors, subject matter experts, and consultants. Other objects include tools, techniques, and supplies such as personal computers, mathematical models, and materials, respectively. All the objects have attributes as well. For example, attributes for people include emotions, strengths, weaknesses, roles, and responsibilities. Still other objects are the processes employed on a project, e.g., change management, configuration management, risk management, planning, status assessment, and resource allocation.

Relationships exist among objects. Some relationships are vertical, e.g., with senior management or a steering committee; others are horizontal, e.g., with team members. Some relationships are external, e.g., with customers and other project managers, while others are internal, e.g., with team members and immediate management. Some relationships are formal, e.g., reporting to senior management; others are informal, e.g., dealing with people in the informal network of a corporation to achieve the goals of a project.

Like all systems, a project faces many constraints, which can include applying a specific methodology; restricting scope; applying a certain technical technique; following a certain type of life cycle, e.g., waterfall or spiral; achieving dictated milestone dates; completing a project within a specific budget; and following policies and procedures. These constraints are formal ones. There are informal constraints that also affect a project, e.g., norms, history of managing projects, politics, risk acceptance or avoidance, and managerial style.

A project has data and signals flowing throughout, internally and externally. These inputs and outputs may include presentations, reviews, minutes, reports, forms, project charter, project announcement, schedules, estimates, contingency plans, and work breakdown structures. Some information can initiate transactional and transformative behavior within a project. Transactional behavior might include transferring data from one stakeholder to another. Transformative behavior might include converting data into information, such as collecting status and generating meaningful reports for a steering committee.

A project can operate in equilibrium when responding to data and signals that arrive from its environment and are generated internally by its elements. Sometimes, data and signals from an environment can push a project into disequilibrium. An example might be when a key team member with very specialized skills decides to depart.

Disequilibrium on a project is often detected via indicators. Indicators include exceeded budget, high defect rate, sliding schedule, greater frequency of negative conflict, and the presence of obstacles and problems.

Of course, a project can adapt to events that shake it into disequilibrium. Decisions and actions related to replanning, corrective actions, and new tools and techniques can all help a project to adapt.

Like all systems, a project is affected and effected by structures. Two common structures are the matrix and projectized types of projects. However, these structures are related more to an external environment. Another way to configure a project is to arrange objects, such as people, either hierarchically or relationally. A hierarchical configuration represents a command and control orientation towards managing a project. The relational configuration represents a more stewardship approach towards managing projects. The integral approach represents a more participative decision-making approach, combining both hierarchical and relational approaches.

Using a systemic perspective, project managers can make changes more easily because they can focus on the "big picture," that is, how all the elements of a project interact. They can make decisions and take actions that leverage the affects and effects on performance. For example, they can identify critical success factors to improve performance of tasks on the critical path, e.g., add people on a task, change working relationships among team members, or increase learning opportunities.

The effect of such changes can be determinable quite easily by reviewing the common indicators associated with project performance, e.g., comparing planned and actual performance, tracking changes to cost performance indices, schedule performance indices, and defect rates. The key point is to realize the importance of tracking the effect of changes via feedback.

## SIMPLE STEPS

Developing a systemic view to lead a project requires following a few simple steps. These steps, however, are not easy to implement because they require a paradigm shift.

1. Identify the major elements of the project. These may be functions or activities performed, key individuals or organizations, and significant relationships among each other.
2. Try to develop an overall sense of the behavior pattern for a system. In this case, it is a project. Typically, a project performs many interrelated functions or processes, such as defining, planning, organizing, controlling, closing, and leading. The relationships frequently interact with each other, depending on the sequence of phases, for example. Some projects might also be on a crashed or fast-track basis, which can affect how the elements interface with one another.
3. Identify the type of systems diagramming approach to apply, e.g., object oriented, process, data, causal, or hybrid. The key is to pick the most comfortable approach for understanding the dynamics and workings of a project.
4. Identify areas in the diagram that can provide key leverage points to influence results. The leverage points will be determined by the topic, issue, or problem to address.
5. Determine the desired decision or action. This determination requires pinpointing where in a system this decision or action begins, which feeds the next step.
6. Determine the downstream effects of a decision or action. Downstream effects may be positive or negative, balancing or reinforcing, or a combination of both.
7. Address anticipated consequences, e.g., downstream impact of a decision or action. Consequences may be explicit or implicit. Also, remember that

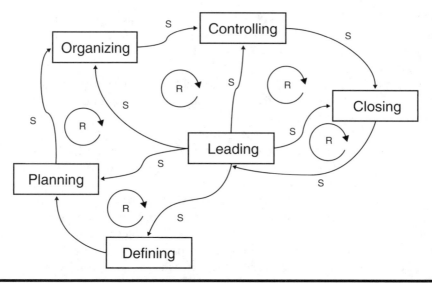

**Figure 5.3**  Systemic View of the Processes of Project Management.

any handling of a consequence may result in additional impacts that could necessitate decision or action.

Causal loop diagramming allows us to see the relationships among different processes or functions of projects and their consequences. By viewing a project from a leadership perspective, the dramatic impact becomes apparent.

For example, Figure 5.3 shows the relationships among the major processes of project management. Leading affects all the processes of project management, from defining to closing. In turn, each process affects other processes, e.g., planning enables organizing to occur more efficiently and effectively. The relationships also reinforce each other, e.g., more efficient and effective planning usually begets more efficient and effective organizing and vice versa.

## SERIOUS LEADERSHIP CONSIDERATIONS

The point is not that project managers must diagram the relationships of their projects. In fact, few project managers do. What is important is that project managers learn to visualize the major elements and relationships of their projects. This ability to do so will enable them to better understand the appropriate decisions and actions and manage the consequences. Few project managers do that, too. This inability to take a systemic view often results in a host of problems, especially people problems, which can negatively affect overall performance.

Project managers must therefore keep the following thoughts in mind when leading their projects.

Too often, project managers focus on individuals. This focus on objects, in this case people, is important but often misdirected. If performance is suffering, this focus lends itself to pointing to an individual as the cause and can result in what I refer to as the "blame syndrome." This, in turn, wreaks havoc on teaming because the focus shifts to one individual who is not likely to change unless he or she can truly realize the impact of his or her thinking and behavior on others. This recognition is often impractical to expect. So project managers exercise a quick fix by removing someone who cannot work well with certain people. Since many project managers lack command and control over many team members, this attempt often fails and leaves a negative residue. Instead, effective project managers try to improve working relationships to further the goals of the project. The emphasis then switches from the individual to the relationships, thus depersonalizing circumstances.

Hence, an important aspect of leading projects is to work on improving relationships among stakeholders. There are two aspects for doing that.

The first one is that focusing on relationships requires you to look at situations from the perspective of different mental models that reflect differences in beliefs, values, approaches, etc. With that knowledge, you will have a better understanding about why people think and feel the way that they do.

The second aspect is that project managers must take a serious look at the structure of their projects. Determining the structure and altering it will inevitably alter relationships among people. Some ways to alter the structure of projects include changing the reporting relationships, altering who works jointly on certain tasks, and assigning people to tasks conducive to their talents and personality.

## SYSTEMS PERSPECTIVE = LEADERSHIP

Project managers must keep their focus on the big picture by constantly asking themselves what the impact of their decisions and actions is on overall performance, e.g., meeting goals and objectives. The best approach for answering that question, of course, is to view a project systemically. To do that, project managers must answer three fundamental questions: Will the decision or actions to address the relationship in question further the goals and objectives of a project? What will be the downstream impacts? Will some additional decisions or actions be required to address downstream impacts, whether positive or negative?

The key point is that project managers must have a good understanding of their projects. Armed with that knowledge, they can respond rather than react to circumstances. They can then harness the energies of their most important potential energy of their projects — people — to achieve goals and objectives.

## CASE STUDY: INTEGRATE

To further his contextual understanding of the project, the project manager immediately developed a systemic view that was used to help determine the key elements and relationships of the project.

This view was formalized in a diagram that showed the major organizations and people, and their corresponding relationships, both internally and externally to the project. The strengths and constraints of each relationship and the overall impact to the performance of the project were also determined. Of particular note was the organizational structure of the entire corporation and the relationships among each of the major organizations and other stakeholders, e.g., business units.

The project manager also noted behavior patterns exhibited by the organizations and key people. These behavior patterns were revealed by how previous projects were managed; the overall managerial style employed; and the emphasis placed on certain metrics vis-à-vis to each other, e.g., cost versus quality versus schedule. Some business units, for example, were very schedule driven while others emphasized cost.

The project manager also identified, via a systemic view, the potential risks. Because the project was "interbusiness unit," the risks concerning relationships among stakeholders were particularly important. Each business unit had its own way of doing business and its own views about how to conduct it. Managing the team was, therefore, very complex. The structure of the project was very important because it determined the reporting relationship to headquarters and its level of control over each team member.

Independence and interdependence were, therefore, two important considerations for this project. Independence was important because each business unit felt its autonomy could be potentially threatened. Interdependence was important because the business units had to work together to develop a common policies and procedures infrastructure, while simultaneously respecting their unique requirements.

The project manager realized, with the support of the executive sponsor and members of the headquarters executive council, that it was extremely important that appropriate representation was on the team and that a common vision served to unite members on the team.

Another important concern was the controls and rules surrounding the project. Since the project altered the content as well as the structure of the policies and procedures, external influences were also important, such as legal compliance with affirmative action and product safety regulations. This determination made it necessary to assign the necessary subject matter experts to the project.

## REFERENCES

1. Fritjof Capra, *The Turning Point,* Bantam Books, Toronto, 1988, p. 267.
2. Dietrich Dorner, *The Logic of Failure,* Perseus Books, Cambridge, MA, 1996, p. 33.
3. Fritjof Capra, *The Web of Life,* Flamingo, New York, 1997, p. 36.
4. Peter M. Senge, *The Fifth Discipline,* Currency Doubleday, New York, 1990, p. 68.
5. Edward De Bono, *Practical Thinking,* Penguin Books, London, 1971, p. 45.
6. Ibid., p. 43.
7. Dietrich Dorner, *The Logic of Failure,* Perseus Books, Cambridge, MA, 1996, p. 5.
8. Russell L. Ackoff, Systems thinking and thinking systems, *Systems Dynamic Review,* p. 175, Summer–Fall 1994.
9. Fritjof Capra, *The Turning Point,* Bantam Books, Toronto, 1988, p. 43.
10. Peter M. Senge, *The Fifth Discipline,* Currency Doubleday, New York, 1990, p. 68.
11. Dietrich Dorner, *The Logic of Failure,* Perseus Books, Cambridge, MA, 1996, p. 39.
12. Ibid., p. 42.
13. Russell L. Ackoff, Systems thinking and thinking systems, *Systems Dynamic Review,* p. 187, Summer–Fall 1994.
14. Peter M. Senge, *The Fifth Discipline,* Currency Doubleday, New York, 1990, pp. 378–390.

# 6

# UNDERSTAND

Contextual understanding of a project is very important to a project manager. The reason is quite simple: By understanding the circumstances about a project, he or she can develop a meaningful plan and respond more effectively to expected and unexpected situations.

## NEGATIVE CONSEQUENCES

Failure to understand context can result in very serious consequences, especially later in a project life cycle.

- *A project manager could adopt an incorrect or unsatisfactory strategy, that is, one inappropriate for the circumstances.* He or she may employ resources, for example, based on an unrealistic scenario, resulting in an inefficient and ineffective execution of the project.
- *It can cause enormous tension, even negative conflict, due to the failure to identify important assumptions and facts.* Teaming with stakeholders may be, for example, especially difficult because everyone operates in a "I thought he or she thought" syndrome. If negative conflict does not arise early, it will surely arise later and with greater intensity.
- *It can result in a lack of commitment and ownership.* A project manager may involve the wrong stakeholders and overlook more important ones. From the very beginning of project execution, he or she may experience resistance for not paying attention to the context.
- *If not enough, unrealistic plans can be the product.* Inadequate assessment of circumstances can easily affect the quality of planning. For example, if

he or she fails to identify assumptions and stakeholders, the negative impacts will appear in the plans and throughout project execution.

- *A poor contextual understanding reflects poor decision making.* Whereas a good contextual understanding of a project can help a project manager make decisions at the right time, a poor contextual understanding provides the opposite; decisions become quixotic, chasing nonexistent or insignificant issues.
- *A poor contextual understanding can result in poor, even no, coordination.* That is because no one, including the project manager, can distinguish between what is and is not important. Consequently, the wrong people focus on the wrong priorities. For example, some stakeholders may consider a schedule important, but others consider quality paramount, and then for some strange reason, the project manager focuses on the budget, which represents his or her contextual understanding.
- *The ultimate consequence of having a poor (or lack of) contextual understanding is that it can cause poor project performance.* People, individually and as a team, immediately become inefficient and ineffective, contributing ultimately to poor schedule and budget performance, perhaps due to rework.

## POSITIVE CONSEQUENCES

Naturally, a good contextual understanding offers many benefits; however, each one is easier to talk about than to achieve.

- *Minimizes negative conflict and fosters positive conflict.* The reason is that project managers will have a good knowledge of the circumstances facing them. If smart, they will encourage positive conflict early to reveal what is and is not important, such as when developing the project charter and planning.
- *Greater teaming becomes a likely result.* Good contextual understanding enables stakeholders as well as project managers to have a realistic appraisal of circumstances and assumptions. This understanding is very important because if something important in the context is not revealed up front, it could prove very costly later during the life cycle.
- *Better communication.* A thorough understanding of project context relies heavily on effective communication among all the stakeholders, especially the important ones. It is safe to state that without good communication, project managers cannot acquire a good contextual understanding. The opposite is also the case.

- *Results in better coordination downstream in the project life cycle.* Project managers and other stakeholders will have a good understanding of circumstances and can respond accordingly and rather reactively.
- *Enables better decision making.* Project managers can make better decisions because they can discern what is and is not important. They will also have more data and information to make decisions.
- *Allows for more ownership and commitment by all stakeholders on a project.* To gain understanding, project managers will need to interact with key stakeholders and work with them to obtain the necessary information. This interaction will, naturally, engender even more commitment and ownership later.
- *Gives others a greater sense of direction.* Everyone will understand what is within the scope and will recognize how their actions add or deviate from scope. Hence, a side benefit is that it provides everyone with more focus.

## MAJOR DIFFICULTIES

There are some major difficulties in obtaining a good contextual understanding. Project managers can never divorce themselves from the environment and obtain a true, objective understanding. In *On Leadership,* John Gardner notes the difficulty quite well, recognizing that leaders cannot divorce themselves from the context in which they find themselves, as they are an instrumental element of the system that they must lead.[1]

This situation, of course, makes it very difficult for project managers to capture and process information to help them strive to obtain a fair, not necessarily unbiased, contextual understanding. Basically, that means having and maintaining a good awareness of what is going on in the general business and project environments. Such awareness is achievable by avoiding jumping to conclusions and becoming more of an observer to understand what is necessary.

Fortunately, recognition is growing about the importance that project managers have a keen contextual understanding to apply the most appropriate leadership style; there appears to be a direct tie.[2] Daniel Goleman says it well in an interview in *PM Network* when he said that project managers must be sensitive to people and the environment.[3]

Contemporary research seems to support him. Martin and Wysocki note three elements that contribute to project success, one being the environmental elements that affect the project team.[4] Opfer, Kloppenborg, and Shriberg also seem to agree and note that individual teams and organizational considerations must be accounted for.[5]

## THE MEANING OF CONTEXTUAL UNDERSTANDING

What does contextual understanding really mean? Basically, it means to look at the setting of a project, such as the influencing factors in the project's environment, as well as major elements and their relationships. In other words, getting a sense of the "overall picture" and how the project fits within it; determining all elements, e.g., facts and assumptions, and ascertaining how they interact; and adopting approaches that enable efficient and effective responses.

## CAVEATS

To enable contextual understanding, project managers should consider the following caveats.

*A truly objective contextual understanding does not and cannot exist.* Project managers are as much captured by their circumstances as everyone else. Being the project manager places you (theoretically) at a "higher" position than many team members, but that does not guarantee objectivity. To deal with this challenge, project managers must consciously understand how they frame their contextual understanding and how others do the same. In addition, they need to involve people with frames or viewpoints that support and deviate from their own. This will counter the tendency of project managers to fall into what I refer to as the "hammer effect," whereby they are like a child with a hammer and everything looks like a nail.

This effect largely reflects the need to be in control, however illusionary, and can result in great costs. In *The Logic of Failure,* Dietrich Dorner agrees and observes that the reason is to augment one's sense of competence and avoid an admission of failure. Besides, such an admission may be perceived as an inadequacy on one's part. So, according to Dorner, conspiracy theories are developed to cover up such inadequacies.[6] These theories limit the view of the world and lead to seeing only what is wanted to be seen.

According to Edward De Bono, one way to obtain a clearer picture of understanding is through a shared explanation. Through a shared explanation, the visibility for understanding becomes clearer.[7] Then, it becomes easier to understand how different perceptions influence progression.

*Constantly remind themselves that a strong tendency exists to see "individual trees before the forest."* A major reason for this tendency is that people often subscribe to what they feel comfortable with, gained either through knowledge or experience. Once project managers lose sight of the big picture, they will find it very difficult to rise to a higher plane. Objectivity becomes even more difficult despite being impossible to attain in the pure sense of the word.

Project managers often become trapped in a perceived way of "how things work" and pursue unrealistic courses of action. According to Dorner, that is because the rules on how things work can constrain the ability to adapt to a changing context, leading to a disastrous result. It is important, therefore, to recognize that everything is in flux and that the ability to adapt is absolutely essential. However, such adaptation is opposite to our desire to develop general, abstract plans.[8] This tendency can lead to an inflexibility that can prove disastrous, at least systemically. Everything in a system is interlinked; inflexibility in one aspect or relationship will permeate a system.[9]

*Recognize the need to distinguish between the tangibles and intangibles by identifying what lies above and below the waterline.* A strong case can be made that an inability to understand the intangible aspects can "sink" a project quicker than the Titanic. Some intangible elements include the informal networks, politics, values, and the overall "atmosphere" enveloping an organization. Frequently overlooked, this inability can result in flawed decisions and actions. The situation does not seem to be improving.

*Recognize the importance of data and information as well as the fragility of both.* Data are, of course, unprocessed facts. Information is processed data that are meaningful to the recipient. Data and information are important because they are instrumental in decision making and for feedback on results. However, data and information are subject to many influences, from handling by developers and providers to the ravages of time. In other words, both data and information are perishable items. Understanding becomes very important concerning these conditions, especially if a desire exists to avoid adhering to and applying irrelevant data and knowledge.

*Not everything has equal value when understanding the context of a project.* Some data and information are critical for better understanding, while others are of minor importance. Unfortunately, this dichotomy poses a very significant problem. What is considered important to one person may not be so to another if operating under a different mental model or paradigm. It is imperative, therefore, that project managers surround themselves with a diversity of thought to avoid falling into a narrow, incorrect understanding of the context. Through understanding the context, it is easier to identify priorities because one can see the bigger picture.

*Encourage open communication right from the start to obtain a contextual understanding.* By encouraging open communication to capitalize on the benefit of different perspectives, they can cross-check the reliability of data and information. They also encourage the early communication of issues and concerns, positive and negative. Such open communication will enable addressing issues early to avoid their downstream impact when they will be more difficult and costly to handle.

However, that is often not easily achieved because of the failure by many project managers to listen. Too often, they arrogantly think they know the answer or solution and then proceed accordingly only to find that the long-term results were not as expected. They would have done well to heed the sage advice of Stephen Covey on two levels: "seek first to understand, then be understood"[10] and "diagnose before you prescribe."[11]

Contextual understanding involves the assimilation of substantial variable information. Such information can reflect the internal and external pressures placed on projects, their types, and their risks. Project managers must organize this information to obtain a contextual understanding and successfully shape their projects. Project shaping means to recognize the different scenarios facing a project and then manage and lead the project accordingly. Of course, this effort is not easy to accomplish since such information is often not readily available.

Diana Lilla, of Diana Lilla Consulting, gave a presentation before the Puget Sound PMI Chapter to discuss the project waterline model.[12] She notes that information is readily observable above the waterline. This information includes stated goals and deliverables. However, some items are below the waterline and, consequently, are not readily available or observable. These items pertain to the people aspects, e.g., informal networks, personal aspirations, and norms, and frequently have a major impact on a project and, therefore, should be acknowledged as best as possible.

What are some considerations that go into acquiring a contextual understanding? The list, of course, can be endless. I think, however, they can be grouped into four categories: people, process, performance, and profit. Each one, in turn, has an external and internal slant.

For *people,* the internal slant involves skills, knowledge, and abilities; formal and informal networks; politics; motivations; values; beliefs; ethics; esprit de corps; and diversity. The external slant relates to similar issues only on a larger scale and from the perspective of influencing performance. They include communication with senior management, management styles, general history and culture of the organization, and relationships with suppliers, vendors, and consultants. What is challenging about determining internal and external slants about people are their subtleties, making it difficult to ascertain their presence and impact.

The internal slant of *process* involves implementing the major disciplines of project management, e.g., defining, planning, organizing, controlling, and closing; administrative or supporting processes, e.g., quality assurance, configuration management, and change management; and additional ones, e.g., portfolio project management. From an external slant, the same processes are involved but on a larger scale. Often, what complicates understanding is their linkage with so many elements within and outside the boundaries of a project.

The internal slant of *performance* centers on measurement, e.g., feedback during all phases of a project. Many tools are available to measure performance. Project management software is the principal tool for comparing expected and actual performance. Earned value management provides a true gauge on schedule and budgetary performance. The external slant again is on a higher level, with the output often feeding data and information to management. The challenges here are providing metrics on what satisfies internal needs while simultaneously satisfying external requirements.

The internal slant of *profit* relates to results achieved and is clearly associated with performance. Its emphasis is, however, more about results that have been achieved rather than the execution of a project. Profit usually relates to internal standards for quality, schedule, and budget. Quality deals with satisfying internal requirements and expectations; schedule, with meeting milestones and finishing on time; and costs, with finishing within budget. The external slant involves the same but with a twist. For quality, it deals with meeting the requirements and expectations of the customer as well as complying with any other externally mandated standards and requirements; schedules, delivering on time to provide a deliverable to another project; cost, satisfying overall budgetary requirements on a program and much larger organizational levels.

## ACTIONS NEEDED

There are several ways to approach acquiring contextual understanding.

One approach is to develop a systemic view of a project. For instance, a project manager might develop, either formally or mentally, a causal loop diagram that identifies what constitutes "the project" and key relationships among all its elements.

Another approach is to view a project in terms of its stage. In my book, *The People Side of Project Management,* I identify the five stages of a project: gestation, growth, independence, decline, and death.[13]

The *gestation* stage represents the birth of a project. It is at this time that a project will or will not become a viable entity. Often, a peeked interest arises because something is wrong, necessitating the project. At the same time, a struggle may ensue — competition with other projects and other priorities. Even with good justification, a project may not survive because the competition and the other priorities may be too strong. Project leadership necessitates the ability to overcome this resistance by proving the project's worthiness. Project managers may find it very difficult to have people take ownership and be committed at this stage.

The *growth* stage is when a project has gained some legitimacy and respectability. In other words, it provides value to key stakeholders. Still, as in gestation, a project must compete to survive, only this time with projects of an equal or better stature. Project leadership requires a style that emphasizes the need to develop and implement an infrastructure that engenders a sense of "sturdiness" in its infrastructure while progressing.

The *independence* stage represents the self-supporting point of a project. It can now compete successfully with other contemporary projects and receive the necessary support to sustain itself. It is the "norming" point of a project. Considerable equilibrium exists in the overall performance of a project. Project leadership involves maintaining a sense of direction and focus.

The *declining* stage is that point when a project moves from being a going concern to nearing goal attainment. It is here that disequilibrium may begin to arise. As the work completes, people begin to focus on other matters, such as finding another project. It is also at this point that rising projects compete to receive attention. Depending on its progress, this stage can be rather euphoric, due to success, or negative, when some people feel the project was a bad investment of their time and effort.

The *death* stage is, of course, the final one. The project loses relevancy to all the stakeholders. In other words, it no longer can sustain legitimacy vis-à-vis other competing projects.

A project can move from the gestation phase to the death stage almost overnight, thereby bypassing the other stages. Or, it can progress through all five stages. The point is that project managers should have a good idea of the phase of the project. This knowledge enables them to make some key decisions and actions pertaining to cost, schedule, quality, and people.

Another approach toward attaining contextual understanding is to determine the category of your project. An excellent approach is the one developed by A.J. Shenhar et al.[14] that they described at the 2002 PMI Research Conference in Seattle, Washington. The idea is that different projects require different management. They developed a matrix that uniquely classifies projects and distinguishes them from one another, referring to the scheme as the strategic/portfolio classification. It consists of projects that are either operational or strategic in nature and the customers as internal or external. Product improvement projects are examples of projects that are operational and external; maintenance, operational and internal; new product development, strategic and external; and research, strategic and internal.

After understanding the classification of a project, the next step is to apply the uncertainty, complexity, pace (UCP) model. Uncertainty is highest at the beginning of a project and reflects scope; complexity consists of a combination of elements, e.g., size and interconnectedness; and pace is the time frame.

Next, identify the product/work distinction, once again reflected in a matrix. The product may be intangible or tangible, e.g., hardware or data, respectively. The work may be intellectual or craft oriented, either new or done earlier, respectively. The combination of two variables, e.g., intellectual and intangible, reflects the degree of risk associated with a project.

According to Shenhar et al., the result of all three models and matrices determines the interest certain stakeholders have in a project. In addition, it determines the overall project management style employed which reflects, in part, how a project manager leads people through the choice of strategies, organization, processes, and tools.[14]

So how do project managers get started in obtaining a contextual understanding? There are several actions or behaviors that they can exhibit; these actions should not be construed, however, as a step-by-step approach. Rather, all of them may occur concurrently and in different order, depending on the circumstances.

Perhaps the most important action to take is a systemic view. A systemic view requires that they look at the project from a particular frame of reference or mental map and identify all the elements and their relationships.

What works for me is an almost ecological systemic view. I identify what I consider all the elements, e.g., objects and relationships, and ascertain how they interact within the contemporary environment. I look for the explicit and implied factors, both within the boundaries of the project and its external environment, and look for linkage. I am particularly interested in the behavior patterns as demonstrated in similar projects from the past and the effectiveness of the processes. Armed with that knowledge, I have a better understanding of the potential risks and actions to take either now or in the future.

There are various ways to obtain this information. Project managers can review documentation, e.g., lessons learned, and data, e.g., earned value, from previous projects. This material may or may not be readily available. Unfortunately, what exists is either too much or too little, both quite paralyzing. If too much, project managers can review the material in a cursory manner to acquire a sense of the challenges, issues, and risks. If necessary, they can convert data into information by developing quality control type charts, e.g., Pareto charts, pie charts.

But if too little material, what can project managers do? The most important action is to meet with stakeholders, direct and indirect. By using effective listening and meeting skills, project managers can get solid insights to help them acquire a good contextual understanding. Remember, the goal is more than collecting data and information; it is to acquire a contextual understanding. In other words, the wisdom of Covey returns — seek first to understand. To a larger degree, acquiring a contextual understanding is like a reconnaissance mission. Data and information may be available, but they may not be reliable or valid. The project manager has to conduct the mission to separate fiction from fact before engagement.

Whether or not the data or information are available, project managers must be critical, not applied, thinkers. Critical thinking, in a nutshell, means to apply judgment, e.g., accept or reject, to the data and information received. Applied thinking means to apply methods, tools, and techniques without really questioning their validity, e.g., calculate the critical path.

When applying critical thinking, project managers must be constantly cognizant that they are immersed in an environment and that obtaining a true objective perspective is impossible. However, this impossibility does not obviate the need for critical thinking but augments it.

There are so many "threats" facing project managers when they exercise critical thinking. These include how projects were managed in the past, group mores and norms throughout an organization, managerial style of superiors, "politics," oversimplification and overcomplication, and availability of data and information sources. If project managers recognize that such threats exist, they can better deal with impacts to their projects.

Naturally, this situation leads to the question of what constitutes critical thinking when trying to acquire a contextual understanding of a project. I think that it requires answering this question with questions like:

- What is my frame of reference?
- What are the frames of reference of other stakeholders?
- Do the data and information reflect facts or assumptions?
- How meaningful or significant are the data and information?
- What are the standards of evaluation to distinguish between fact and assumption?
- Is feedback clear and concise to avoid erroneous judgments?
- What are implicit factors influencing the performance of a project?
- What are the inferences and conclusions drawn from the data and information?
- What is the logical thinking behind inferences and conclusions?
- How can the inferences and conclusions be verified to avoid basing them on inaccurate data and information?
- Has judgment been suspended before the data and information are used?
- What are the consequences of using data and information that are received?

■ What are some contradictions in the data and information received and the methods employed to seek clarification and resolution?

■ How will the data and information be compiled and organized to reduce bias?

Answering the above questions is not easy. However, they do provide project managers with the opportunity to get their bearings, especially during the early phases and stages. Too often, project managers fall into the same trap as other professionals. They treat assumptions and theories as facts and, even in some cases, as truisms. They rely on inaccurate or incomplete data. Many examples exist due to an inability to develop an accurate contextual understanding; assumptions, data, and information are often unreliable or invalid. This blind acceptance complicates leading a project because what was used and accepted up front permeates the life cycle, creating downstream challenges.

## IMPORTANT ROLE

Perhaps the most important insight about contextual understanding is the role people play, not simply facts, data, and assumptions. Project managers often fail to recognize this reality. They tend to rely exclusively on research or documentation reviews. However, projects are about bringing people together to achieve a common goal and satisfying individual ones. Project managers are well positioned, formally and informally, to make "things happen" and the best way to do that is to have a solid contextual understanding. Leading them becomes the focus, not planning and execution, as they adopt an appropriate leadership style.

## CASE STUDY: UNDERSTAND

The project manager immediately attempted to acquire an understanding of the project. This understanding helped to not only appreciate the scope and scale of the project, but also the potential major stakeholders and their relationships. One of the first steps, therefore, was to sit with the senior executive sponsor and try to obtain an understanding of the expectations for the project from the executive council and acquire some preliminary assumptions, facts, and data. Using that information, the project manager took a cut at the initial stakeholders from each business unit on who would participate on the team.

The project manager also conducted an inventory of information about the circumstances surrounding the project. Some areas of interest included major stakeholders and their relationships with each business unit as well as assumptions, facts, and data about the current policies and procedures infrastructure. In addition, the political considerations were reviewed to identify what each stakeholder had to lose or gain from the change and understand why. This information enabled the project manager to anticipate obstacles and objections to change and prepare appropriate responses to justify the project.

Another important piece of information for understanding the project was to distinguish between what was significant and what was insignificant. The project manager was then able to focus energies on the key issues and concerns, thereby avoiding a "shot gun" approach when getting started. This was accomplished by interviewing people associated with the project, e.g., subject matter experts and other executives, as well as reviewing the history of what existed on similar projects that previously failed.

An interesting note was that two similar projects were conducted in the past. They failed to make significant progress, thus creating a need for this project. The project manager investigated the reasons for the failure to learn the lessons and avoid the same pitfalls.

The project manager understood that the gestation phase of the project was going to be the most difficult and soon realized and expected that the team members of each of the business units could potentially see the project as a threat to their autonomy both on a short- and long-term basis. The key, therefore, was to get the right stakeholders involved in formulating the vision and plan for the project.

## REFERENCES

1. John W. Gardner, *On Leadership,* The Free Press, New York, 1990, pp. 38–47.
2. Warren A. Opfer, Timothy J. Kloppenborg, and Arthur Shriberg, Project leadership: setting the stage, in *Proceedings of PMI Research Conference 2002,* Project Management Institute, Newtown Square, PA, p. 417.
3. Jeannette Cabanis-Brevin, The human task of a project leader, *PM Network,* p. 39, November 1999.
4. Warren A. Opfer, Timothy J. Kloppenborg, and Arthur Shriberg, Project leadership: setting the stage, in *Proceedings of PMI Research Conference 2002,* Project Management Institute, Newtown Square, PA, p. 417.
5. Ibid.
6. Dietrich Dorner, *The Logic of Failure,* Perseus Books, Cambridge, MA, 1996, pp. 69–70.
7. Edward De Bono, *Practical Thinking,* Penguin Books, London, 1971, p. 34.
8. Dietrich Dorner, *The Logic of Failure,* Perseus Books, Cambridge, MA, 1996, p. 98.
9. Fritjof Capra, *The Turning Point,* Bantam Books, Toronto, 1998, p. 273.

10. Stephen R. Covey, *The Seven Habits of Highly Effective People,* Simon & Schuster, New York, 1990, p. 237.
11. Ibid., p. 243.
12. Diana Lilla, Navigating the waterline, Presentation at Puget Sound PMI Chapter, March 11, 2002, pp. 1–17.
13. Ralph L. Kliem, *The People Side of Project Management,* Gower, Aldershot, Hampshire, U.K., 1992. pp. 20–26.
14. A.J. Shenhar, D. Dvir, T. Lechler, and M. Poli, One size does not fit all, Presentation at PMI Research Conference 2002, July 15, Seattle, WA.

# 7

# DECIDE

Making decisions is a key skill for leaders. Most project managers face a flurry of activities that constantly pressure them to make decisions that have considerable impact on the execution of their projects.

## MANY THEORIES

Leadership theorists in project management now recognize the importance of decision making by project managers. Jurgen Hauschildt, Gesche Keim, and John W. Medcof conducted a study on selecting and developing project managers. They identify a classification of project managers who are known as "stars," with above-average ability in decision making.[1]

Greg Skulmonski, Francis Hartman, and Roch DeMaere also conducted a study on the competencies of project managers and came to similar conclusions, observing that what distinguished superior project managers from participants was the former's competencies of decisiveness and delegation.[2]

## CHARACTERISTICS OF POOR DECISIONS

Despite this recognition of decision making by project managers, many project managers often make poor decisions. "Poor" decisions by project managers often share characteristics.

*A failure to consider the behavioral consequences of their decisions.* When they do, they take inappropriate action to mitigate the consequences. For example, some project managers decide unilaterally to change a course of action.

Under certain circumstances, making such a decision may be appropriate. In other words, it can cause people to perform rework or seek additional skills. Failure to account for such consequences can deteriorate morale and esprit de corps.

*Adherence to a short-term perspective.* Because many projects move fast, such as fast-track development projects, project managers feel pressure to succumb to a quick fix. Sometimes, however, the quick fix may lack wisdom and represents a failure to consider looking at downstream impacts, e.g., rework and delays. Impacts augment frustration and tension to an already frustrating and tense experience. In *Why Decisions Fail,* Paul Nutt describes the consequences quite clearly in the general context of decision making. He says that people who make decisions often grab the first idea and then try to make it a reality.[3] Ian Mitroff agrees and notes that it is a serious shortcoming of management in general, and observes that most management errors are predicated on addressing either the wrong issue or an unclear one.[4]

*An inability to distinguish between major and minor issues and information.* Some project managers consider everything equal when in reality that is not true. Not surprisingly, these projects fall into an analysis paralysis mode, awaiting definition and verification of everything. When making a decision, it becomes an anachronism, losing its relevancy and significance.

*A failure by some project managers to focus on the goals and objectives of their projects.* When focus is lost, the opportunity for "scope creep" increases. Scope creep is the inadvertent expansion of goals and objectives; it often occurs by accident rather than design. Failure to direct decision making from the context of the original goals and objectives can have disastrous effects on performance, e.g., excessive overtime, burn out, and missed milestones.

*Introduction of bias.* Bias can come from the project manager alone or from other stakeholders, such as senior management or a customer. The impact of bias can be tremendous and can result in overlooking essential information; failing to consider different, perhaps more important alternatives; and being overly optimistic or pessimistic. What complicates bias is the difficulty in detecting it, especially personal bias. Whether detectable or not, biases can cause silence when people should speak up; overlook important information; and play "favorites" among team members. Stephen Covey observes quite correctly the powerful influence of bias in decision making and the problems accompanying it once it was in the form of a paradigm. He says that everyone has "maps" within their brains that divide everything into what is and what should be. The maps are very powerful because people interpret everything with them and they are seldom questioned. All subsequent attitudes and behavior reflect these maps.[5]

*Failure to seek feedback on effectiveness.* Without feedback, project managers will be unable to ascertain effectiveness. Too often, many project managers not only make snap judgments, but also fail to conduct follow-up. If they do, they frequently do so to support their own decision. In other words, they allow bias, either by design or fault, which is a common problem in other management levels. Paul Nutt says that some decision makers will continually re-evaluate with the intent of defending their decision to show that it is feasible or that it was the right one. Such efforts can prove costly in terms of time and money.[6]

## CHARACTERISTICS OF GOOD DECISIONS

"Good" decisions have certain characteristics, too.

*Based on a pursuit for objectivity despite being virtually impossible to attain.* Project managers who make good decisions seek to identify and consider "facts and data" before making a judgment. If they involve assumptions, project managers identify and recognize them as such. They do not try to fool anyone, including themselves.

*Recognize that not all facts, data, and assumptions are equal; some are more important than others.* Rather than wade through minutia, they distinguish between what is and is not important and leverage the former to further decision making and action.

*Consider short- and long-term impacts of a decision.* They recognize the need to ensure that the project progresses. They do so by thinking about the present through the "eyes of the future." This unique perspective then enables a response rather than a reaction. The reason is that they can anticipate and prepare for what will likely happen in the future.

*Look at the context of their decision by considering the environment and its major influences.* They have a good idea of the issues, pressures, and stakeholders, for example, and understand their influence on project activities.

*Consider, with time permitting, many viewpoints or perspectives.* They recognize that they may be held captive to a paradigm that "colors" their views. Involving others in decision making not only generates commitment, but also encourages the opportunity to consider additional information and alternatives in their decision making. They receive a more balanced view that enables them to make an appropriate decision for dealing with a situation. Leaders should look through different "lenses," says Max De Pree in *Leadership Jazz*. He adds that it should be from the perspective of followers, through a "new reality" and experience, as well as unfairness.[7]

*Not place the "horse before the cart" by determining a solution first.* Instead, they define an issue or problem first, determine alternatives, select the best one, and collect feedback to determine any necessary adjustments. This approach forces project managers to think before ramming a solution into implementation. Ian Mitroff says that a nested relationship exists among problem definition, actions taken, and justifications. It becomes very important, he adds, to raise questions about all three.[8]

If considered an important activity, a feeling will likely arise by some stakeholders that a solution is being forced on them; they will lack commitment and ownership when implementing it. Since most project managers lack command and control over team members, for example, determining the solution first can place them in an adversarial position with the very people who must execute it.

*Be ever mindful of the "traps" into which decision makers fall prey.* John Hammond, Ralph Keeney, and Howard Raifa observe that decision makers often fall into several traps that include emphasizing considerable importance to the amount of information, supporting the status quo, justifying sunk costs, and confirming existing views.[9]

*Avoid falling into the analysis paralysis trap.* Instead, they seek an appropriate, not perfect, solution. The search for a perfect solution in project management can consume much time and resources, resulting in an anachronistic decision. In other words, a point of diminishing returns arises. Project managers should seek effectiveness, therefore, and not perfection. Here are two good reasons: enough facts and data are never available and both are frequently incomplete. If making a decision, they often feel forced into it. Being a perfectionist is dangerous, particularly when making decisions. Worry can take over and lead to a desire to avoid making a decision for fear of failure or waiting for someone else to make it. Otherwise, the person makes a decision by default.[10]

## CAVEATS

When making decisions, project managers should heed the following caveats.

*Recognize that enough facts and data will never be available.* Project managers will never reach a point of completeness, regardless of how much a perfectionist they might be. They can "drill down" into databases, interview a host of people, and review piles of documentation and still feel uncomfortable with the degree of facts and data. Besides, a point of diminishing returns may arise when pursuing more facts and data. It will also add to the angst of facing ambiguity, even intensify the feelings. Edward De Bono agrees and notes that it is virtually impossible to obtain complete details. In fact, he adds, a person can seek so much detail that it may decrease clarity.[11]

*Acknowledge the role of emotion as well as logic in decision making.* Decisions are a human endeavor. In an effort to think and appear objective, many project managers strive to be objective but ignore the emotional side. However, their emotions — from anger to fear — will be meshed with their logic; it is part of the human condition. This emotion will be reflected largely in their response to the circumstances. Emotions will determine not only what they consider facts and data, but also what they select and process. It will also influence their selected response to a situation. Our moods powerfully affect our thinking in general and decision making in particular. Hence, a good mood will encourage us to do something risky while a negative mood leads us to be cautious.[12]

*Decisions often involve a choice of values, reflecting a subjective, not objective, exercise.* What a person deems important versus unimportant often reflects their preferences and biases built up over the years either through learning or experience. When project managers are in a decision-making position such influences affect, either overtly or subtly, the choices made. They will affect the ability to define the issue or problem, identify alternatives, select the best solution, and implement it. Some overt influences include vocation and experience. Some subtle influences include attitude, limited knowledge, education, and risk acceptance level.

All decisions have consequences. Project managers do not operate in a void. By virtue of their position, they influence just about everything on a project, as they are essentially linchpins. They are in the locus of decision making. It is important, therefore, that project managers realize the impact of their decisions.

These impacts of decisions can be classified in several ways.

1. Impacts can be short or long term. A short-term impact affects activities early on, e.g., during the current phase of a project's life cycle. A long-term impact might be felt much later on.
2. Impacts can be explicit or implicit. An explicit impact is easily tangible, e.g., reducing rework resulting from the efforts of a specific task. An implicit impact is very hard to detect, e.g., a decrease in morale or esprit de corps. Implicit knowledge may be even more meaningful despite not being quantifiable.
3. Impacts can be positive or negative. A positive impact furthers progress, e.g., a decision to adopt a new process. A negative impact retards progress, e.g., a decision to change scope without coordinating with people.

Naturally, a decision can be a combination of all three categories. For example, the impact of a decision can be explicit and positive, like a reward for performing a task well. Or, it can be long-term, implicit, and negative, like a decision not to perform a process at the time because it seemed unimportant but later causes rework and schedule delay.

*Decisions are neither "right" nor "wrong" per se.* Many project managers want to "make the right decision." The reality is that there is no right decision and that many decisions may be right or wrong only from the perspective of the frame of reference or mental model of the decision maker. This desire for being right and correct often leads to premature decision making because people jump to a conclusion. Consequently, project managers are often at constant war with their circumstances by imposing decisions and then "selling and marketing" them. In reality, many decisions do work that way, each with its unique consequences. What project managers should strive for is to identify options to address and selecting the best, not the right, one.

*Decisions must consider the context of an environment.* While seemingly straightforward, this is often ignored. Many project managers make decisions as if inside some egg, immune from the outside world, e.g., isolating themselves from daily project activities. Effective project managers act like open systems, however, attuned to activities and events whether internal or external. To lead effectively, they must factor such considerations into their decisions.

*Decisions are rarely, if ever, isolated acts by a project manager.* Yet, many project managers make decisions exactly that way. They unilaterally make decisions, ignore input, or do not consult with others. They fall into an "Ivory Tower" trap and issue impractical and unenforceable declarations on large projects. The reality is that decisions require both information about circumstance and notification about the need for decision making. Still, many project managers act unilaterally only to find their decisions often flawed, failing to achieve effectiveness, and creating constant tension. They need to consider the scale of consultation and participation in decision making. Of course, project managers need not consult every stakeholder on every decision. It is a matter of circumstance. As Thomas Gordon notes: Everyone on a team needs to be involved and then be available when needed.[13]

*Sometimes not making a decision is the best decision, if intentional.* Some project managers feel they have to make a decision. However, occasions arise that necessitate making a decision under different circumstances or at another time. Many project managers rush to judgment even without defining exactly the issue or problem under consideration or the relevancy of the facts and data. Instead, they exercise a "fire, ready, aim" rather than a "ready, aim, fire" attitude.

Sometimes this approach will work but project managers need to recognize when it is best to "shoot from the hip" rather than "shoot from the head" and vice versa. When the former, it is always wise to consult with someone, if warranted, to avoid creating a bigger problem or issue than the original one.

*Decisions often deal with problems or issues of gray rather than black or white.* This point is related to the last one. Many project managers simplify for ease of decision making. Simplification may make decision making easier, but it may also result in an inappropriate decision that lacks scalability, that is, appropriateness to circumstances or "one size fits all" orientation. This approach can lead to "absolutionism" and may create problems with stakeholders.

Other project managers do just the opposite. They complicate an issue or problem and, in turn, do the same for decision making. The result is a "bird's nest" of facts, data, and assumptions that leads only to greater confusion and frustration.

What project managers need to recognize is that decision making often deals with issues and problems on a gray scale. They must define issues or problems clearly and then tailor the decisions by consulting with other stakeholders, even those who do not share the same views. This approach will help prevent over-simplification or overcomplication of an issue or problem and decision making.

This approach requires, therefore, that project managers challenge their own assumptions and those of others. For reasons of security, such challenges are often difficult to face because they may mean admitting being wrong or incomplete.

A decision has two parts: making the decision and its execution. While this sounds like common sense, it is often not exercised. Most project managers make decisions throughout the life cycle of projects, but many of them fail to perform follow-up. Large, complicated projects may pose a problem in this regard. However, on small- or medium-sized projects, this appears to be a smaller problem due to scalability. Nonetheless, project managers must converse with stakeholders to determine whether a decision has been actually executed. Simple declaration is not enough. Stakeholders get occupied with other issues; time passes between the decision and its implementation, and people simply forget about it. Project managers may not have communicated the decision very effectively or people simply did not speak up. Regardless, project managers must constantly follow up on their decisions.

*All decisions usually involve trade-offs, that is, sacrificing something to achieve something else.* For example, a decision may require sacrificing one goal or objective for another as it relates to cost, schedule, quality, and scope. Of course, in times of unlimited resources this circumstance may not exist. Such moments are few and far between. More often than not, project managers must make trade-offs because resources are scarce — whether time or money. There is an acronym to describe this scenario: TANSTAAFL, for There Ain't No Such Thing As A Free Lunch. Such trade-off decisions, of course, present substantial challenges to project managers because they will invariably dissatisfy or satisfy certain stakeholders. It is imperative, therefore, that project managers do not, unless circumstances warrant it, make unilateral decisions. They should also effectively communicate their decisions.

*Decisions should be made from the perspective of a vision for a project for two major reasons.* The first is that it will help prevent scope creep, that is, the tendency to take on additional work that goes beyond what was originally defined. The other reason is that it eases "selling" a decision, as it is relatively self-explanatory. People will tend to find it more acceptable, especially if they did not participate in a decision.

*Decision making requires both sides of the brain, left and right.* True, analytical, linear thinking (left brain) is important. However, to decide on problems or issues, integrated relational thinking is also important. Overlooking the importance of an integrated perspective can lead to tunnel vision and negative downstream effects on a project.

*Use flexibility when adapting different approaches towards decision making.* Some project managers may find that elaborate mathematical calculations are preferable to select the best alternative, particularly when time is available. Or, they may take an intuitive approach that emphasizes "gut feel." To be reliable, however, intuition depends largely on experience Another option is to use an experiential approach. Instead, project managers rely on experience, which allows them to recognize patterns and identify key issues or drivers to "visualize" effects.

With these caveats in mind, it becomes easier to understand and deal with the human side of decision making. People add complications to the decision-making process. Leadership is about dealing with the human side.

## DECISION-MAKING STEPS

The following steps are common among all decision-making models and will be discussed at length from a project leadership perspective: Define the problem or issue; determine the facts, data, assumptions, and other relevant information regarding the problem or issue; develop different alternatives; determine the best approach; plan for execution and feedback; and execute the decision and adjust accordingly.

## Define the Problem or Issue

Defining a problem or issue is perhaps the most important step in decision making. Unfortunately, it is often the most neglected. Way too often project managers develop a solution before fully defining a problem or issue. They develop and implement a decision, perhaps only partially effective, and it is "pushed rather than pulled" into acceptance by stakeholders.

The key for defining a problem or issue, of course, is to determine its type. Three basic types of problems or issues exist: descriptive, normative, and prescriptive.

1. A descriptive problem or issue centers on questions related to "how," that is, those that deal with applied rather than critical concerns. An example might be: How do I build this network diagram?
2. A normative problem or issue centers on questions of what must be done "right." They address concerns about doing things correctly. An example is: Is the network diagram constructed correctly?
3. A prescriptive problem or issue centers on questions about doing the right things. They raise issues or problems of what ought to be done. An example is: Should we build a different type of schedule?

Most project managers deal and feel comfortable with descriptive and normative issues and problems. Few have the same perspective about the prescriptive ones. Their avoidance is understandable. The first two are less controversial and require a more methodical approach. The third one requires that the project manager challenge the basis of action, e.g., whether something should be done and, if so, should be done differently. That is the nature of critical, not applied, thinking skills.

Nevertheless, once project managers classify a problem or issue, they can begin a definition process. This approach is not easy, but is absolutely crucial because defining a problem or issue will influence the selection of an approach and the subsequent chain of events to address it. In fact, it will determine what is considered and in what context.

So when defining a problem or issue, project managers must understand the context. This understanding includes the category of the problem or issue discussed; availability of facts, data, and assumption; scope or boundaries; stakeholders directly and indirectly involved; and other factors.

When defining the problem or issue, project managers face many challenges. In *Smart Thinking for Crazy Times,* Ian Mitroff refers to Type III problems.

These problems include picking the wrong stakeholders, setting a scope too narrowly, phrasing a problem incorrectly, and failing to think systematically.[14]

From a leadership standpoint, such challenges can tremendously impact the quality of a definition. In fact, those just described can pose several challenges.

A common challenge is to define an issue or problem satisfactorily and know when it is satisfactory. There are various factors that affect the quality of such a definition.

On an individual person basis, factors include lack of knowledge and experience, deliberate introduction of bias, having incomplete data and information, misconstruing assumptions as facts and data, being impatient with the time and effort required to develop a satisfactory definition, and being "intellectually ignorant," or more politely, knowing the right answer before really knowing the issue or problem.

On a group basis, the challenge is conformity, more specifically, Groupthink. Groupthink is caused by pressure placed on individuals to modify or suppress thoughts and feelings to "get along." Decision-making processes become negatively skewed to the point of failing to make realistic decisions.

Groupthink can severely restrict essential cognitive abilities to make qualitative decisions. This challenge can permeate throughout an entire decision-making process of a group.

Obviously, the quality of a decision depends on the quality of the definition for issues and problems. How do project managers improve the quality of their decisions and the processes behind them?

- Be aware of the influences that adversely affect a definition, e.g., individual bias and Groupthink.
- Involve people who think differently about a problem or issue. They could provide a balanced perspective about an issue or problem.
- Avoid rushing to judgment; that is, jumping to a solution before sufficiently defining an issue or problem.
- Explore different ways to look at a problem or issue. Shifting paradigms and not project managers should do that. Also, encourage others to do the same by identifying the different ways and looking at ranges, possibilities, and combinations.
- Develop multiple definitions of a problem or issue by experimenting. Chances are the definition will be a hybrid.
- Although impossible, strive for an objective definition. Remove adjectives and adverbs, keep the definition of the problem or issue to one or two sentences, and avoid value-laden words. If people perceive a definition as biased, then emotion will prevail and influence the results.

Because mental models, paradigms, or perceptual maps influence the way people see and interpret reality, project managers must strive not so much to achieve objectivity, but to offset the negative affects of subjectivity. The best approach is to have the participation of people with different backgrounds to offset negative influences. At the same time, project managers must be attuned to their own subjective tendencies. Through both actions, project managers will increase the likelihood of developing meaningful definitions of problems or issues.

## Determine the Facts, Data, and Assumptions Regarding the Problem or Issue

All three are very important for contextual understanding of a problem or issue. Some descriptions about all three are necessary.

Data consist of facts that provide the ingredients to develop meaningful information. Data alone are meaningless. Collection of data means nothing, but provides the basis to generate information. Hence, the result of processing data gives information.

Assumptions, often mistaken as facts, are subjective determinations. According to the Project Management Institute, they are construed as being real, certain, or imagined. In other words, some people view them as facts while others view them as opinions.

In the end, what we determine as facts, data, assumptions, and information are subjective. People cannot extricate themselves from their environments or their paradigms. What one project manager thinks is an assumption, another might view as fact and vice versa.

In addition, we can never really know if we have identified the necessary facts, data, and assumptions and their significance. Our mental model distorts our view of what exists by filtering and affecting our perceptions, resulting in either deliberate or accidental deception. Add emotion and it seems almost impossible to distinguish fact from fiction.

Project managers have few options, therefore, to ascertain relevant facts, data, and assumptions.

One option is a systemic approach. A systemic approach requires that they apply mental maps, which are subjective determinations of the "way things work." Despite the subjectivity, they help us to ascertain what one would consider facts, data, and assumptions. More importantly, they help us to identify the relationships among all three.

Much of the facts, data, and assumptions can be drawn in a diagram. An important advantage of diagramming is that project managers can more easily communicate with other stakeholders, thereby furthering understanding and getting consensus, if not agreement, over facts, data, and assumptions for a particular issue or problem. The type or form of diagram does not matter; that is not the purpose. What is important is the employment.

Another option, potentially for use with the last one, is to seek key stakeholders' confirmation over the facts, data, and assumptions regarding an issue or problem. After receiving confirmation, project managers have the basis for dialog on just about any issue or problem.

Stakeholders vary in knowledge, experience, values, and expectations about the dimensions of facts and data. These qualitative aspects include their reliability, accuracy, completeness, timeliness, consistency, and currency. Naturally, great variability often exists among stakeholders regarding the degree that facts and data satisfy these dimensions. Adding to the complication are problems associated with facts, data, and assumptions that arise, e.g., loss, insufficiency, meaningless, and incorrectness.

There are also "grander" factors influencing the dimensions of facts and data. These are what are referred to as potholes. In an excellent article in IEEE's *Computer* magazine, Diane Astrong, Yang Lee, and Richard Wang identify three major potholes: information production, e.g., multiple sources of information that produce different values; information storage, e.g., information distributed among many different and incompatible systems; and information utilization, e.g., conflicts that restrict access to information.[15] These potholes have significance because they determine the quality and quantity of facts and data available to make decisions. They also lead to very subjective evaluations about facts and data in decision making. It is very important, therefore, to involve key stakeholders to help determine facts and data as well as assumptions; their desired qualitative and quantitative dimensions; and how to overcome potholes.

Because decision making is frequently a very information-intensive process, project managers cannot ignore the above issues. Otherwise, their decisions will be flawed because the facts, data, and assumptions are flawed. Unfortunately, project managers never really know how much is enough and whether what they do have is unequivocally valid and reliable. Therefore, they need stakeholder involvement to provide the checks and cross-checks to preclude having the "GIGO effect" of decisions. (GIGO is an information technology term for Garbage In, Garbage Out.)

Of course, project managers should be cautious about relying too much on groups to help define necessary facts, data, and assumptions. Groupthink can play a powerful role in twisting or suppressing facts, data, and assumptions; project managers must control this dangerous aspect. Ways to prevent the effects of Groupthink are to meet with pertinent stakeholders on an individual basis; verify the validity and reliability of stated facts, data, and assumptions through research; and seek people in a group who hold contrary views.

## Develop Different Alternatives

Armed with a consensus or agreement on defining an issue or problem and the facts, data, and assumptions, project managers can begin the arduous and creative task of developing alternatives to make decisions.

One of the biggest challenges with determining the alternatives is resisting the tremendous pressure to "know the answer" right away. Many decision makers simply jump to a decision and implement it right away.[16] What are the consequences for doing this? Decision makers then impose the decision that reflects a limited search for alternatives.[17]

This challenge has considerable influence on the quality of the decision-making process on projects.

For one, it may force an inappropriate solution. Indeed, the decision may become more problematical than not making the decision at all. The reason is that the solution may prove inadequate when the project manager tries to ram it into existence, despite the fact that it does not fit the circumstances. Project managers could then find themselves constantly on the defensive, trying to impose or sell a decision due to a lack of acceptance.

For another reason, such a solution can create unanticipated consequences because it is based inappropriately on the short- and long-term circumstances. Project managers will find themselves in a reactive mode by attempting to "put out fires" caused by the wrong decision.

If not enough, jumping to a solution can mean overlooking key considerations due to a narrow focus. Project managers with a background in a narrow discipline often fall into this trap. Their decisions have a financial or technical orientation because they rely on what they know and, consequently, feel comfortable with. There are consequences. In the short run, they may feel confident and comfortable. In the long run, however, they may have to deal with the negative impacts of being comfortable and confident.

Another reason is the poor application of resources. Even an appropriate solution consumes resources. In time, an appropriate solution will require re-work, and reflect not only that it was inappropriate, but also perhaps that it partially or completely wasted resources. This circumstance can result in exceeding a budget as well as sliding a schedule but, most importantly, it can increase frustration levels for everyone.

A final consequence is the lack of buy-in and ownership when adopting an inappropriate solution. Pursuing a solution can be the result of an arbitrary decision by one person or group. By developing alternatives, subjective preferences can give way to a more objective analysis. Then, through careful assessment of alternatives with input from stakeholders, a solution can be made that has at least the appearance of objectivity, thereby avoiding the possibility of problems during its implementation.

What can project managers do to ensure alternatives will be developed?

First, they can *apply more common approaches to develop alternatives.* Brainstorming is one of them and has been around for a while. Its goal is to develop many alternatives prior to evaluation. Every effort is made to record as many alternatives as possible, regardless of impracticality or silliness. Alternatives can be "piggybacked" on other ones to generate more. The idea is to lower social and mental barriers that obstruct thinking. Project managers should use caution to avoid influencing or swaying a brainstorming session.

Brainstorming is not restricted to group levels. Project managers can also exercise it personally. They can generate their alternatives on a sheet of paper and apply techniques like mind mapping to freely generate alternatives, reducing the effects of prejudice.

Whether brainstorming alone or with a group, project managers must allow the freedom to consider many alternatives. That means delaying judgment to develop a complete list.

Another effective approach for defining a problem or issue is a technique called synectics. Synectics is a group approach that capitalizes on the power of analogous thinking. It uses four categories of analogous approaches: personal, direct, symbolic, and fantasy. Using one of the categories, a "client" presents an issue or problem that is refined and restated several times. The group then proposes multiple solutions to the problem or issue and after several iterations and exchanges the session ends after a time period and a corresponding solution results.[18]

Synectics is different from brainstorming in that the freedom in brainstorming is not present because the effort is to satisfy someone, e.g., a client. It also requires considering both the pro's and con's of each alternative or solution, not suspending evaluative judgment to the end.[19]

Developing alternatives is very difficult because of explicit and implicit factors that influence the quality and quantity of results. Explicit factors include past working relationships, historical experience, policies, procedures, and reporting relationships. Implicit factors include mores, norms, values, and informal networks. Project managers must strive to suspend the influences of both factors when generating alternatives. Failure to appreciate these influences can result in unsatisfactory alternatives to consider and eventually a similar decision.

Second, they can *apply creative thinking techniques.* Sometimes brainstorming and synectics are not enough. Project managers and their stakeholders sometimes need a catalyst to proceed forward to generate alternatives.

An excellent way to generate alternatives is to follow the insights and thoughts of Edward de Bono, an author of numerous books and articles on creativity. De Bono developed the idea of lateral thinking, which is a creative way to break the shackles of patterned thinking. He does that by considering different perspectives to generate new ideas and techniques. According to de Bono, the human mind is a self-organizing system that develops patterns of thinking. Over time and exposure, the patterns become more permanent and more difficult to change. It is quite clear that this mental behavior can serve as both an asset and a liability. As an asset, for example, it can organize and store information. As a liability, it hardens one or more patterns of thinking, thereby limiting the ability to think more creatively.

De Bono contrasts lateral thinking with vertical thinking. The former is more open to new ideas to generate different alternatives. The latter is more closed, focused on finding the right answer while moving in a specific direction. Lateral thinking is a "journey," which allows for an exploratory, nonlinear approach; vertical thinking is a "trip," which requires a focused, linear one.

Lateral thinking is a way, therefore, to challenge patterned thinking to develop different ideas, thoughts, and techniques. De Bono refers to it as "provocative." As De Bono observes in his landmark book, *Lateral Thinking,* especially from the perspective of generating alternatives, the goal is to look at things differently from multiple perspectives or ways, and then, using lateral thinking, rearranging and restructuring the information to derive new alternatives.[20] Some suggestions that he provides to generate alternatives are to set a quota, challenge assumptions by asking why, and suspend judgment. These and other approaches help to further the aim of lateral thinking that he says is taking multiple perspectives, restructuring patterns, and developing different alternatives.[21]

De Bono offers an additional way to break the pattern of thinking, only this time with groups. He developed an approach called Six Hats Thinking. Using the analogy of wearing different colored hats, people, individually or as a group, can change thinking via role playing.

According to De Bono, each hat has a different color to allow different thinking and, consequently, develop more alternatives. When people wear a White Hat, they think neutrally and objectively; with a Red Hat, emotionally; with a Black Hat, negatively and pessimistically; with a Yellow Hat, positively; with a Green Hat, creatively; and with a Blue Hat, they think in a controlled and organized way.[22]

The six hats approach can enable project managers to break the restraints of patterned thinking when generating alternatives. For example, during brainstorming team members may not be receptive to new ideas. Project managers can assign someone to wear a Yellow Hat to be more positive and a Green Hat to develop more alternatives to counter resistance.

Third, project managers can *seek diversity in thinking styles.* Too often, project managers surround themselves with people who think the same way or are assigned people who "see the world" the same way. Although it may make cooperation on a project easier and minimize negative conflict, "sameness" does not guarantee creativity. Even when everyone applies creative approaches like brainstorming and six hats, if everyone is alike the chance to generate creativity will likely not occur.

Project managers must, therefore, embrace diversity. In this context, I am not talking about race or religion. Diversity here is in terms of thinking.

Fourth, *remove the barriers to develop alternatives.* Unfortunately, so many barriers face the development of alternatives. Basically, the barriers can be classified as explicit and implicit. Examples of explicit barriers when developing alternatives include formal policies and procedures, managerial direction, accepted practices, availability of tools, acceptable techniques, and scope restriction. Implicit barriers, too, can often prove just as restrictive. Examples of implicit barriers are politics, norms, beliefs, values, history, culture, and managerial style.

It is easier to determine the best ways to remove explicit barriers when developing alternatives. Project managers can seek or grant permission to suspend policies and procedures, for example, or apply different tools and techniques. It is more difficult to remove implicit barriers. However, they can do some things. They can hold a session to develop alternatives at a location away from the project location. They can involve external or internal consultants or other people that do not have a stake in the outcome. They can even ask management to emphasize the importance of developing innovative alternatives.

A popular approach is to conduct an offsite meeting. The meeting is held in a distant location, giving people the physical and mental freedom away from the explicit and implicit barriers confronting them in their workplaces. Project managers must use discretionary judgment about invitees to the offsite meeting. If senior management or the wrong people attend the session, then discussion could be inhibited and thereby limit alternatives.

## Determine the Best Approach

This step tends to be the least exciting to some project managers despite its importance. The reason is that the related alternative will positively or negatively influence a project in the future. When selecting the best alternative, project managers should consider the following caveats.

*Strive for objectivity when selecting the alternative even though subjectivity will creep into the process.* The key is to be cognizant of the potential influence of subjectivity when selecting an alternative.

Individually, bias may enter via a tendency to quickly discount alternatives either by preference or intuition. The consequence is that a few people will perceive, rightly or wrongly, that project managers are merely "going through the motions" to present the mere appearance of objectivity.

On a group level, bias may be from Groupthink. Groupthink can quickly lead to an erroneous selection of an alternative that a group may feel comfortable with, but that may generate resistance by key stakeholders.

*Avoid making exceptions to the rules used to select an alternative.* By resisting the urge to waive criterion, a greater opportunity arises for subjectivity to prevail. The likelihood will increase for people to protest a decision during implementation. Most people will be less likely to resist a decision if an effort to be objective has been made when selecting an alternative.

If circumstances permit, involve key stakeholders when selecting an alternative. Get their participation in the process to garner sufficient support for a decision. People will be less resistant to a decision if they feel they had involvement in its selection. Of course, this involvement depends on circumstances. In an intense, fast-paced environment such involvement may be impractical. More often than not, however, circumstances allow for such involvement. The key is to determine whether circumstances permit the desired level of involvement.

Paul Nutt identifies four levels of participation in decision making: comprehensive, complete, delegated, and token. Comprehensive participation involves full delegation to a group. Complete participation involves only interested parties, or stakeholders, with some restriction. Delegated participation involves representatives of interested parties to make the decision. Token participation involves restricting involvement and is the least effective.[23] Naturally, the level of participation depends on the style of a project manager.

*Recognize that selecting an alternative will have a negative or positive impact, immediately or later or both, and will likely require trade-offs.* A decision will likely have a positive impact, e.g., furthering schedule progress. It may also have a negative impact, e.g., causing rework to address a quality issue. Project managers must identify both positive and negative impacts to capitalize on the former and deal with the latter.

A decision will also have short-term impacts, positive or negative. For example, it may require an increase in team size. The additional expertise may accelerate a schedule but increase costs.

A decision may involve trade-offs. A trade-off, or "satisficing," is choosing to further one goal or objective at the expense of another. For example, it might include sacrificing a budgetary goal by having people work overtime to meet a major milestone. The important point is that selecting an alternative will likely reflect the concept of TANSTAAFL.

A decision must be communicated. People need to know about it. While common sense, this point is sometimes overlooked, which explains in large part why many a decision persists and nothing changes. The communication should include the decision itself as well as the purpose and rationale.

A decision must "go back to the drawing board" if the selection criteria reveal that alternatives failed to meet minimum standards. Often, some project managers select an unsatisfactory alternative that results in negative consequences; this circumstance may substantiate the notion that no decision may prove more valuable than having one that fails.

When making a decision to select an alternative, a project manager can take several approaches.

*They can use their intuition.* Sometimes, the criteria to select an alternative may not be very definitive. When that occurs, intuition may be the best approach, based on high-level criteria and a "gut feel." While intuition can prove effective, it has certain drawbacks.

In their book, *Decision Traps,* J. Edward Russo and Paul J. H. Shoemaker note that intuition has its flaws, e.g., inconsistency. They add that it is also susceptible to intangible factors like fatigue, boredom, and, yes, relationships with a spouse.[24]

*They can apply a methodical approach.* Many of these types of decision making approaches exist. Russo and Shoemaker identify two types, subjective and objective linear models. Subjective linear models use weighting approaches to which one or more people assign a value and result in identifying the best alternative. Objective linear models are used for repetitive decisions and sufficient data are available to make statistical calculations. While objective linear models have greater reliability than the use of intuition, they rely on past performance to make a decision about the future.

*They can use heuristics, or rules of thumb.* Heuristics, like intuition, provide a shortcut to make decisions. Russo and Shoemaker note that the goal is to reduce the "overhead" for developing the right answer. However, they caution, heuristics are wrought with danger because a heuristic may be inappropriate for a situation.[25]

In my experience, the type of decision-making approach is less important than the ability to determine the circumstances when most applicable. For example, a fast-paced environment would likely have less time available for an objective, even subjective, methodical approach. Intuition and heuristics may be a project manager's only option.

Regardless of the approach taken, project managers must be willing to perform the next step.

## Plan for Execution and Feedback

Perhaps obvious, this step is frequently overlooked. Many project managers declare a decision and think people will execute it unwittingly. This is a naïve, unrealistic notion for several reasons.

A project manager often lacks formal command and control over people. This fact alone makes it very impractical to believe that people will merely "follow orders," especially if a decision is nonaligned with their interests.

Also, the immediacy of "getting the work done" often outweighs the abstract thinking behind a decision. Even routine work can overshadow a decision. The result is that deploying a decision can be overshadowed by the interests of other stakeholders. Small wonder that many project managers express frustration when implementing a decision.

In addition, many people do not understand a decision that favors an alternative. They may have a narrow discipline, e.g., information systems or accounting, and do not appreciate a particular alternative that was selected. This situation especially becomes a challenge for people whose life experience is within the paradigm of a specialized field.

Additionally, executing a decision requires a sense of ownership so people trust it and care for its implementation. People who implement a decision must see it from the perspective of both the overall interests of a project and their own. The decision must be framed in the context of trust and meaning; trust that a decision is in the interest of furthering a project and meaning in the sense that it satisfies individual needs.

Finally, few project managers realize the importance of feedback. They assume their decision is right. Circumstances can quickly change, however, and make all or part of a decision irrelevant. Feedback is important to ascertain if a decision is relevant. Nothing can cause more havoc with morale and esprit de corps than implementing an irrelevant decision. Positive and negative feedback are necessary to avoid this situation.

Here are some steps that project managers can perform to plan for execution and obtain feedback.

*Define the mechanics of a plan and its execution early.* This step requires answering the who, what, when, where, why, and how for executing a decision. In other words, project managers must think in advance about what needs to be done, not only the answers regarding execution but also the feedback.

*Avoid developing a plan in a vacuum.* Doing so unilaterally can only add difficulty during execution, especially if a decision is perceived as one of imposition. By gaining involvement in execution and feedback, project managers can expect less resistance even when a decision is unpopular. If circumstances require little or no participation, they should consider consulting with key stakeholders even casually to ascertain the degree of receptivity. That way, they can adjust accordingly.

*Communicate the plan, not just once, but several times.* By communicating it continuously, project managers reiterate its importance. It helps avoid, like many plans, becoming "out of sight out of mind." Through continuous communication, a plan becomes ingrained in the activities of the project.

*Seek feedback on a plan.* Because project managers often find themselves making decisions, simple and complex, a tendency exists to ignore the importance of feedback.

This feedback entails two key questions: Is the plan being executed as envisioned? Is it achieving desired results?

Many project managers assume that if schedule and budgetary performance improve then the relevant decision has been effectively executed. While a good indicator, the contributor for improvement may or may not be the plan. Something else may be improving performance.

Obtaining feedback requires considerable attention, much more than many project managers realize. Russo and Shoemaker refer to the complications associated with obtaining feedback as a failure to learn. They identify serious traps with feedback that project managers should heed. These traps involve "fooling yourself about feedback," to include rationalizing, claiming credit for success (and not failure), and hindsight bias.[26]

So how can project managers ensure feedback will be useful? While plenty of attention is on desired results, as much attention should be given to how the feedback is obtained. The focus should be on how to execute the process.

Project managers need, therefore, to apply two categories of processes for obtaining feedback, formal and informal. A formal method could be to hold one-on-one sessions or team meetings to determine the effectiveness of a plan. They can collect metrics, too.

Informal methods are just as useful, perhaps even more so, at least from my experience. These methods might include holding ad hoc, one-on-one discussions with stakeholders affected by a plan or picking up signals from team members, e.g., complaints or concerns expressed, which inadvertently arise during plan execution. Project managers, like functional managers and executives, can learn much by practicing "management by walking around," or MBWA.

## Execute the Decision and Adjust Accordingly

In other words, turn a decision into reality. This step is perhaps the most difficult because, like planning for an entire project, a gap may arise between the ideal and the actual. Of course, this gap poses serious challenges to project managers.

One challenge is that a tendency might exist to deviate from a plan due to "fires" that need to be extinguished. Or, higher priorities may exist that deserve more attention.

Another challenge is that executing a plan may require adjustments to deal with realities facing a decision. This challenge can create higher levels of frustration and impatience by disillusioned individuals. Support often begins to wane for decision and plan alike.

A final challenge that project managers may confront is selective hearing regarding feedback related to a plan's execution. Project managers and others may only hear what they want to hear, affirming that their decisions are the right ones and are being implemented as planned. They may not be interested in genuine feedback about negative ramifications, e.g., increasing rework or plummeting morale, which may be arising as a result of the decision or plan.

What can project managers do to prevent or mitigate the impacts of these challenges?

*Involve people while implementing a plan.* If done correctly, they should involve people earlier when developing a plan. This involvement should include taking responsibility for specific actions and providing feedback on their progress.

*Encourage an atmosphere of openness and trust.* This atmosphere will encourage a freer flow of data and information on progress about implementing a plan. Feedback will then be more useful and meaningful, and will enhance the decision-making process.

*Seek feedback continuously, not ad hoc.* Through continuous feedback, project managers can ascertain ongoing effectiveness of a decision and take appropriate action before something negative happens. This feedback, too, should require telling project managers what they need to hear, not what they want to hear.

*Apply active and effective listening skills.* These skills will help the project manager determine what is and is not important as well as avoid filtering data.

*Be aware of explicit and implicit signals that often accompany feedback.* Explicit signals can be positive or negative and the effects can be reflected in schedule and budgetary performance. Implicit signals, also positive or negative, are less quantifiable and more qualitative. These include people who feel that they have been forced into compliance and, as a result, conduct subterfuge through complaining.

## LEADING DEMANDS DECISIONS

Project managers must make decisions constantly. If they fail to do so, their projects will likely not progress. If they do make decisions, they must make those that further the vision of their projects. Successful project managers, therefore, are individuals who make the "right" decision at the right place and right time. However, they do not do so in a vacuum. They know that they need input from others, especially from the people who must implement their decisions if they hope to avoid quixotic results. Involvement by others ensures that the people who implement decisions are committed to translate them into meaningful action and take corrective action.

## CASE STUDY: DECIDE

Nothing can hurt a project manager more than an impasse over a key decision. The momentum for the project slows and then it becomes very difficult to regain activity in the desired direction. The project manager immediately laid the groundwork to avoid this situation.

An issues management process was developed. This process identified different categories of issues and a response for dealing with each category. Throughout the project, the project manager kept a "pulse" on the key issues to ensure follow through and worked hard to ensure open communication. Frequent status review and assessment meetings were held to ensure that issues or problems requiring decisions received sufficient visibility.

During decision making, the project manager always focused on the facts, data, and assumptions while simultaneously focusing on the goals and objectives of the project. This approached helped avoid the typical traps of decision makers, e.g., jumping to a solution before truly understanding the problem or issue, viewing circumstances in black and white or according to prejudices, or taking a short-term perspective.

Throughout the life cycle of a decision, a concerted effort was made to review effectiveness based on feedback. That was achieved with periodic inquiries at meetings about decisions and one-on-one sessions with those stakeholders affected by a decision. Every effort was made to ensure the decision's "visibility" in order to guarantee its implementation and achieve the desired results.

Because decision making is often "tarnished" by values and prejudices, every attempt was made to define an issue or problem clearly, to identify and evaluate different alternatives to deal with it, to consider different viewpoints, and to foresee possible consequences of each alternative and viewpoint.

Finally, the project manager performed an extensive risk assessment for the project. All the key stakeholders were involved in the session, identifying all the risks, the likelihood of occurrence and impacts, and possible courses of action. The important point was that the project manager involved key stakeholders and encouraged ownership to monitor them.

## REFERENCES

1. Jurgen Hauschildt, Gesche Keim, and John W. Medcof, Realistic criteria for project manager selection and development, *Project Management Journal,* p. 30, September 2000.
2. Greg Skulmonski, Francis Hartman, and Roch DeMaere, Superior and threshold project competencies, *Project Management,* 6(1), 14, 2000.
3. Paul C. Nutt, *Why Decisions Fail,* Berrett-Koehler, San Francisco, 2002, p. 5.
4. Ian Mitroff, *Smart Thinking for Crazy Times,* Berrett-Koehler, San Francisco, 1998, p. 7.
5. Stephen R. Covey, *The Seven Habits of Highly Effective People,* Simon & Schuster, New York, 1990, p. 24.
6. Paul C. Nutt, *Why Decisions Fail,* Berrett-Koehler, San Francisco, 2002, p. 6.
7. Max De Pree, *Leadership Jazz,* Dell, New York, 1992, p. 8.
8. Ian Mitroff, *Smart Thinking for Crazy Times,* Berrett-Koehler, San Francisco, 1998, p. 18.
9. John S. Hammond, Ralph L. Keeney, and Howard Raifa, The hidden traps in decision making, *Harvard Business Review,* pp. 47–58, September–October 1998.
10. Monica Ramirez, The perfect trap, *Psychology Today,* p. 34, May–June 1999.
11. Edward De Bono, *Practical Thinking,* Penguin Books, London, 1971, p. 32.
12. Daniel Goleman, *Emotional Intelligence,* Bantam Books, New York, 1995, pp. 85–86.
13. Thomas Gordon, *Leadership Effectiveness Training (L.E.T.),* Bantam Books, Toronto, 1980, p. 38.
14. Ian Mitroff, *Smart Thinking for Crazy Times,* Berrett-Koehler, San Francisco, 1998, p. 19.
15. Diane M. Astrong, Yang W. Lee, and Richard Y. Wang, 10 Potholes in the road to information quality, *Computer,* pp. 38–46, August 1997.
16. Paul C. Nutt, *Why Decisions Fail,* Berrett-Koehler, San Francisco, 2002, p. 49.
17. Ibid.
18. Gerard I. Nierenberg, *The Art of Creative Thinking,* Cornerstone Library, New York, 1982, pp. 197–199.
19. James L. Adams, *Conceptual Blockbusting,* 2nd ed., W.W. Norton, New York, 1979, pp. 137–139.
20. Edward De Bono, *Lateral Thinking,* Perennial Library, New York, 1990, p. 63.
21. Ibid., p. 131.
22. Edward De Bono, *Six Thinking Hats,* Little, Brown, Boston, 1985, pp. 199–207.
23. Paul C. Nutt, *Why Decisions Fail,* Berrett-Koehler, San Francisco, 2002, p. 108.
24. J. Edward Russo and Paul J. H. Shoemaker, *Decision Traps,* Fireside Books, New York, 1989, p. 120.
25. Ibid., p. 81.
26. Ibid., pp. 173–188.

# 8

# MOTIVATE

A major theme of this book is that leading a project is, first and foremost, about people — involving them actively to achieve goals and objectives. Without their involvement, no project is possible. Effective project managers know how to make this happen and the secret is motivation. The importance of motivation is often overlooked or trivialized, causing needless frustration and anger, even for project managers. As William Cohen observed in *The Art of the Leader,* leaders often fail to understand what motivates their followers and, if they do, they misconstrue what the real motivation is.[1]

Many project managers hold a common feeling that they lack power over people and, therefore, cannot get people to do their bidding. Nothing could be further from the truth. Project managers have considerable power to influence, although not necessarily control, people. Even seasoned executives with substantial power will admit that the more one tries to control in the traditional sense, the less they actually do.

## INFLUENCING, NOT COMMANDING

One of the biggest failures by project managers is to not consider the "people factor" very seriously. Ultimately, this failure results in sliding schedules, exceeding the budgets, and poor quality of output. However, these are only indicators of a poor understanding of people. What is the real contributor? It is a mismatch of a person with his or her task and relationship with peers. In other words, no synchronicity occurs among personality, commitment, and assigned work.

Some consequences are quite common, some controllable and others not. A common consequence is a prevalence of negative emotions, e.g., fear, anger, frustration, and anomie. These emotions lay the seeds for "bad" performance, such as rework and needless oversight, greater turnover, and sick time. In time, the stress can mount to a point that involvement declines. On a much larger scale, negative conflict destroys teaming and power struggles arise over tasks, even for the position of project manager.

## UNDERSTANDING PEOPLE PAYS OFF

So what happens when project managers have a good understanding of people?

Managing a project becomes easier, not harder. Project managers do not have to exercise close oversight or apply negative techniques to "force" people to perform. They recognize and apply the techniques that get people "synchronized" with the work to perform by seeking a greater match between the personality, talents, and abilities of the individual and their work. When this occurs, people have greater confidence, ownership, and accountability as well as experience more enjoyment on a project. It is almost a guarantee that less turnover, rework, and negative conflict, e.g., power struggles, will occur. A greater tolerance will arise for other people and their ideas because people will feel unthreatened. Naturally, better schedule and budgetary performance will result as well as improved quality of work.

What is meant by motivating positively? In a nutshell, project managers subscribe to McGregor's Theory Y rather than Theory X approach towards managing people. Under Theory X, project managers negatively perceive people, viewing them as unmotivated and lazy as well as requiring close supervision. Under Theory Y, project managers take a positive perspective, viewing people as self-motivated and who like to work without close supervision.

Most management theorists of today subscribe to the Theory Y approach. But the question is: How do project managers make that happen?

Synchronicity. They match a person to the right tasks to feel good about their work and their performance. Project managers achieve synchronicity by enabling people to self-actualize, to use Maslow's term, and have a sense of "flow" that Mihaly Csikszentmihalyi discusses in his works about creativity. Flow, according to Csikszentmihalyi, is an optimal experience when people feel a sense of enjoyment and excitement in what they do.[2]

Project managers will not find this effort easy because it requires an integration of the personality and motivations of each team member with the goals and objectives of their projects to give people meaningful participation. Understanding people presents some tough challenges to project managers. The biggest challenge is to get "inside the heads of other people" and figure out "what makes them tick." No way exists to do that unless you are a psychologist or psychiatrist and even then considerable disagreement exists. However, project managers can employ some models to help them understand people better.

*Avoid stereotyping or "boxing in" people.* Few people fall completely into one category or another; they usually fall on a continuum. The different classifications of people and their talents and abilities described in this chapter are only tools to help project managers to deal with other people in a general sense. This insight, however, does not lessen their value. These models serve as a means to an end to manage the complexity behind human behavior that is multidimensional.

*Recognize that people are dynamic, not static.* Each person is a complex organism that changes to a degree. People behave consistently with their personality, manifested via belief, values, and action. However, over time and circumstance, people can change but not easily. As living, open systems, people must interact with their environment and other people. Such interaction can reinforce as well as alter human behavior.

*Assume the "best in people"; look for opportunities to help people exercise their strengths while pursuing mutually beneficial goals and objectives.* Look for opportunities for people to apply their talents, skills, and knowledge in a manner that garners contributions towards achieving the goals of a project. Project managers must not force people — over whom they often have no direct control — but influence them. They achieve that through involvement up front and sustain it throughout the life cycle of a project.

*Encourage people to step beyond their "protected wall."* These walls, a term popularized by the psychologist Carl Rogers, can be mental maps, paradigms, or psychological blocks. Whatever the form, project managers need to encourage people to "take one step out" to "see things differently." This task is not an easy one, but project managers can achieve it by coaching people while navigating into the unfamiliar, by taming, training, and emphasizing the need to focus on the "big picture."

*Accept diversity as the norm rather than the exception.* Diversity goes beyond the physical characteristics of people. It also includes how people think and perceive reality. The importance of diversity is frequently overlooked, and does more damage to morale and esprit de corps than a budget cut or impractical schedule. Lack of acceptance of diversity often results in intolerance, arrogance, and a loss of opportunity to capitalize on the different strengths people bring to a project.

*Build an atmosphere of openness and trust; allow people with different thoughts and talents to contribute to overall goals and objectives.* If this openness and trust fails to exist, people will retreat behind their walls. This retreat results in inefficiency and ineffectiveness as well as people "holding back." Project managers end up with an "army of soldiers" rather than an "army of warriors." The difference is that the former merely follow orders to do the minimum while the latter take the initiative.

*Influence, not coerce, people to take on tasks.* For good reason, as Cohen notes, by saying that domination does not guarantee anything but recognition of not being the leader. Trust, so crucial to leader-follower relations, can crumble.

## USING DIFFERENT MODELS AND THEORIES

One interesting theory about people is the one by Howard Gardner. He developed the idea of multiple intelligences, which defines intelligence as having the ability to solve or create something of value for a culture or community. According to Gardner, seven categories of intelligence exist (at least at the time of his book, *Multiple Intelligences*): linguistic, logical-mathematical, spatial, musical, bodily-kinesthetic, interpersonal, and intrapersonal.

Linguistic intelligence is reflected in using words, e.g., talking, verbalizing, speaking. Logical-mathematical intelligence is reflected in using numbers and logic, e.g., calculating, analyzing, classifying. Spatial intelligence is reflected in using pictures and images, e.g., painting, mapping. Musical intelligence is reflected when developing or conducting rhythms and melodies. Bodily-kinesthetic intelligence is reflected via physical action, e.g., sports as well as the physical act of balancing and sorting. Interpersonal intelligence is reflected through understanding and working with people, e.g., communicating, empathizing, motivating. Intrapersonal intelligence is reflected through the understanding of one's self, e.g., feelings, inner thoughts.[3]

This theory has profound implications for project managers. By understanding which intelligence is developed in team members, they can assign people to tasks that capitalize on their strengths and avoid assigning them to those that may sap their intelligence. Or, if they assign a task to someone who has not developed the necessary intelligence, they can assign another team member to compensate for the weakness. Or, they can send a person for training to augment his or her skills.

The point is not that project managers can improve a person's intelligence. Chances are it will be impossible. The real point is that project managers can capitalize on people's strengths, compensate for their weaknesses, and take some remedial action.

Another popular theory is the whole brain thinking by Ned Herrmann. His theory is based on the concept that the human brain can be divided into left and right sides. It would be instructive before discussing whole brain thinking to provide an overview of the capabilities of the left and right side of the human brain.

According to contemporary theory, a human brain is divided into two halves, left and right. Each side provides a given set of thinking capabilities.

The left brain is associated with the ability to think logically and sequentially, as well as concretely, rationally, and objectively. People who are left-brain dominant, therefore, are good with numbers, problem solving, and defining goals. The right brain is associated with emotions. People who are right-brain dominant are visual, intuitive, and think metaphorically and spontaneously.[4]

Ned Herrmann developed a more holistic view of the human brain by taking an integrated perspective of the two halves, calling it "whole brain thinking." Viewing the mind as a circle, he identifies four quadrants of thinking. The first quadrant deals with thinking logically, analytically, and quantitatively. People who fall in this quadrant, for example, think realistically and like to calculate numbers. A second quadrant deals with thinking in an organized, sequential, detailed manner. People in this quadrant, for example, like to establish procedures and develop plans. These two quadrants are closely related, forming the left side of the brain. A third quadrant deals with thinking holistically and intuitively via synthesizing and integrating. People who fall in this quadrant, for example, tend to take risks and are spontaneous. A fourth quadrant involves feelings and emotions. People in this quadrant, for example, tend to be emotional and like to teach. These two quadrants are closely related, forming the right side of the brain.[5]

Herrmann had some interesting insights that can prove useful to project managers. His research reveals that patterns can be reflected in "spider charts" to indicate a person's dominance in certain quadrants and less so in others. This dominance has implications for a preferred managerial style, chosen vocation, and decision-making style. People who fall in the first (upper left) quadrant are problem solvers. People who fall in the second quadrant (lower left) are planners. People who fall in the third quadrant (upper right) are holistic thinkers. People who fall in the fourth quadrant (lower right) are interpersonal.[6]

Another one of the more popular approaches for understanding people is the Myers-Briggs Type Indicators. These indicators reflect a person's personality in terms of degree. Based on Jungian psychology, four categories of type indicators exist: Extraversion and Introversion, Sensation and Intuition, Thinking and Feeling, and Perceiving and Judging.

Extraversion and Introversion are the first category. A person in the Extroversion category sees people as a source of energy whereas a person in the Introversion category prefers to be alone. The former is typified through sociability and many relationships; the latter tends towards concentration and fewer relationships.

Sensation and Intuition are the second category. A person in the Sensation category prefers facts and perceives himself or herself as being rooted in the here and now. A person in the Intuition category is imaginative and focuses on the future. The former is typified through emphasis on experience and practicality; the latter tends toward speculation and inspiration.

Thinking and Feeling are the third category. A person in the Thinking category strives to be objective, even impersonal. A person in the Feeling category emphasizes values over facts and does not favor rule-based decision making that the thinking types would prefer. The former is typified through emphasis on analysis and criterion; the latter tends towards subjectivity and persuasion.

Perceiving and Judging are the final category. A person in the Perceiving category tends to resist deadlines whereas a person in the Judging category looks at options, selects one, and sets deadlines. The former is typified by being spontaneous and adaptable; the latter tends towards planning and being fixed.[7]

According to a popular book on the subject, *Please Understand Me* by David Keirsey and Marilyn Bates, not everyone is an "either/or" type. Instead, most people fall on continuum. Nevertheless, the four categories of type indicators create sixteen combinations of temperaments INFP, ENFP, INFJ, ENFJ, ISFP, ESFP, ISFJ, ESFJ, INTP, ENTP, INTJ, ENTJ, ISTP, ISTJ, ESTP, and ESTJ.

Interestingly, the authors note that the temperament will have an influence on the way people lead. SP combinations tend to be good negotiators and troubleshooters as leaders. As team members, they tend to be process oriented, concentrating on what is realistic and getting "things in motion." SJ combinations tend to be stabilizers as leaders, setting up regulations and routines. As team members, they are industrious and product oriented. NT combinations tend to be principle oriented, questioning everything on the basis of those principles. As team members, they function as designers or architects, building models. NF combinations tend to be transactional and democratic as leaders. As team members, they are personal in their dealings, being transactional.[8]

Another popular approach is the Enneagram, a well-received but not scientifically based approach for understanding one's own personality and others. However, this fact should not discredit it because the Enneagram is concerned with normal rather than pathological behavior. It is also easy to apply one's self and others.

The Enneagram identifies nine personality types that are interconnected and reflect dynamic movement from one type to another. The nine are: Perfectionist,

Giver, Performer, Tragic Romantic, Observer, Devil's Advocate, Epicure, Boss, and Mediator.

Perfectionists believe that there is only one way to do things; they tend to be critical of others and, sometimes, of themselves as well as being practical and rigid. Givers focus on meeting other people's needs, satisfying their need for affection and approval as well as being demonstrative. Performers are the competitive types who focus on achievement in a comparative manner vis-à-vis others; their efficiency and persuasiveness enables them to progress. Tragic Romantics are idealistic, attracted to what may be unrealizable, and tend to be dramatic and creative. Observers like to maintain their distance emotionally and concentrate on keeping their privacy by behaving in a detached manner. Devil's Advocates emphasize thinking over action, more out of fear and doubt; they are constantly questioning and vigilant. Epicures avoid commitment and depth, acting superficial and more like dilettantes. They tend toward optimism but find it difficult to commit to anything. Bosses are the "take charge" kind of people, being protective and combative; although very territorial, they are also very protective of people within that territory. Mediators see all viewpoints, looking for agreeableness among everyone; this requires considerable patience on their part.

The nine personality types are based on nine features of emotional life. These nine features are anger, pride, deceit, envy, greed, fear, gluttony, lust, and sloth, and they play a key role in our motivations and the preoccupation of one prevents people from other activities.

The Enneagram applies to all people because everyone has the potential for all nine types; however, most people identify with only a few. Helen Palmer says that the Enneagram is dynamic, not fixed.[9]

From a project management perspective, the principal advantage of the Enneagram is that it provides the ability to see reality from various perspectives, e.g., from the "lens" of a Perfectionist or Tragic Romantic. An ancillary advantage is that it helps project managers to become aware of their own biases during planning and execution of their projects. This awareness can help them to obtain a more balanced perspective, especially during decision making.

In her book *The Drama of Leadership,* Patricia Pitcher develops an approach to look at people from an emotional perspective exhibited through behavior, thought processes, and temperament. Using the research described by Antonio Damasio in *Descartes' Error,* she identifies three types of people: Artist, Craftsman, and Technocrats.

Artists focus on people, providing imagination and inspiration. They are the visionaries of the three categories. Additional words to describe them are intuitive, emotional, and exciting.

Craftsmen are the experts, rooted in the world of practicality. They "know their stuff" and are hardworking and responsible. Additional words to describe them are trustworthy, well balanced, and open minded.

Technocrats are very analytical, the least emotional of the three types, and tend to be determined and uncompromising. Additional words to describe them are intense, methodical, and detail oriented.[10]

Each category has their strengths and weaknesses, reflected in the way they lead. Artists provide the vision, but they also can be emotionally unpredictable. Craftsmen, albeit predisposed to structure, tend to be more sensible. Technocrats have the expertise, but tend not to be very personable or compromising.[11]

An entertaining yet useful way to identify a person's personality is to use the color approach of Taylor Hartman that he discusses in his book, *The Color Code*.[12] He provides a four-color typology to identify and understand human behavior that is based on needs and wants. Each color represents a set of strengths and weaknesses, with most people having a primary and a secondary color. The four colors are: red, blue, white, and yellow.

Reds are individuals who are quite independent in thinking and action but do not allow others the same latitude. They want to strive for action and produce results right away. They are motivated by power via technical proficiency.

Blues are individuals who are oriented towards being a "people person." They want to be appreciated and are driven by value and conscience. They are motivated by intimacy via moral goodness.

Whites are individuals who seek tranquility by avoiding confrontation and keeping a low profile. They are motivated by peace, especially internally.

Yellows are individuals who are the "party animals" of the four categories. They desire attention, especially the center of attention. They are motivated by fun via social presence.

Each color has its weaknesses. Reds, while being very active and productive, can be highly critical and impatient. Blues, while passionate about work and people, can be perfectionists and distrustful. Whites, while being diplomatic and tolerant, can be indecisive and noncommunicative. Yellows, while being and radiating enthusiastic, can be undisciplined and superficial.[12]

From a project leadership perspective, the color code can prove quite useful. There are times in the project life cycle when reds can prove useful, e.g., a project has a slow start, and blues can be brought on for empathetic talents to bring people together at the beginning of a phase. Yellows can come to bring levity to an intense phase, e.g., implementation. Whites can bring the virtue of patience, e.g., when a project begins too quickly without concurrence from principal stakeholders.

The DiSC Model, which has been around for a while, is useful for understanding human behavior through dimensions. DiSC is an acronym for Dominance, Influence, Supportiveness, and Conscientiousness. It is a powerful tool to explain what occurs when a personality of one of the dimensions must deal with its environment. It provides people with the ability to respond with an appropriate dimension to a specific situation. If a situation changes, a person can exhibit a different dimension.

Dominance pertains to directness and assertiveness. It consists of elements like daring, forceful character, and competitiveness. Their strengths are being self-starters, go-getters; those who seek and take action. Their weaknesses include being abrupt, intimidating, and impatient. People with a high dominance "factor" are the hard chargers and tend to prefer to be in charge. They excel when given the autonomy, in a fast-paced environment that requires results.

Influence is for inducing and expressing an interest in other people. It consists of elements like persuasiveness and attractiveness. Their strengths are working with other people and being positive. Their weaknesses include overlooking important details and being sensitive to the behavior of others. People with a high influence factor take selling or persuasive approaches rather than forcing people into compliance. They excel, too, in fast-paced environments that provide recognition and the opportunity to be creative. They excel in environments that are informal and collegial.

Supportiveness is for submissiveness. It consists of elements like willingness and nonaggressiveness. Their strengths include being reliable and practical. Their weaknesses include a rigidity in thinking and slow adaptation to change. People with a high supportiveness are people who proceed cautiously as they study a subject thoroughly.

Conscientiousness is for being compliant. It consists of elements like resignation and harmony. Their strengths include being detail oriented and following procedures. Their weaknesses include being unreceptive to criticism and insecure. People with a high compliance factor emphasize the importance of order and proceed cautiously. They excel in environments with sufficient resources and are conservative.[13]

The prevalence of a particular dimension will be reflected in the overall style of an organization. A Dominant organization, such as a project, will be decisive, direct, competitive, and action oriented. An Influence organization will be collegial, with plenty of socializing and little discipline in terms of procedures and schedules. A Supportiveness organization is one with little conflict, that emphasizes loyalty and cooperation. A Conscientiousness organization is one that emphasizes detail, formality, and being methodical.[14]

All of the above approaches to understanding human behavior tell us much about people. What they do not tell us much about is how people respond to adversity and difficult situations. Paul Stoltz[15] developed the concept of the Adversity Quotient (AQ) to address this issue. According to him, people have different capacities or abilities for dealing with adversity, e.g., setbacks. A person's AQ is reflected in how resilient and optimistic they are when dealing with adversity. A person's AQ is a pattern that has been developed and is exhibited in thought, emotion, and action.

The capacities for dealing with adversity consist of four dimensions: Control, Ownership, Reach, and Endurance. Control deals with a person's response to adversity, either delayed or spontaneous. Ownership is the extent a person feels he or she can improve the situation. Reach is the degree to which adversity is allowed to permeate his or her life. Endurance reflects how he or she perceives adversity and, therefore, is willing to persist through it. An overall AQ score determines one's capacity to deal with adversity. In *Adversity Quotient @ Work,* Stoltz says that a CORE response to an event reflects one's perception of it. Hence, the higher one's AQ, the greater the likelihood of a person perceiving an event as positive. Likewise, the lower the AQ, the probability increases that a person will view it as negative.

Stoltz identifies three categories of people reflecting their response to adversity using the metaphor of mountaineering: climbers, campers, and quitters. Climbers are people who continue on their ascent, learning along the way, but not turning away. Campers, when faced with adversity, retreat into their comfort zones to feel secure. Quitters cease, even retreat, thus avoiding the negative aspects of an ascent; they simply give up.[15]

## DEALING WITH DIFFICULT PEOPLE

Project managers, by virtue of their position, have the opportunity to work with all types of people. While people are a pleasure to lead the majority of the time, some can be downright frustrating, especially if noncooperative for whatever reason. Indeed, many fellow colleagues have told me that being project manager would be great if not for the people!

One category of difficult people are procrastinators. Procrastinators, of course, are people who do not act unless something impels them to do so.

In an excellent book by Linda Sapadin with Jack Maguire, titled *It's About Time,*[16] the authors identify six styles of procrastinators: Perfectionist, Dreamer, Worrier, Defier, Crisis Maker, and OverDoer.

Perfectionists are the people who must do everything according to their high standards or it is not worth doing. If rattled with fear, they will probably never start. Why? They hold such high expectations for themselves that they do not want to dash them with imperfection. Dreamers are speculators. They never get beyond the idea or vision. They are, essentially, masters of hyperbole. Worriers have a constant need for security. They may find it difficult to move forward because it means taking them from their comfort zones. So they specialize in avoidance. Defiers are rebels. They break all the rules and the first one to break is the person in authority. They see everything as a threat to their autonomy and individuality. They do not act simply because project managers want them to. Crisis Makers are notorious for turning a "mole hill into a mountain." They turn everything into high drama, to the point of crisis. They overreact, placing great stress on themselves and others around them. The emotion gets so intense that they are unable to act. The OverDoer is someone who cannot and will not make choices or establish priorities. To them, everything is of equal importance and they cannot say "no." They have a "mountain of things to do" and, of course, nothing gets done.

According to Sapadin and Maguire, each style exhibits three fundamental characteristics. First, they do not understand why they act the way they do. Second, they rationalize or excuse their behavior. Third, they feel regret.[16]

So what must a project manager do? Wait around for them to act?

Perhaps the best approach is for a project manager to shift the burden to procrastinators. They can have the procrastinators provide options to move forward and have them select the best one. If they refuse to select one, explain the impact of their delay on others and on the overall project. If they still refuse to select an option, call a meeting with other stakeholders, raise the issue, and let peer pressure do the work. It has never failed me. Also, once the procrastinator makes a commitment, give it the widest visibility.

Failure to deal with procrastinators has severe consequences on morale and esprit de corps. It tends to drag others down. It frustrates others who depend on a procrastinator's work as well as delays progress.

By far the best work on dealing with a wide variety of "less than pleasant people" is Robert Bramson's *Coping with Difficult People.*[17] He identifies seven patterns of difficult people. The first category is the Hostile Aggressive, consisting of three subsets: Sherman Tanks, Snipers, and Exploders. As their names imply, they seek to dominate or destroy. The second category is the Complainers. They "bitch and moan" constantly. Nothing is satisfactory and they take no responsibility to resolve complaints. The third category is the Super-Agreeables. They are the people who are the "nice guys" who "put up a front." They will agree, but do not expect them to follow through with their agreements. The fourth category are the Negativists. Close cousins to the Complainers, they are the nay-sayers who insist that, no matter how good something is, it will not work. The fifth category is the Know-It-All Experts. They think of themselves as being the best and the brightest and, by God, they will let you know it. Naturally, they are arrogant and condescending. The sixth category is the Indecisives. These people are direct kin of the procrastinators. They cannot and will not make a decision. The seventh category is the Silent and

Unresponsives. They respond to project managers with a terse response or none at all.

Bramson states that people in general must learn to cope with a person who fits in one or more of these categories. Otherwise, the balance of power will be in their court, for example, not the project manager's.[17]

Whatever pattern of behavior dealt with, ways exist to cope with it. People, project managers in our case, can avoid letting their own behavior escalate the negative behavior pattern of the other person. They can then more readily cope with the person exhibiting the unpleasant behavior. They can, for example, pick and choose the moment to execute their plan to cope. They can also follow through on the effectiveness of their coping.[18]

## MEANING

An area often overlooked by project and functional managers alike is the importance of meaning, defined as providing people with a sense of purpose in whatever they do.

Meaning is often lacking on projects for several reasons. People are often assigned to tasks that they do not enjoy, that do not meet their expectations, or that do not satisfy their own goals. The importance of meaning is often overlooked. It is the one ingredient that entices people to accept difficult tasks and weather the most deplorable conditions. Project managers must do a better job in this regard if they wish to be more successful. As Margaret Wheatley notes, people prefer leaders who offer or create meaning behind whatever we do and we tend to respond accordingly.[19]

Whatever the reason, meaning is often lacking, resulting in tremendous costs for a project. Morale and esprit de corps suffer, causing a decline in project performance in terms of cost, schedule, and quality. Why? The team lacks the necessary emotional commitment to complete their work. To them it is just another job.

Inculcating meaning is no easy task because project managers control few variables. Nevertheless, it is an important topic because emotional attachment is often the key to success, making the difference between marginal or outstanding results. Ideally, project managers should inculcate that sense of WOW! that Tom Peters talks about in his books, which he describes as something significant and fills people with zest.[20]

Essentially, it boils down to a question of control, not by the project manager, but by the individual. A person needs to have a sense of his or her own destiny, not one dictated by some extraneous force. This is the desire that the poet David Whyte (in *The Heart Aroused*) discusses in which people desire to imbue their soul in their experiences.[21]

To get that sense of WOW! or control is really the desire to provide people with the opportunity to have an intense personal, emotional involvement in their work. Abraham Maslow and Mihaly Csikszentmihalyi adeptly described the importance of personal, emotional involvement in work.

Maslow called it the peak experience and describes it as the B-love or mystic experience when people fulfill themselves in whatever they do.[22] People who can have this experience are the ones who self-actualize, which is at the top of his Hierarchy of Needs Theory. In a nutshell, Maslow described five basic needs arranged in a hierarchy. These needs are physiological, safety, love, esteem, and self-actualization. For each individual, his or her needs can be satisfied to various degrees. In general, however, if the basic needs are satisfied, then self-actualization plays a salient role. Through self-actualization, people can have the peak experience.

Csikszentmihalyi discusses the peak experience from the context of creativity. However, the concepts are fairly similar and deserve discussion. According to Csikszentmihalyi, creative people achieve "flow," which he describes as an optimal experience. He calls it flow because it involves circumstances whereby a person's attention is invested in pursuit of their goal.[23] According to the author, achieving flow requires focusing psychic energy. This focus is important because it provides the necessary energy to do work and, in doing so, gives an opportunity to release it.[24]

Through flow, meaning becomes possible by providing emotional concentration necessary for goal attainment. Csikszentmihalyi agrees and observes that by providing a challenging goal, people receive the significance that they want.[25] In addition to purpose, meaning also involves intending to achieve a goal and fitting a person's activities with his or her needs. It is the latter point that is important, especially when harmony exists among thoughts, feelings, and behavior, both internally and externally.[26]

Whether calling it a peak experience or flow, project managers must provide the opportunity for it to happen. The only question is: How?

*Exhibit a positive attitude towards people.* They should subscribe to a Theory Y perspective, accepting at face value that people want to contribute meaningfully to projects. If project managers hold a positive perception, people will perform accordingly. If negative, they will also perform accordingly. This connection between perception about people and the consequent results is known as the Pygmalion Effect, or self-fulfilling prophecy. Paul Hersey and Kenneth Blanchard stress the importance of people having positive assumptions about followers. These assumptions can translate into growth for followers.[27]

Part of this positive attitude toward people is to treat them with respect by understanding their need for dignity and self-worth. As Cohen writes, being respectful towards people builds supporters and increases success.[28]

*Give people the opportunity to determine their destiny on a project.* Enable them to take ownership of the work to do. Project managers can make that happen by allowing people to determine requirements and assume personal responsibility for results. Hence, they allow people to develop their portion of the work breakdown structure, develop estimates, identify task sequences, and determine appropriate criteria of quality. This approach will almost guarantee a sense of meaning by team members because it is their tasks, estimates, and responsibilities. The peak experience or flow then has a greater opportunity to happen.

The key is to get people to think for themselves. Of course, project managers must use judgment. Not everyone will be ready to perform every task for which they volunteer. They must have a level of readiness to perform it. Hersey and Blanchard identified two components of an individual's readiness to perform a task, ability and willingness.

Ability, according to the authors, is the background and skills of a person assigned to do work. Obviously, the more the depth of the background and skill level, the more likely it will be that he or she can perform a task. Willingness is the level of self-confidence and motivation that a person has to perform a task. Obviously, the more self-confidence and motivation one has to perform a task the better. Ideally, a person assigned to a task is willing and able. More often than not, however, the person is sometimes willing and not able or able and not willing or unable and unwilling.[29]

Naturally, project managers want team members, for example, to be willing and able but more often than not they must deal with the other combinations. How can project managers increase the likelihood of people being both willing and able? The answer again is involvement. Project managers can get the involvement by allowing people to participate in planning and even managing aspects of their projects. Examples include having people explode their own portions of the work breakdown structure, determine their own time estimates, and choose to be responsible for the quality of deliverables. People tend to be more committed to whatever they have had a "say."

Admittedly, some people choose a task to perform because they are willing to perform but lack the ability. Project managers, however, can compensate for that situation by teaming the person with someone with more experience or sending him or her to training.

Because they often lack formal power over individuals, project managers must avoid the common tendency to do everything unilaterally and tell everyone what to do by a specific time. This approach makes project management more difficult and can demotivate a team. Again, I cannot overemphasize — involvement, involvement, involvement.

*Fuse logic and emotion when dealing with people.* People are the only creatures who think logically and emotionally. They are ruled by the heart and the mind; each affects the other.[30]

Too many project managers think logically, and assume everyone else does too. They fail to realize that logic often reflects the deep emotional needs of individuals. Hence, project managers must be attuned to emotional and logical needs when assigning tasks. While assigning a task to a person may make good logical sense, for example, it may not make good sense from an emotional perspective. That person may not be the right one because of emotional considerations of which the project manager is often unaware. So these project managers find themselves in a struggle between the heart and the head. If project managers assume that people operate on emotion and justify their actions with logic, their task becomes easier. And the best way to fuse the two is to give people the opportunity to determine their own destiny.

*Get to know stakeholders, particularly team members, on a personal level.* Strive to understand their paradigm or mental maps, their expectations about the project, and the type of work they enjoy doing.

An effective approach is to meet with each person individually. Applying active and effective listening skills, project managers can learn much about a person. They have a better chance of learning what people are willing and able to do or not willing and able to do. They will also gain insight into what truly drives a particular person and their overall attitude. The goal is to learn as much as possible about a person with the idea that project managers can provide the best opportunity to involve that person. Of course, project managers should keep all aspects of the interchange confidential to maintain trust.

When trying to get to know a team member or another stakeholder, a key goal is to empathize, that is, to see and feel the project from their world. Empathy not only furthers relationships but also increases one's social awareness. According to Goleman, Boyatzis, and McKee, the most effective means for increasing social awareness is empathy. They define empathy as knowing how people feel at a particular moment and responding in a way that mitigates and improves feelings.[31]

This approach offers several advantages. People garner a more personal relationship with project managers. They no longer feel like a "cog in a project machine." People begin to feel that they have an opportunity to grow through participation. Project managers also gain. They get to learn more about the people they must work with in order to achieve project goals. They have a better understanding of what motivates people. They have a greater confidence in dealing with the most difficult part of a project — people.

*Apply good conflict management.* All project managers face this situation when people do not want to cooperate with you or disagree with you. Procrastinators and other difficult people will appear and the larger the project, the greater likelihood of their presence. When that happens, conflict management on a one-on-one basis is very important to overcome a potential problem on a project.

If there is one issue that frustrates project managers more than anything, it is dealing with difficult people. I believe, however, the reason that it creates so much frustration is the approach that many project managers take. Rather than treating conflict as an opportunity to open doors between two people, it turns into a power struggle between project manager and stakeholder, often a team member. Many project managers, who often lack formal command and control over people, act as if they have it. Many project managers, in turn, attempt to "force" a person into submissive response. A submissive response, according to Robert Bolton, in *People Skills,* occurs when a person demonstrates a lack of respect for their own needs and rights. What results, of course, is compliance, not commitment.

Sometimes project managers do not get submissive but aggressive behavior, reflecting the more they push the more reaction returned. Bolton says people who exhibit aggressive behavior tend to be abusive, sarcastic, and often hold a grudge.[32] If an aggressive person does accept a task, it often results in poor quality or work or noncooperation.

Ideally, project managers want people to willingly accept the tasks assigned and not be forced to do them. When conflict does arise when assigning tasks, even after people provide their input, project managers should seek a Win-Win agreement — a person feels that their needs are being satisfied while, at the same time, fulfilling the needs of a project.

Whenever dealing with conflict, project managers should remember three useful insights that Bolton identifies in his book:

- Treat the other person with respect. Avoid forcing people into submission or rebellion.
- Listen to the other person. Strive first, as Covey notes, to understand before being understood. This involves not only understanding them logically, but emotionally.
- State their own views, needs, and feelings as well. The exchange between project managers and stakeholders is reciprocal; both parties need to understand where the other is coming from and what their needs are.[33]

There is a final insight on how managers should address conflict and it is from the perspective of solving a problem. In *Leadership Effectiveness Training*

*(L.E.T.)*, Thomas Gordon identifies six steps that can lead to a Win-Win result. They follow closely the approach taken to make decisions that was described in an earlier chapter. The steps are: (1) identify and define the problem, (2) generate alternatives to solve the problem, (3) evaluate the alternatives, (4) make a decision on the best alternative, (5) implement the solution, and (6) conduct the follow-up.[34]

Of course, this approach is very logical when solving the problem. There is also an emotional side to consider. The key is to keep the locus of responsibility for solving a problem in the hands of the stakeholder. This approach will provide a person with the opportunity to commit to tasks. It also encourages people to exhibit assertive, not submissive or aggressive, behavior. Bolton describes assertive behavior as one that affirms a person's sense of value and dignity.[35]

## HORSE SENSE

There is a popular saying in American folklore: "You can lead a horse to water but you can't make it drink." The analogy fits well for people: You can assign them to a project but you cannot force them to perform. At least that is the case for project managers, who often lack formal authority over people. Project managers, therefore, must provide the incentives for people to achieve the vision for their projects. The best way to make that happen is to encourage involvement in a manner that generates sustained commitment.

## CASE STUDY: MOTIVATE

One of the more difficult challenges is to motivate team members to want to complete a project successfully. As mentioned earlier, two previous attempts to change the policies and procedures infrastructure failed because team members from the business units feared relinquishing the independence of their organization.

To motivate team members, the project manager allowed each one to develop a portion of the work breakdown structure for which they would be responsible for executing, completing, and providing status. They were allowed to identify the dependencies among tasks as well as provide time estimates. Of course, the project manager ensured that they understood that their output must fall within the parameters in the project charter.

By allowing team members to generate their own work breakdown structure (a generic one to follow had been provided), the project manager engendered a feeling among team members that the project was — at least to some degree

— their project and that they willfully participated. In other words, the project manager took ownership and led by influence rather than by command.

Another important approach for motivating was to meet with each team member personally. One-on-one sessions were held to learn more about interests, cares, and concerns related to the project. The project manager knew that during these sessions, plans could be developed that would satisfy many of their needs and help overcome shortcomings.

Of course, the project manager had to deal with some difficult people, particularly individuals from the one business unit that had historically resisted any attempt to cooperate on previous projects. The project manager, therefore, made every attempt to build bridges, not walls, between himself and members from the "uncooperative" business unit. Some of the approaches that worked successfully to overcome resistance included assigning tasks requiring each member of the different business units to work together, holding meetings at the uncooperative business unit location, profiling the work of its members on the project, and having team members speak frequently at these sessions. The idea was to encourage more involvement, physical and psychological, to the point that the project became meaningful to everyone on the project.

## REFERENCES

1. William A. Cohen, *The Art of the Leader,* Prentice Hall, Englewood Cliffs, NJ, 1990, p. 139.
2. Mihaly Csikszentmihalyi, *Flow,* HarperPerennial, New York, 1990, pp. 1–8.
3. Howard Gardner, *Multiple Intelligences,* Basic Books, New York, 1993, pp. 15–26.
4. Jacquelyn Wonder and Priscilla Donovan, *Whole Brain Thinking,* Ballantine Books, New York, 1984, pp. 3–19.
5. Ned Herrmann, *The Whole Brain Book,* McGraw-Hill, New York, 1996, pp. 15 and 23.
6. Ibid., p. 272.
7. David Keirsey and Marilyn Bates, *Please Understand Me,* Prometheus Nemesis, Del Mar, CA, 1984, pp. 13–26.
8. Ibid., pp. 129–166.
9. Helen Palmer, *The Enneagram,* HarperSanFrancisco, San Francisco, 1991, pp. 7–41.
10. Patricia Pitcher, *The Drama of Leadership,* John Wiley & Sons, New York, 1997, pp. 15–49.
11. Patricia Pitcher, Artists, craftsmen, and technocrats, *Training and Development,* pp. 30–33, July 1999.
12. Taylor Hartman, *The Color Code,* Fireside Books, New York, 1998, pp. 43–124.
13. Ibid., p. 68.
14. Tom Ritchey and Alan Axelrod, *I'm Stuck, You're Stuck,* Berrett-Koehler, San Francisco, 2002, pp. 19–117.

15. Paul G. Stoltz, *Adversity Quotient @ Work,* William Morrow, New York, 2000, pp. 19–77.
16. Linda Sapadin and Jack Maguire, *It's About Time,* Penguin Books, New York, 1997, pp. 6–14.
17. Robert M. Bramson, *Coping with Difficult People,* Dell, New York, 1981, pp. 4–7.
18. Ibid., pp. 159–179.
19. Margaret J. Wheatley, *Leadership and the New Science,* Berrett-Koehler, San Francisco, 1994, p. 135.
20. Tom Peters, *The Project 50,* Knopf, New York, 1999, p. 15.
21. David Whyte, *The Heart Aroused,* Currency Doubleday, New York, 1994, p. 17.
22. Abraham H. Maslow, *Toward a Psychology of Being,* 2nd ed., Van Nostrand, Princeton, NJ, 1968, p. 73.
23. Mihaly Csikszentmihalyi, *Flow,* HarperPerennial, New York, 1990, p. 40.
24. Ibid., p. 33.
25. Ibid., p. 216.
26. Ibid., p. 217.
27. Paul Hersey and Kenneth H. Blanchard, *Management of Organizational Behavior,* 6th ed., Prentice Hall, Englewood Cliffs, NJ, 1993, p. 189.
28. William A. Cohen, *The Art of the Leader,* Prentice Hall, Englewood Cliffs, NJ, 1990, p. 142.
29. Paul Hersey and Kenneth H. Blanchard, *Management of Organizational Behavior,* 6th ed., Prentice Hall, Englewood Cliffs, NJ, 1993, p. 191.
30. Antonio Demasio, *Descartes' Error,* Avon Books, New York, 1994, pp. 191–196.
31. Daniel Goleman, Richard Boyatzis, and Annie McKee, *Primal Leadership,* Harvard Business School Press, Boston, 2002, pp. 5–6.
32. Robert Bolton, People Skills, *Touchstone,* New York, 1986, p. 123.
33. Ibid., pp. 218–222.
34. Thomas Gordon, *Leadership Effectiveness Training (L.E.T.),* Bantam Books, Toronto, 1980, pp. 194–197.
35. Robert Bolton, People Skills, *Touchstone,* New York, 1986, p. 125.

# 9

# TEAM

Building a team is critical to achieve the goals and objectives of any project, as most project managers will tell you. Unfortunately, few project managers build effective teams. Instead, they treat their project as a committee; members meet, do what they have been told, and depart. Synergy is lacking.

## DEFINITION OF A TEAM

What is a team? One common definition is that a team is a group of people with each one having a narrow set of skills, knowledge, and interests that are applied to achieve a common purpose.[1] This definition, like many others, is incomplete. The team is viewed like a machine. The emotional and psychological aspects are missing.

The best definition is one that appears in *The Wisdom of Teams* by Jon Katzenbach and Douglas Smith where they define a team as a small group of individuals with complementary skills that are applied to achieve a common goal by which everyone is held accountable.[2] The operative words in this definition are complementary, common, committed, and accountable.

*Complementary* means that a team consists of people with different skills. *Common* means that people share a destination and path when applying their complementary skills. *Committed* means that they have a personal stake in activities and outcome. *Accountable* means that their participation contributes not only to their own success but also to that of others and the entire project.

Why does a team prove more valuable than individual efforts? It is the synergistic quality. According to Katzenbach and Smith, teams are the "basic unit of performance" that reflects the composition of many skills, experiences, and judgment. In other words, a team is more than a mere collection of people, e.g., committee. In addition, teams are more adaptable and productive than other organizational units because they often have clearer goals, which lead to better performance.[3]

## MAKING TEAMWORK

A team, however, does not just happen. It requires teamwork, which is the collaboration of different people seeking to achieve common goals and objectives.

Team building must be nurtured and that occurs when the team leader exhibits leadership. Without leadership, a team does not or barely exist(s); teamwork becomes next to impossible. The team leader's job is to provide the "spark" that encourages people to want to achieve goals and objectives.

What do team leaders do? Five things.

1. *They seek to build a committed, cohesive group so everyone feels like they are part of something much greater than themselves.* In other words, they build esprit de corps and cohesion through involvement and grant autonomy in decision making. People end up feeling like owners.
2. *They encourage collaboration.* They build collaborative and cooperative environments. They are respectful of others in terms of needs and interests, making everyone winners.
3. *They treat all people as important.* Leaders recognize the importance of mutual respect by creating an atmosphere that builds and sustains self-esteem and self-confidence.
4. *They strive to align personal and group needs.* Leaders "earn their stripes" via satisfying the needs and hopes of a group's membership.
5. *They build synergy.* That is, leaders recognize that they need to cement the relationships with the members of their groups in a way that goes beyond the achievements of a single individual.

## INDICATORS OF POOR TEAMING

Unfortunately, teams, team building, and team leadership are rare occurrences, as demonstrated by some common problems existing on teams. A team in trouble often exhibits the following characteristics.

- *It is riddled with negative conflict.* Members think only of their needs to further their own agendas. Some team members, for example, prefer one approach towards executing a project while another seeks a different one; neither side yields and progress stalls.
- *Members are full of cynicism and distrust.* No one trusts each other whether in thought, words, or deeds. As a result, people are hesitant,

even afraid to speak, either out of fear or to gain advantage. They do not bother to communicate or share information.

■ *A team pursues unclear goals and objectives.* The reason for existence becomes unclear to the members. People start to focus on what is important to themselves rather than on the overall goals and objectives of the project. Team cohesion becomes nonexistent as the atmosphere becomes one of "every man for himself."

■ *It lacks energy.* Since most or all members lack enthusiasm, the entire team lacks it. Ideally, a team should exhibit substantial energy, at levels much greater than the sum of its members. What energy that does exist gets dissipated.

■ *Members are misaligned, both internally and externally.* A team may be internally misaligned with its very own reason for existence, manifested by doing insignificant and irrelevant activities. A team may be externally misaligned with higher goals and objectives by doing activities that do not accomplish the goals and objectives of a parent organization. Team members frequently exhibit "busy work."

■ *A team lacks leadership, either by the leader or other team members.* Instead, the team floats according to the circumstances that direct it. Its leadership lacks involvement for whatever reason; meaningful output rarely results.

From a project management perspective, these conditions can seriously impact cost, schedule, quality, and overall performance. Some indicators are unrealistic schedules and estimates; quality problems, e.g., rework and last minute "patches"; people problems, e.g., miscommunication, dashed expectations, failure to complete their tasks.

## REASONS FOR POOR PROJECT TEAMS

So why do such conditions exist on projects?

*Many project managers do not provide team members with well-defined goals, roles, and responsibilities.* They should facilitate a definition of what to produce and perform. Unfortunately, the norm is often only a vague idea of the product and tasks. In addition, they fail to encourage a greater understanding of why their contributions matter in the first place.

*They fail to develop an integrated plan.* Instead, they assign work that creates busy work, that is, tasks that do not further goals and objectives. The team resembles a bag of different colored marbles that fall to the floor and scatter in different directions. An overall sense of direction is missing.

*Many project managers fail to manage conflict effectively.* Instead, they treat it as irrelevant, like all "people issues." Yet the consequences of this failure are all too real, reflected in the presence of back stabbing, domination by certain personalities at meetings, a lack of meaningful contribution of others, and no consensus over how to proceed. Conflict can also occur interfunctionally, meaning that people with different disciplinary backgrounds cannot resolve their differences.

*They often fail to develop a well-rounded balance of skills and talents on a team.* Instead, their teams are often overrepresented with people of certain skills and talents while people with other vital talents are lacking. As a result, everything is interpreted through the lens of people who have similar or the same backgrounds, leading to serious oversights and misinterpretation that can lead to poor decision making. The team's work often becomes incomplete, due to overlooking important issues. This situation often manifests itself in meetings with one-sided discussions, e.g., emphasizing a particular discipline at the expense of others. The team, in other words, lacks a multidisciplinary perspective.

*Many project managers often misallocate resources.* They allocate resources to people without a need, while others that do have a need go without. They may allocate too much of the wrong resource and too little of what they need. Naturally, the misallocation of resources creates the opportunity for considerable infighting, which ultimately results in frustration and poor performance. Competition can then become intense for resources, causing dissension and resentment.

*They often fail to align the efforts of their projects to anything meaningful.* They do not provide meaningful goals and objectives or provide the opportunity to develop them. Instead, their projects are adrift, causing people to move in different directions. This misalignment, of course, reduces any opportunity for a team and its individual members to provide meaningful contributions, giving it a weak sense of direction.

*Many project managers often fail to seek support from the key stakeholders.* The fact that they lack sufficient resources and have nonexistent or ill-defined goals reflects this lack of support. This circumstance eventually leads to morale and esprit de corps problems. In addition, the team can quickly become subject to the harmful effects of hostility or indifference regarding resources.

## CHARACTERISTICS OF GOOD PROJECT TEAMS

A high-performance team has several characteristics, reflective of high morale and esprit de corps.

*They encourage a sense of community among all members, direct and indirect.* In his book *On Leadership,* John Gardner recognizes the importance of a sense of community, noting that its creation is one of the most important skills of a leader.[4] He then identifies conditions for generating this sense of community. Although Gardner talks in the context of public service, I believe his conditions apply just as much to business in general and projects in particular. These conditions include a shared culture, trust, teamwork, and good communication.[5]

*They encourage collaboration, willingly and constantly.* The team leader, however, has the responsibility to lay the groundwork and sustain it. As Kouzes and Posner said, it is about people working together; however, they add, such collaboration requires that leaders and, indeed, team members continually invest effort and energy to sustain it.[6]

According to Edward Marshall, in his book *Transforming the Way We Work,* the basis for collaboration is principles and values.[7] He identifies what he calls collaboration values, such as consensus, integrity, ownership, and respect.[8]

*They encourage a strong sense of commitment by all team members.* Without this feeling of commitment, overall performance will likely be marginal. To be lasting and effective, however, this sense of commitment must be shared by everyone; the way to achieve that is through a compelling goal. Common commitment is necessary; otherwise, a group is merely a composite of individuals.

*They focus on results, defined as the achievement goals and objectives.* However, there is a catch. Both the goals of the team and individuals require alignment. Without alignment, or misalignment, the commitment will be tepid and wane over time, causing a loss of synergy and effectiveness. Peter Senge notes the importance of alignment, observing that lack of alignment leads to waste whereas alignment results in focus and harmony.[9]

*They openly share ideas, information, and feelings.* Openness is not a weakness but an expectation and a strength. To a large extent, the issue is not so much one of openness, but one of emotional intelligence exhibited not only by individuals but the entire team. In *Primal Leadership,* Goleman, Boyatizis, and McKee observe that the emotional intelligence of groups consists of the same elements as an emotionally intelligent person.[10] This emotional maturity is reflected in the way a team interacts as Vanessa Druskat and Steven Wolff note in *Harvard Business Review.* They say that emotionally intelligent teams are willing to confront difficult circumstances and seek external advice and consultation on performance.[11]

*They recognize that everyone on a team has leadership potential, not just the team leader.* A team leader can enable that to happen by allowing team members to "rise to the occasion" if a situation warrants.

Of course, some team leaders construe this behavior as relinquishing their leadership responsibilities. That really is an inaccurate assessment. It is really more of a balancing act that relies on the team leader's judgment, as Katzenbach and Smith observe. They note that the balance is often between such considerations as guidance and control as well as creativity and discipline. Unfortunately, they say, traditional hierarchies yield to the pressure that favors control and discipline, for example.[12]

*They provide the basis to create what Katzenbach and Smith describe as a high-performance team and Bennis and Biederman describe as a Great Group.* The core of creating such a team is the meaning or the reason for its existence.

This sense of meaning or mission is reflected by the high energy radiating from the team, as Bennis and Biederman further observe. According to them, such teams thrive on deadlines, like high drama, and prefer action.[13]

A direct relationship exists between effective project management and effective teams. Indeed, just about all the practices of project management are correlated with all the practices of building effective teams.

Francis Hartman and Greg Skulmonski identify characteristics of highly effective teams that also apply to project teams, e.g., open communication, ownership of work, creativity, and trust.[14]

H. Dudley Dewhirst in *PM Network* notes practices like staffing, chartering, obtaining feedback, and managing performance. He also notes, however, that it involves more than the "mechanics" of project management. It also involves "soft issues," such as authority issues, relationships with customers, facilitating communications, seeking agreement and consensus, and encouraging feedback.[15]

He further implies that performing such activities makes the difference between the categories of teams described by Katzenbach and Smith: Star, Effective, Pseudo, and Name-only teams. Star teams are the best, followed by Effective, Pseudo, and Name-only, respectively. A Star team reflects the definition of a team provided by Katzenbach and Smith described earlier in this chapter. Effective teams are hampered by organizational constraints but still manage to "get the job done." Pseudo teams lack many of the mechanics of project management. Name-only teams lack the mechanics as well as leadership.[16]

According to Hans Thamhain and David Wilemon, a high-performing new product team, which is really a project team, has many characteristics of a high-performance team: low conflict, high commitment, involved people, and good communication.[17] What seems to increase the likelihood of having a high-performance project team? Project leadership, they add, prefers action, provides resources, directs plan development and implementation, and addresses important issues.[18]

## BUILDING THE PROJECT TEAM

What, then, are some actions that project managers can take to build teams that will help them be effective team leaders?

## Acquire a Solid Understanding of Team Dynamics by Taking a Systemic View of a Team

From that perspective, a team is a system consisting of elements and their interrelationships with one another and their surrounding environment. Teams, therefore, consist of objects or people, who interact with one another to pursue a common purpose.

There are several quantitative and qualitative factors to consider as well. Qualitative factors include skill, knowledge, experience, education, and grade. Quantitative factors include the number of people with applicable qualitative factors, e.g., the number of people with requisite skills.

Relationships among people also have qualitative and quantitative factors. Qualitative factors include being formal or informal, positive or negative, and direct or indirect. Quantitative factors include the number of interactions among specific stakeholders and the number of people reporting to a project manager to reflect span of control.

Of course, conditions can also affect project performance. Although too numerous to list completely, there are some salient ones that can impose constraints on a project team. These conditions include economic, e.g., availability of money to finance the project; political, e.g., support by upper management and the customer; and technical, e.g., maturity of the technology used on the project. Conditions can have positive, negative, and neutral impacts on a project.

There also are constraints placed on a team that can be overt or subtle. Some examples of overt constraints include monetary restrictions, policies and procedures, resource (e.g., people) availability and expertise, and mandatory dates in schedules. Subtle constraints are more difficult to ascertain, but their influence can be considerable. Examples of subtle constraints include norms and mores for conducting business, motivation of stakeholders, informal networks, learning curves, informal roles and responsibilities, perceptions of individuals and the team, and working and power relationships.

Another important action is for project managers to understand that building a team is not easy. A team has many opportunities for entropy and disintegration to occur unless project managers, as leaders, actively involve themselves in orchestrating a reversal.

In addition, project managers must appreciate and accept the reasons for building a team. Quite a few project managers do not look favorably on teams. Instead, they rely on select individuals because, they feel, it requires less time and is more efficient and effective. Efficient perhaps, but more effective?

That may be more a misperception. Building an effective team reflects less on the effectiveness of teaming per se and more on a lack of effectiveness by a project manager to function as a leader. For example, consider the "team traps" identified by Alan Slobodnik and Kristina Wile in *The Systems Thinker* and it becomes quite clear that most of them represent a failure in leadership. These traps include inability to reach closure, lack of mutual accountability, left out stakeholders, and uneven participation.[19]

Project managers must also recognize that as many different types of teams exist as do varieties of projects. For example, Katzenbach identifies three types of teams: those that provide recommendations, those that take action, and those that perform operations.[20] In the *Team Members Survival Guide,* Jill George and Jeannette Wilson also identify four categories of teams: cross-functional quality improvement, functional work team, multifunctional empowered, and virtual.[21]

Project managers need to match the type of team with the goals and objectives of their projects. Failure to recognize the type of team can result in the application of an inappropriate approach for leading a project, which may cause an "out of sync" condition between activities and goals and objectives of a project.

Finally, project teams are conflict prone (by their very nature) and project managers must prepare themselves to deal with it. Conflict can occur between two team members or throughout an entire team. Goleman, Boyatizis, and McKee note that failure to deal with conflict can have dire results. It is the team leader, say the authors, who build harmonious and collaborative teams. He or she must inculcate a sense of being positive and optimistic in personal and group behavior.[22]

To deal effectively with conflict, especially negative conflict, project managers must recognize its sources. These sources include unclear goals and objectives, ineffective resource distribution, different approaches and values, unreasonable expectations, and diversity in ethnicity and thinking.

Failure to recognize such sources can have severe consequences. Perhaps one of the best perspectives on the relationship of viewing a team as a system and the resulting conflicts that can arise is the article by Slobodnik and Wile. They identify four categories of team systems: closed, with a strong hierarchy; synchronous, with vision and values; random, with a degree of tolerance for individuality and autonomy; and open, with a degree of openness and collaboration. Each one can lead to conflict, manifested overtly or covertly. For example, a team that is synchronous might have conflict that is covert, e.g., not sharing information. A team that is open might have overt conflict, e.g., failure to reach a consensus.[23]

## Understand That Like Human Beings, Teams Progress Through Phases

These phases are not, however, the same as the project life cycle phases.

The Tuchman Model is a popular perspective on building teams often taken by experts. The four phases through which a team progresses from start to finish are: Forming, Storming, Norming, and Performing.

The Forming phase occurs when team members get acquainted and gain familiarity with the team's purpose. The Storming phase is a time of "jockeying" for position and authority as well as resolving issues. The Norming phase occurs when the team acquires a sense of cooperation and organization. The Performing phase occurs when all efforts of a team are focused on the achievement of goals and objectives.

Project managers can help to "smooth out" the trials associated with each phase. For the Forming phase, they can encourage people to know each other better and identify ways for people to understand clearly the purpose of the team. For the Storming phase, they can clarify issues about roles and responsibilities and seek agreements and consensus over important issues. For the Norming phase, they can capitalize on people's strengths and compensate for their weaknesses. For the Performing phase, they can help a team to adjust to change in a manner that minimizes disruption in performance as well as protects it from red tape. Ideally, of course, project managers want to reduce the negative aspects of forming, e.g., exactly reforming, and lessen the impact of storming.

Another view of the phases of a team is the one by George and Wilson in the *Team Member's Survival Guide:* Pre-team, New, and Mature. The Pre-team phase occurs, of course, before forming a team and, like the Forming phase in the Tuchman Model, when an unclear purpose and roles exist. The New team phase occurs when a team clearly identifies its purpose, defines team members' roles, and encourages a sense of working together. The Mature team phase occurs when a team becomes essentially a going concern, having the ability to adapt to changing circumstances, e.g., additional responsibilities.[24] Naturally, project managers must involve themselves in all phases, but especially during the Pre-team and New phases because actions taken then affect the overall performance of the team through the remainder of the project life cycle.

## Build Commitment Through Involvement

As mentioned earlier, commitment is extremely important, especially from a motivational standpoint. It can make the difference between mediocre and high performance. In *The Wisdom of Teams,* Katzenbach and Smith observe that high-performance teams are filled with commitment. They also tend to involve a limited number of people who have the requisite background. Of the two, commitment seems to have the biggest impact.[25]

Who is responsible for laying the groundwork for engendering commitment by all stakeholders to the project? The project manager, of course. The question is: How?

The key to garnering this commitment is to involve stakeholders, both physically and emotionally. This involvement is achievable through participation by team members during decision making by using tools like brainstorming and nominal group technique. They can determine performance measurement approaches and standards. They can encourage greater functional representation on the team. Without involvement, stakeholders will likely exhibit inadequate or unequal levels of commitment.

Of course, threats to obtaining and sustaining commitment will arise and project managers should always be cognizant of them. These threats include lack of focus, recognition, management support, and trust; insufficient resources; unrealistic milestone dates; extensive overtime due to poor workmanship; too much conflict; inappropriate managerial style; and no sharing of information. In the end, however, a team and its members can be highly committed even when facing such threats if the team and its members feel tied to the team. It is the team as a whole that must act decisively and feel in control.[26]

## Inspire, Not Perspire, People

Use less command and control over people and encourage others to apply their knowledge, skills, and abilities to achieve goals and objectives. It also requires augmenting strengths and offsetting weaknesses.

To enable others through inspiration, a project manager acts as a steward or servant leader, similar to what Peter Block and Max De Pree describe. In that role, he or she acts more as a facilitator, coach, sponsor, or healer than someone directing and controlling.[27] The behavior exhibited by a project manager, therefore, includes one of trusting: candid, respectful, caring, and encouraging.[28] As Bennis and Biederman observe, leaders "encourage and enable."[29]

To enable others to perform their best, a leader capitalizes on what people do best and accounts for their weaknesses. In other words, a project manager seeks to inspire others to complement one another, involving a full spectrum of technical, functional, and interpersonal talents and skills. To have teams of people who complement each other, project managers must have a good knowledge about their talents and skills. That requires building a trusting relationship with them through greater involvement in identifying and directing work. This approach will not only engender a greater sense of ownership and accountability, but also meaningful involvement. Work becomes less of a "job" and more of a "responsibility" because people find it enjoyable and meaningful. Consequently, burn out and complacency become less of an issue.

Another side exists to this issue of enabling others to actualize by complementing each other. It is developing a diverse team rather than one that "parrots" a project manager's style. As Hersey and Blanchard note, having similar styles is not the key. The key is that everyone understands each other's roles, shares common goals and objectives, and complements each other.[30]

## Provide Unity of Direction

One of the hardest challenges facing a project manager is to move a group of people towards a focused direction, especially if he or she lacks formal, functional control over people. Most project managers face this type of challenge.

Without appropriate leadership, a project team can move in many directions, especially one not originally intended. It becomes even more challenging when the people on a team are talented and independently minded. By virtue of their roles, project managers must have team members focus, especially when leading a high-performance team or a Great Group. As Bennis and Biederman note, it is not easy leading a Great Group. The key is to provide such a group with a meaningful sense of direction.[31]

A major ingredient to ensure that a team obtains and maintains focus is for project managers to provide clarity of purpose, that is, to define exactly what a project team must accomplish. Failure to do so can result in individuals and/or the whole team performing inefficiently and ineffectively.

It is important, therefore, for project managers to set direction — but not necessarily unilaterally. They need to involve key stakeholders to garner the commitment through their guidance. They play an instrumental role by ensuring direction in several ways: helping the team define its vision; identifying desired results, e.g., objectives; determining critical success factors; collecting performance data; and developing a plan. With a team's involvement, its members are more committed and, therefore, less inclined to deviate.

## Foster Collaboration Through Cooperation to Achieve a Common Purpose

Collaboration, of course, does not often arise through happenstance. Many reasons stand in the way, e.g., limited availability of resources, poor communication, different values and beliefs, and conflicting policies and procedures.

"Subjective elements" especially make collaboration very difficult as they, but not their effects, are hard to detect. Perceptions and emotions are examples that have a dynamic impact on people and how they go about achieving results.[32]

Fortunately, some people are available who can lay the groundwork to surmount obstacles to collaboration. These people are project managers who function as social architects, according to Thamhain and Wilemon, who understand how behavioral and organizational considerations influence the degree of negative conflict that occurs.[33]

An important area that project managers must address is building in mutual accountability for results. This accountability is very important if project managers hope to avoid the "every man for himself" syndrome. In fact, no team can really call itself a team until mutual accountability exists.

Mutual accountability cannot, however, be commanded. It can only occur if project managers lay the groundwork through a well-defined vision and a path to get there. Katzenbach and Smith say that mutual accountability can be inculcated through trust and is a by-product of shared goals and approaches.[34]

Another important area is managing conflict. Failure to manage conflict constructively can result in stalemates, noncooperation, and, ultimately, poor performance.

In *PM Network,* Erik J. Van Slyke identifies several actions to tackle conflict on a team basis. These are very similar to those discussed about dealing with one-on-one conflict, but still deserve mentioning. These actions are: (1) preparing for interaction by taking a big picture perspective; (2) initiating exchange through confrontation, involvement, and problem solving; (3) facilitating relationships by being open and demonstrating trust; (4) understanding interests regarding why they feel the way that they do; (5) examining the solutions by determining options; and (6) reaching consensus so everyone can live with the result.[35]

Conflict is not all bad, of course, and the absence of it may indicate something. Consensus is not the absence of disagreement but because of it, a fact seldom recognized.

In today's project environment, two major challenges exist that project managers face when building a truly collaborative team; failure to address either one can add to conflict and destroy mutual accountability. These challenges are virtual teams and globalization.

Virtual teams are often geographically disperse teams, thanks to advances in technology. Under these circumstances, encouraging collaboration is difficult because of geography and time differences. The way to address this challenge is to develop a "real" team through a common vision and interdependence.

Globalization is the other challenge, and perhaps, the more difficult of the two. It involves bridging cultural differences to achieve a common vision. Each culture has a different perspective on how the world operates; this difference increases the opportunity to lose the chance to collaborate. The seriousness of this circumstance is clearly articulated by Karen Bemowski in *Quality Progress,* noting that what she calls "cultural archetypes," or cultural patterns, affect people's perceptions of a circumstance and how they react to it. She says that the best way to handle an archetype is to identify it and react accordingly.[36]

Perhaps the best way to overcome these two challenges, and others, is for project managers to set the norm for collaboration, right from the start. As Druskat and Wolff observe in *Harvard Business Review,* a team needs to adopt norms that establish and build trust and identity. By doing so, members, individually and as a group, get emotionally involved in the work.[37]

## Liberate, Not Subjugate

A constant theme in this book is that project managers must do less controlling and more involving. Otherwise, they will execute their roles and responsibilities with great difficulty. The way to avoid that situation is for project managers to facilitate the work of others by reducing or eliminating constraints on performance.

Countless constraints on performance exist, formally and informally. Formal examples include policies, procedures, and accepted tools and techniques. Informal constraints include politics, senior management, influence, and expected managerial styles. Both formal and informal constraints can be very bureaucratic.

Whatever the constraint, however, project managers must mitigate or remove their impacts so individuals can effectively apply their talents and skills. Removing or mitigating the affects of constraints will enable people to team more effectively without feeling controlled or punished.

This ability of project managers to liberate team members and an entire team from constraints, especially external ones, is an important one by leaders of Great Groups. Such project managers provide considerable autonomy while they focus the entire team's energies on a goal. According to Bennis and Biederman in *Organizing Genius,* talent rises to the surface in a Great Group.[38]

Project managers can liberate individuals and their entire team in several ways. They can encourage open sharing of ideas and information, be "boundary busters," look for opportunities to encourage formal and informal interaction among stakeholders, invite different people with diverse insights to team meetings, regularly challenge the modus operandi, build an atmosphere of trust, communicate honestly, share power and delegate, emphasize teaming on tasks, promote team decision making, and reward and recognize creativity as an important ingredient for project success.

Through liberation, an additional benefit arises that is often overlooked: the ability to adapt to a changing environment. If constraints become too rigid and actions inflexible, a team will fail to adapt and that is an all too frequent occurrence. This inflexibility is quite evident when taking a systemic view; dysfunctional behavior and subsequent results manifest themselves clearly and repeatedly.[39]

Project managers need to release the potential energy that resides within a team. Too often that energy, both on individual and group bases, are wasted or applied in an unfocused way. As leaders, project managers must remove the barriers to release that energy and direct it in laser-like fashion toward the vision of their projects.

### Create a Sense of High Drama

A major earmark of a high-performance team or Great Group is a sense of excitement that permeates an entire team. The intensity is so great that when these projects end, the members tend to have an emotional crash.[40]

If any problems are associated with high drama on a project, there are two main examples. Burn out is the first. Team members may be so enthusiastic about their project that they are willing to work long hours and endure grueling conditions to succeed. Conflict is the other potential problem. Due to the intensity, team members may be so consumed with emotion that they do not want to yield. Why? They have a high emotional relationship with the outcome, mixing personal best with team best.

Regardless, the benefits of high drama outweigh the problems, if managed properly. There are many ways to do so: have frequent milestones in the schedule, constantly and consistently collect and communicate status, give as much visibility as possible to intermediate results, meet frequently to discuss significant issues, recognize outstanding performance, emphasize the magnitude of the challenge repeatedly, and allow complacency to be the exception rather than the norm.

## HARD AS STEEL

A team is more than a collection of individuals. It is more like an alloy, whereby strength is increased through the merging of talents and skills rather than people functioning separately. Project managers must meld the individuals together to build strength and compensate for weaknesses. Essentially, people — as a team — become a single unit that achieves results beyond what any committee, for example, can do.

## CASE STUDY: TEAM

Because of the history of autonomous behavior by the business units in the corporation and the challenge of everyone to work together on company-wide projects, the project manager paid particular attention towards building a team. He knew that each business unit had its own way of doing business, its unique history, and preferences about what was and was not important.

During the vision workshop, the groundwork was laid to overcome the complexities and travails associated with the first two phases of a team under the Tuchman Model, forming and storming. The project manager also stressed the importance of sharing best practices, insights, and comments as well as formulating a common vision. He also used the workshop as a means to show-case situations where cooperation occurred between two or more business units.

Throughout the project, the project manager emphasized and practiced a focus on the overall picture, which was the vision described in the project charter and other documentation. This emphasis on interpreting and responding based on the perspective of the overall vision helped the project manager and others to avoid "turf battles" and disagreements over petty issues. It also provided an effective means for managing conflict positively by justifying decisions and actions based on achieving the common vision.

The project manager looked at opportunities for team members from different business units to work together to overcome potential division that could threaten team unity. People were assigned to tasks that created deliverables that all business units could share, e.g., criteria to identify policies and procedures no longer accurate and to select a common tool to author and display policies and procedures. This approach created a sense of interdependence among team members as well as encouraged information sharing.

## REFERENCES

1. Karen Bemoski, What makes American teams tick?, *Quality Progress,* pp. 39–40, January 1995.
2. Jon R. Katzenbach and Douglas K. Smith, *The Wisdom of Teams,* Harvard Business School Press, Boston, 1993, p. 45.
3. Ibid., p. 15.
4. John W. Gardner, *On Leadership,* The Free Press, New York, 1990, p. 118.
5. Ibid., pp. 115–118.
6. James M. Kouzes and Barry Z. Posner, *The Leadership Challenge,* Jossey-Bass, San Francisco, 1987, p. 134.
7. Edward M. Marshall, *Transforming the Way We Work,* Amacom, New York, 1995, p. 4.
8. Ibid., pp. 27–36.
9. Peter M. Senge, *The Fifth Discipline,* Currency Doubleday, New York, 1990, p. 234.
10. Daniel Goleman, Richard Boyatizis, and Annie McKee, *Primal Leadership,* Harvard Business School Press, Boston, 2002, p. 177.
11. Vanessa U. Druskat and Steven B. Wolff, Building the emotional intelligence of groups, *Harvard Business Review,* p. 85, March 2001.
12. Jon R. Katzenbach and Douglas K. Smith, *The Wisdom of Teams,* Harvard Business School Press, Boston, 1993, p. 132.
13. Warren Bennis and Patricia W. Biederman, *Organizing Genius,* Addison-Wesley, Reading, MA, 1997, p. 214.
14. Francis Hartman and Greg Skulmonski, Quest for team competence, *Project Management,* 5(1), 14, 1999.

15. H. Dudley Dewhirst, Project teams: what have we learned?, *PM Network,* pp. 35–36, April 1998.
16. Ibid., pp. 33–34.
17. Hans J. Thamhain and David L. Wilemon, Anatomy of a high performing new product team, in *Proceedings of the Project Management Institute Seminar/Symposium,* October 8–10, 1984, Philadelphia, PA, Project Management Institute, Newtown Square, PA, p. 147.
18. Ibid., p. 149.
19. Alan Slobodnik and Kristina Wile, Taking the teeth out of team traps, *The Systems Thinker,* 10(9), 1, 1999.
20. Jon R. Katzenbach and Douglas K. Smith, *The Wisdom of Teams,* Harvard Business School Press, Boston, 1993, pp. 43–46.
21. Jill A. George and Jeannette M. Wilson, *Team Members Survival Guide,* McGraw-Hill, New York, 1997, p. 5.
22. Daniel Goleman, Richard Boyatizis, and Annie McKee, *Primal Leadership,* Harvard Business School Press, Boston, 2002, p. 184.
23. Alan Slobodnik and Kristina Wile, Taking the teeth out of team traps, *The Systems Thinker,* 10(9), 5, 1999.
24. Jill A. George and Jeannette M. Wilson, *Team Members Survival Guide,* McGraw-Hill, New York, 1997, pp. ii–iv.
25. Jon R. Katzenbach and Douglas K. Smith, *The Wisdom of Teams,* Harvard Business School Press, Boston, 1993, p. 65.
26. Ibid., p. 132.
27. Edward M. Marshall, *Transforming the Way We Work,* Amacom, New York, 1995, pp. 77–78.
28. Oren Harari, The dream team, *Management Review,* pp. 29–31, October 1995.
29. Warren Bennis and Patricia W. Biederman, *Organizing Genius,* Addison-Wesley, Reading, MA, 1997, p. 26.
30. Paul Hersey and Kenneth H. Blanchard, *Management of Organizational Behavior,* 6th ed., Prentice Hall, Englewood Cliffs, NJ, 1993, pp. 175–176.
31. Warren Bennis and Patricia W. Biederman, *Organizing Genius,* Addison-Wesley, Reading, MA, 1997, p. 54.
32. Alan Slobodnik and Kristina Wile, Taking the teeth out of team traps, *The Systems Thinker,* 10(9), 2, 1999.
33. Hans J. Thamhain and David L. Wilemon, Anatomy of a high performing new product team, in Proceedings of the *Project Management Institute Seminar/Symposium,* October 8–10, 1984, Philadelphia, PA, Project Management Institute, Newtown Square, PA, p. 149.
34. Jon R. Katzenbach and Douglas K. Smith, *The Wisdom of Teams,* Harvard Business School Press, Boston, 1993, p. 43.
35. Erik J. Van Slyke, Resolving team conflict, *PM Network,* pp. 85–87, June 2000.
36. Karen Bemoski, What makes American teams tick?, *Quality Progress,* p. 39, January 1995.
37. Vanessa U. Druskat and Steven B. Wolff, Building the emotional intelligence of groups, *Harvard Business Review,* p. 82, March 2001.

38. Warren Bennis and Patricia W. Biederman, *Organizing Genius,* Addison-Wesley, Reading, MA, 1997, p. 30.
39. Barry McGibbon, High performance through team building, *Object Magazine,* p. 57, November 1997.
40. Warren Bennis and Patricia W. Biederman, *Organizing Genius,* Addison-Wesley, Reading, MA, 1997, p. 109.

# 10

# TRUST

One topic that is seemingly overlooked, yet plays an important role in managing projects, is credibility.

## WHAT IS CREDIBILITY?

Credibility is one of those abstract terms that is difficult to define but quite apparent when lacking. For purposes of this book, credibility is defined as behaving consistently with beliefs and expectations. Without consistency, a credibility gap can arise. Also, one's credibility will constantly be on trial. Credibility is very hard to get and very fragile.[1]

## KEY INTERRELATIONSHIP

Ethics, trust, and integrity are interrelated. A breakdown in ethics, for example, can lead to a decline in trust that will result in a loss of integrity. The linkage can occur in different sequences. However, that is not the key point. The key point is that whatever order they influence one another, a breakdown in one ultimately leads to a breakdown in credibility.

When credibility falls, many problems can arise that affect goal attainment. Some problems include a lack of teaming; reluctance or unwillingness to share information; poor communication, both vertically and horizontally; lack of coordination; no creativity; and self-absorption. The overall consequence is that a goal is not achieved or marginally so.

Credibility is a very important topic from a project leadership perspective for several reasons.

1. Project managers often lack formal, functional control over team members. They must establish credibility very carefully and maintain it to be effective.
2. Project managers must communicate constantly by virtue of their roles. The slightest action that negatively affects credibility will cause people to question the veracity and reliability of their communications.
3. Once credibility is lost, managing other projects can prove quite difficult because the reputation often precedes them. Loss of credibility, therefore, can be a career-limiting event for project managers.

General leadership theorists recognize the importance of credibility. In their classic work *Leaders,* Warren Bennis and Burt Nanus note that credibility has great value nowadays and is constantly being watched.[2] This scrutiny makes credibility very important; it may be the number one quality of leadership. That is why Kouzes and Posner emphasize the need to protect it.[3]

Credibility like fame, of course, can be fleeting. Indeed, credibility must be built continuously because the opportunity to tarnish it always exists. Charles Handy observes that credibility is also very situational, depending on one's constituency.[4]

Credibility should not be taken lightly, therefore, because it impacts a leader's effectiveness now and in the future. It is perhaps the most important factor in determining whether or not a leader will be followed.[5]

The public agrees. In 1996, Kouzes and Posner conducted a survey of 15,000 managers across the globe. The survey was on the characteristics of the "most admired" leaders. Honesty finished number one.[6]

Although literature lightly covers credibility and project management, some acknowledgment of its importance exists.

In his monumental classic *Project Management,* Harold Kerzner notes that credibility is a key variable when dealing at least with senior management.[7] In the *Project Management Journal,* Dean Sitiriou and Dennis Wittmer cite that integrity is an important "influence method" when tied with project expertise.[8] Albert Einsiedel identifies five qualities of an effective leader, ranking credibility first.[9] In *Project Management,* Skulmoski, Hartman, and DeMaere observe — in a study of threshold and superior competencies — that trust appears in both, writing that both project managers and team members need competencies in open communication and trust.[10]

Credibility of project managers is important for several reasons.

1. Stakeholders need to feel comfortable that their project managers are trustworthy. That is, that they will provide honest information and feedback.

2. Stakeholders need to know they are not being used for some "hidden agenda." They want to rely on project managers for honest feedback and to be "above the board" even at times when their projects face difficulties.
3. People just need to trust their project managers. Without trust, they will be less inclined to share information and maintain open communication among themselves and with their project managers.
4. People want someone to count on to lead them through difficult situations. If people lose credibility in their project managers, they will be less inclined to follow them through difficult times, simply because they are unable to trust them.

Project managers, due to their position and responsibilities, constantly feel the pressure to sacrifice their credibility. Yielding to the pressures can result, intentionally or accidentally, in causing credibility to erode because everything they do pertains to ethics, trust, and integrity to one degree or another.

Project managers face pressures to satisfy cost and schedule as well as to meet quality standards. These pressures can be so intense that they can yield very easily to the temptation to over- or underreport status as well as "massage" feedback to create an inaccurate impression.

They also face the pressure to get along with stakeholders because they need the cooperation of people over which they lack formal control. Sometimes this pressure can be so severe that they will sacrifice credibility to obtain that cooperation. This only results in lowering the respect of the project managers.

Project managers find themselves in a difficult position. They must report on what is supposed to occur, e.g., expectations, and what actually happens. Either way, the temptation is to skew feedback or "spin" in a way that will eventually cause credibility problems for them. Once they become "spin masters" and then other stakeholders do the same, credibility between everyone deteriorates.

Identifying the key elements of credibility is also very important. This task is difficult, but Kouzes and Posner[6] have done so on an abstract level, recognizing that credibility is really a composite of honesty, competency, inspiration, and the ability to be forward looking.[11]

Their insights can be translated into three essential ingredients of credibility: ethics, trust, and integrity. Breach any one and leaders will lose and tarnish their credibility.

## ETHICS

Ethics means adhering to values that determine the right decision or action. The decisions and actions of the project manager should be intended to achieve the best for the team and the project. Ethics, of course, depend on beliefs that act as "moral compasses" to make decisions and take action. They also reflect overall attitude towards people and their work.[12]

Max De Pree identifies three essential ideas that associate leadership with ethics. The first is that ethical leadership does not mean much without justice. It is the leader asking: What do I owe to the group? The second is celibacy. Leaders behave as stewards, by continually exercising personal restraint. The third is when both ethics and leadership are on behalf of an entire group.[13]

Not surprisingly, De Pree derives two types of relationships that leaders create and develop in their environment. These relationships directly impact the level of importance. The first type is a contractual relationship. It is based on transactions; providing a quid pro quo in exchange for a service, for example. The other type is a covenantal relationship; a shared commitment exists to ideas, values, and tolerance. The key between the two is focus.[14] The former deals with means, whereas the latter concerns itself with ends.

In *Leadership,* James MacGregor Burns distinguishes similarly between two categories of leadership styles and their relationship to ethics. The first category is ethics of responsibility, which involves an approach to decision making and rational behavior. It requires more of a choice over the means to achieve some practical ends. It tends to deal with everyday needs and wants. The other category is ethics of ultimate means, which means to be motivated by some "higher" purpose, often idealistic and abstract.

The distinction is important, particularly in relationship with the two fundamental concepts of leadership by Burns that was discussed in an earlier chapter: transactional and transformational. According to Burns, the ethics of responsibility is associated with transactional leadership and the ethics of ultimate means with transformational leadership.[15]

Covey et al. take a very similar perspective to a covenantal and transformative leadership style regarding ethics, but call it stewardship instead. They define stewardship as trusting a person to be accountable for another person or cause much more than oneself.[16]

Project managers must always act ethically, therefore, by doing what is right. While most project managers would never disagree, the reality is that few really understand the meaning from a leadership perspective. Ethics must play a central role and there are ways for that to happen.

*Project managers must lead by example.* They must act according to the expectations and standards that they expect others to follow. In other words, they should not establish a "double standard"; nothing can kill the effectiveness of project managers faster. Ethics and leadership are closely tied together.[17]

*They must emphasize ethical behavior in all dealings with stakeholders.* If they compromise ethics on small issues, they will lay the groundwork for lapses of ethical behavior when dealing with larger, more important concerns. De Pree says the big challenge is to apply ethics with people daily.[18]

*Project managers must reduce or eliminate the conditions that encourage lapses in ethical behavior.* These conditions include setting an atmosphere of fear, discouraging open communication, not dealing with issues on sincere levels, and punishing the messengers. They are reflected in behavior like inconsistent messages, false feedback, and lack of trust in others.

Of course, conditions exist that project managers cannot handle directly. These conditions can make leading projects very difficult. By acknowledging their sources and impacts, they can adapt better. These conditions include the negative effects of globalization, takeovers, automation, restructuring, and corporate fraud.

*They must create a positive atmosphere at work.* For example, they remove bureaucratic red tape that may hinder people. This action may become an issue, because people start taking shortcuts to achieve results not in accord with ethical behavior.

Project managers must identify and eliminate as many barriers as possible without shortcoming ethics. If a conflict between the two arises, project managers must always grant ethics the highest priority.

*Project managers must encourage accountability for results.* A good way to do this is to have people responsible for specific tasks and deliverables in a manner that will encourage ownership. Such accountability will encourage people to pursue an ethical route simply because the effects of their work can be traceable to them. For this to happen, project managers must empower team members to encourage and support ethical behavior. That is an ongoing activity between leader and follower involvement; participation is critical.[19]

*They must focus on "doing the right things" rather than "doing things right."* Everyone should ask: "Is this the right thing to do?" Failure to ask that fundamental question can lead to oversights in ethical behavior as people concern themselves with details. Consequently, people may find themselves inadvertently "doing the wrong work in the right way."

A principle-centered orientation makes the job easier. In *Principle-Centered Leadership,* Covey says that principles serve as a "compass" for pointing in the right direction, especially during times of confusion and conflict.[20]

Trouble brews when ethics, for whatever reason, get suspended. Opportunism and self-centeredness through protection and deception become the rule. Such behavior causes what Paul Nutt describes as "ethical decision traps." These traps are usually reflected when people are reluctant to admit the suspension of ethics by placing them on an equal level with rational justification.[21]

## INTEGRITY

Integrity means to be genuine and open about decisions and actions. It is about what is professed and demonstrated through behavior and action in all dealings and situations.

Integrity is the cornerstone to generate trust. Like trust, people must earn it. Until it is earned, a leader will have a hard time performing, if at all. Covey and the Merrills agree, noting further that it involves dogged determination to achieve a goal. It also involves an open relationship.[22]

One of the hallmarks of a leader is that he or she exhibit integrity in everything done, whether at work or somewhere else. Leaders exhibit integrity in private and public, observe Kouzes and Posner, and base it on a set of values for making consistent choices under different situations.[23] These values are the ingredients for a leader to act with integrity, even when facing tremendous costs and risks.

In a very significant way, integrity has three parts to it: emotional honesty, practical intuition, and applied integrity. Emotional honesty requires a serious consideration of instinct or gut feelings. Practical intuition means to have an innate feeling about doing what is right. Applied integrity means to have the courage to take action in accord with emotional honesty and practical intuition.[24]

Essentially, integrity reflects the important "chain" of belief, commitment, action, and results. In other words, believing in what is right and committing to what is right by taking action to achieve results consistent with beliefs. This chain creates the basis for the other two cornerstones of credibility: ethics and trust. It cannot be contrived or faked; it is a fundamental part of a person's character.[25]

Integrity does not just happen. Project managers must exhibit integrity constantly. A lapse can wreck effectiveness as a credible leader. Fortunately, project managers have some very effective ways to exercise and maintain integrity.

*They must consistently exercise integrity.* They must demonstrate it on all issues, making no exceptions. If making exceptions, stakeholders can no longer ascertain whether project managers are straightforward. Project managers with integrity, therefore, exercise it "on and off the field"; their actions are in concert with their beliefs at work and at home. Failure to have consistency will likely permeate actions on a project and credibility will quickly be hurt or destroyed.

*Project managers must be reliable; they must follow through.* They say something and demonstrate it through action. They do not make impossible promises or fail to keep them, but rather deliver to the expectations they set. Establishing and maintaining credibility allows for no exceptions.

*They must act consistently with expectations set and held by others.* Project managers function in a role with certain expectations that they and others have. These role expectations are very similar to those that Henry Mintzberg identifies for managers in general. He identifies three roles that managers assume: interpersonal, which includes performing as the leader and liaison of the group; informational, acting as a spokesperson and disseminating information; and decisional, allocating resources and negotiating.[26] If they fail to meet expectations with these roles, project managers may find themselves losing credibility.

*Project managers must act consistently with their professed beliefs.* They should understand the chain discussed earlier: beliefs, commitment, action, and results. If a discontinuity occurs between beliefs and results, people will not know what to expect because they are unpredictable. In other words, alignment must exist from thought through results; otherwise, no one will take a project manager seriously.

*They must communicate openly.* Project managers must avoid being a spin master or others will be spin masters with them.

Two major challenges, which make open communication difficult, occur on projects that cause project managers to become spin masters. The first challenge is the desire to get along. This desire for acceptance can cause people to become experts at "coloring" information to avoid upsetting others. The other challenge is the desire to want to please the customer. While it is good to focus on a customer, this desire can generate a strong belief that not pleasing a customer will mean the project is a "failure." Naturally, people with such desires will reluctantly communicate openly with the customers or even managers, thereby providing disinformation and misinformation.

*Project managers should strive for objectivity.* Although strict objectivity is unattainable, they should identify facts and data as much as possible and use both as a means to assess situations. Facts and data, as opposed to assumptions and perceptions, allow project managers and others to base their evaluations and actions on what is right. If project managers lose even the perception of objectivity, however, people will accuse them of being unfair and displaying favoritism. People will be less inclined to condemn project managers over an error in judgment than over an error of intent.

*They must be open and approachable, so people are willing and wanting to communicate on just about anything with them.* This communication should include negative and positive information. Too often, project managers hear only what they want to hear, or selectively hear. When that occurs, people and project managers often sacrifice integrity. Project managers can best obtain openness by meeting with stakeholders frequently either in a group or one-on-one basis. During meetings, they can obtain openness by encouraging tolerance for diverse ideas or comments different from their own.

*Project managers must be honest in all dealings.* They must "tell it like it is," the negative as well as the positive. They should also expect the same of stakeholders. Only through honesty can anyone better understand the efficiency and, more importantly, the effectiveness of their projects. Failure to deal honestly, on small and large scales, can result in a serious credibility gap.

*They must follow and apply consistently a personal set of beliefs and values.* That is, they must demonstrate continuity from idea to results. If results diverge from espoused beliefs, their credibility can crash and recovery will be very difficult. Stephen Covey stresses the need, therefore, for leaders to establish ethical standards to guide their actions.[27]

Beliefs and values are extremely valuable for project managers who face ambiguous situations. They serve as a "compass" to guide project managers to make the right decisions. They also give people the necessary confidence in their project managers because predictability is reflected in their behavior.

## TRUST

Trust means follow through. It is a combination of a perception of character and a reflection of character itself. It is also an instinctual feeling; that a leader can be relied on regardless of circumstances. The core of trust is predictability on the part of the leaders.

Different levels of trust exist, however, according to a *Harvard Business Review* article by Robert Galford and Anne Seibold Drapeau. Strategic trust is the type people have in their senior leadership to make the right decisions. Personal trust is the type people have in their immediate managers. Organizational trust is the type that people have in their institution.[28] Project managers, of course, should concern themselves with developing and maintaining personal trust. However, the quality of strategic and organizational trust can also impact how well people trust their project managers.

Generating trust, of course, does not often arise spontaneously. It is earned by the leader and can be accumulated as it is earned.[29] Trust is also earned through personal interactions.[30]

Leaders must not only earn the trust of subordinates, but they must also demonstrate their trust in others. They will gain an important benefit by their willingness to trust others. They will become more tolerant of different ideas and actions. Leaders who demonstrate trust will consider many perspectives and will be willing to allow others to influence their decisions.

Trust is the third cornerstone of credibility and, in the end, the most important of them. If project managers violate trust bestowed by stakeholders, their credibility can decline quite rapidly. Fortunately, project managers can earn and sustain trust in many ways.

*They must be straightforward with all stakeholders in all dealings, that is, "tell it like it is."* People trust others, especially leaders, who reveal their positions and act with thorough-through, thereby building trust.

If a project cannot meet all its goals and objectives, for example, project managers should be honest about the circumstances. Unfortunately, for reasons of pride or to avoid complicating relationships, many project managers will not admit a problem exists. Instead, they may present explanations that create a facade that everything is fine when, in reality, nothing is going well. Often, they rationalize to themselves that "things will improve with time." The danger is that improvements in performance may not occur, surprising stakeholders at the last minute. Once that happens, project managers lose the trust granted to them.

*Project managers must empower and delegate.* To gain and maintain trust, project managers must also exhibit trust in others. They must avoid controlling too closely, or micromanaging, others, e.g., "looking over their shoulders." That means leaders must create an environment that augments people's confidence that, in turn, encourages risk taking. The emphasis can then shift from blaming to learning.[31]

Project managers, instead, must empower team members and delegate tasks to them. Failure to do so only exhibits their distrust in others that, in turn, generates distrust. Effective project managers must demonstrate trust in others if they want to be trusted.

*They must be fair in all dealings.* They must avoid even the appearance of taking sides. Otherwise, they will reduce their opportunities to strive for objectivity and receive the active contributions from team members. Unseasoned project managers often find themselves viewing stakeholders as "good vs. bad guys." When that happens, cooperation breaks down and marginal contributions of team members follow. Even more importantly, they and everyone else lose trust.

Two of the best ways to maintain fairness in dealings with stakeholders:

1. Focus on the goals and objectives of their projects. When a contentious issue arises, project managers should frame it from the context of the goals and objectives.
2. Concentrate on facts and data that relate to an issue. Project managers must avoid treating assumptions and values as facts and data; otherwise, some stakeholders will view projects managers as taking sides.

*Project managers should respect all stakeholders in dealings.* Project managers should recognize that everyone has an important role, albeit small, on a project. While some stakeholders contribute more than others, project managers should avoid ignoring and even disregarding the work of others who may not be major contributors. Making people feel that they are unimportant or insignificant often generates negative consequences, e.g., treating performance or deliverables in kind. If project managers have respect for others and their work, stakeholders will exhibit more trust because they will feel more comfortable in trusting them with their insights and comments.

*They must manage themselves as well as others.* Project managers must "walk the talk." They must exhibit what they say if they hope to earn trust. There is wide agreement among leadership experts in this regard. In *Leaders,* Bennis and Nanus note that not managing oneself can harm a leader's effectiveness and that of others.[32] Michael Abrashoff agrees and further observes that people look on leaders as role models. As such, a leader must exhibit strengths reflective of courage, integrity, accountability, authenticity, and good judgment.[33]

If project managers do not "practice what they preach" they will be seen as people who heed their own words because it raises the simple question — if project managers are not consistent in action, then how can they be trusted in other matters, e.g., being truthful with oneself. Project managers must live by the very beliefs and values that they expect others to hold if they expect people to trust them.

*Project managers must maintain confidentiality.* Nothing is worse than telling someone something in confidence only to find that it has been leaked to other people. If people are to disclose needs and feelings, leaders must create a "climate of trust" through caring.[34]

For example, a team member talks to a project manager about the performance of a colleague. The project manager then talks to someone else about the discussion in such a way that reveals the identity of the person who raised the issue. When that happens and becomes known, people will reluctantly share any other thoughts or information with the project manager. Trust collapses over this incident and likely for the remainder of the project.

*They must respect people's needs and wants via personal understanding.* Covey says that helps to overcome barriers to performance on individual and group levels. The reason is because it encourages openness.[35]

Project managers who understand the importance of this facet of respect will see people placing their faith and trust in them. They will likely share information and go to them on other issues; they see the project manager as someone to approach rather than to avoid. In other words, to use a phrase popularized by the psychologist Carl Rogers, project managers are seen as builders of bridges, not walls.

## BOTTOM LINE: TRUST IS EVERYTHING

Project managers must establish their credibility. However, they must do more than that. They must maintain credibility to the very end. A crucial ingredient for establishing and maintaining credibility is trust that, in turn, requires consistent and ethical behavior in all aspects of a project. Project managers must not only get people to trust them, they must also learn to trust others. When such levels of trust exist, all people can exhibit leadership.

## CASE STUDY: TRUST

The project manager made every attempt to establish credibility with all team members knowing that most business units held a high level of distrust towards headquarters when it instituted company-wide projects. The prevalent suspicion by business units was that headquarters was always trying to impose control or doing so via other business units.

To help break down this wall of suspicion, even the mere appearance of unfairness was avoided by focusing on the overall vision for the project and considering facts and data during decision making. The project manager also strove to be tolerant and receptive to different viewpoints on issues and problems, regardless of whether they supported or opposed his own preferences.

In addition, he strove to appear and act consistent in his approach when dealing with issues and problems. He sought to avoid making exceptions for individuals and did so in the interests of the overall project and communicated his rationale. If necessary, he sought approval from the others. This collaboration encouraged a sense of fairness and buy-in.

The project manager also employed positive confrontation — dealing with an issue or problem openly — when dealing with issues or problems. That was accomplished by encouraging dialog and avoiding the dangerous charge of operating according to a hidden agenda.

By allowing team members to develop their own portion of the work breakdown structure, estimates, and dates (within the confines of the project charter), the project manager demonstrated his trust in them. He instilled, without them realizing it, a sense of responsibility and accountability. To ensure their commitment, he published the results of all work on the web site.

Finally, he demonstrated ethical behavior throughout the project by reporting negative as well as positive news about cost, schedule, and quality performance. This approach augmented stakeholders' trust in him and his overall leadership of the project. In other words, he avoided "sugar coating" results and did not succumb to pressures, especially from senior managers who had a track record of "shooting the messenger."

## REFERENCES

1. James M. Kouzes and Barry Z. Posner, *The Leadership Challenge,* Jossey-Bass, San Francisco, 1987, p. 24.
2. Warren Bennis and Burt Nanus, *Leaders,* Perennial Library, New York, 1985, p. 11.
3. James M. Kouzes and Barry Z. Posner, Ten lessons of leadership, in *A Systems Approach to Small Group Interaction,* 6th ed., Stewart L. Tubbs, Ed., McGraw-Hill, Boston, 1997, p. 196.
4. Charles B. Handy, *Understanding Organizations,* Penguin Books, New York, 1986, p. 137.
5. James M. Kouzes and Barry Z. Posner, *The Leadership Challenge,* Jossey-Bass, San Francisco, 1987, p. xvii.
6. James M. Kouzes and Barry Z. Posner, *Credibility,* Jossey-Bass, San Francisco, 1993, p. 14.
7. Harold Kerzner, *Project Management,* Van Nostrand Reinhold, New York, 1995, p. 496.
8. Dean Sitiriou and Dennis Wittmer, Influence methods of project managers: perceptions of team members and project managers, *Project Management Journal,* pp. 12–20, September 2001.
9. Albert A. Eisensiedel, Profile of effective project managers, in *Leadership Skills for Project Managers,* Jeffrey K. Pinto and Jeffrey W. Trailer, Eds., Project Management Institute, Newtown Square, PA, pp. 4–6.
10. Greg Skulmoski, Francis Hartman, and Roch DeMaere, Superior and threshold project competencies, *Project Management,* 6(1), 14, 2000.
11. James M. Kouzes and Barry Z. Posner, *Credibility,* Jossey-Bass, San Francisco, 1993, p. 21.
12. Stephen R. Covey, *The Seven Habits of Highly Effective People,* Simon & Schuster, New York, 1990, p. 255.
13. Max De Pree, *Leadership Jazz,* Dell, New York, 1992, pp. 130–139.
14. Max De Pree, *Leadership Is an Art,* Dell, New York, 1989, pp. 58–60.
15. James M. Burns, *Leadership,* Harper & Row, New York, 1979, pp. 45–46.
16. Stephen R. Covey, A. Roger Merrill, and Rebecca R. Merrill, *First Things First,* Simon & Schuster, New York, 1994, p. 129.
17. Max De Pree, *Leadership Jazz,* Dell, New York, 1992, p. 125.
18. Ibid., pp. 125–126.

19. James M. Kouzes and Barry Z. Posner, Ten lessons of leadership, in *A Systems Approach to Small Group Interaction,* 6th ed., Stewart L. Tubbs, Ed., McGraw-Hill, Boston, 1997, p. 198.

20. Stephen R. Covey, *Principle-Centered Leadership,* Summit Books, New York, 1991, p. 19.

21. Paul C. Nutt, *Why Decisions Fail,* Berrett-Koehler, San Francisco, 2002, pp. 206–226.

22. Stephen R. Covey, A. Roger Merrill, and Rebecca R. Merrill, *First Things First,* Simon & Schuster, New York, 1994, p. 146.

23. James M. Kouzes and Barry Z. Posner, *The Leadership Challenge,* Jossey-Bass, San Francisco, 1987, p. 301.

24. Robert K. Cooper and Ayman Sawaf, *Executive EQ,* Audio-Tech Business Book Summaries, Willowbrook, IL, November 1997, pp. 2–9 (Booklet).

25. Stephen R. Covey, A. Roger Merrill, and Rebecca R. Merrill, *First Things First,* Simon & Schuster, New York, 1994, p. 204.

26. Henry Mintzberg, The manager's job: folklore and fact, *Harvard Business Review,* pp. 54–59, July–August 1975.

27. Stephen R. Covey, *The Seven Habits of Highly Effective People,* Simon & Schuster, New York, 1990, p. 300.

28. Robert Galford and Anne S. Drapeau, The enemies of trust, *Harvard Business Review,* pp. 89–95, February 2003.

29. Warren Bennis and Burt Nanus, *Leaders,* Perennial Library, New York, 1985, p. 153.

30. James M. Kouzes and Barry Z. Posner, *The Leadership Challenge,* Jossey-Bass, San Francisco, 1987, p. 151.

31. James M. Kouzes and Barry Z. Posner, Ten lessons of leadership, in *A Systems Approach to Small Group Interaction,* 6th ed., Stewart L. Tubbs, Ed., McGraw-Hill, Boston, 1997, pp. 197–198.

32. Warren Bennis and Burt Nanus, *Leaders,* Perennial Library, New York, 1985, p. 56.

33. Abrashoff, Michael D., Playing to win: ten principles of grassroots leadership, *Seminar for Living Leadership,* 2003, p. 63.

34. James M. Kouzes and Barry Z. Posner, Ten lessons of leadership, in *A Systems Approach to Small Group Interaction,* 6th ed., Stewart L. Tubbs, Ed., McGraw-Hill, Boston, 1997, p. 197.

35. Stephen R. Covey, *The Seven Habits of Highly Effective People,* Simon & Schuster, New York, 1990, p. 151.

# 11

# COMMUNICATE

One of the great ironies of project management is that project managers spend considerable time communicating. Yet, few can do so very well.

If project managers want to lead, not just manage, they must acquire and exercise good communication skills. This is a prime activity of an effective leader who expects to successfully complete a project involving the participation of other people. As John Gardner notes, two-way communication is an important ingredient in establishing and sustaining the relationship between leaders and followers.[1]

## LEADERS

Leaders must not only establish good communication, but also sustain it. In *People Skills,* Robert Bolton agrees and acknowledges the importance of open, clear communication and says that when it deteriorates, it has negative consequences on the leader-followers.[2]

The job is not, however, getting done effectively. As Hersey and Blanchard observe, despite the fact that managers in general are doing so much, there seems to be so much room for improvement at the same time.[3] A report by the Canadian Manufacturers and Exporters agrees, observing that improvement is needed in three areas: problem solving, communication, and teamwork.[4]

The importance of communication is substantiated in other research as well. For example, a survey of managers by *Training* magazine with The Center for Creative Leadership found that communication was the second most important leadership challenge.[5] *Training and Development* magazine identified ten skills that managers need to be a success, at least from a Human Resource manager's perspective. All contributed to success to various degrees. The skills were inter-personal, listening, persuasion and motivation, presentation, small group commu-nication, advising, interviewing, conflict management, writing, and reading.[6]

At first glance it would appear that communication is important only to senior executives. Nothing could be more misleading. It also has a great level of importance for leading projects. In *Project Management,* Harold Kerzner observes that communication on projects is critical.[7]

My experience supports this assertion. It is one failure or shortcoming common to projects in trouble. If project managers do not exercise good communication on an individual and group basis, their projects will have a lesser chance of success. If they do succeed, then they will do so with great effort. Hence, the responsibility for establishing and maintaining effective communication rests directly with project managers.

Project managers must make a conscientious effort to encourage and sustain communication among all stakeholders. It is the responsibility of the project manager to lay the groundwork and manage it throughout his or her project.[8]

## BASICS OF COMMUNICATION

Project managers need to have a good understanding of the communication process. What follows is a high-level description that occurs on group and person-to-person levels.

All communication has a sender and a receiver. The sender develops and forwards a message to a receiver who interprets it and makes a decision based on the contents. At first glance, it appears this is a simple one-way process; but, in reality, it is not. The receiver responds or reacts to the message reflected in a signal that he or she returns to the sender in the form of feedback. This exchange can occur many times under different situations according to some signal.

What happens during this exchange is that both parties are encoding and decoding based on factors like perceptions, values, and emotional states. The messages exchanged then get modified according to interpretation.

The exchange of messages can occur over different media or channels. For example, a sender may elect to communicate a message through oral commu-nication and the receiver may respond in the same mode or through e-mail. Each medium has its pluses and minuses. Sometimes, a message is distorted by the medium through noise, or interference, when being transmitted.

Of course, several quantitative and qualitative characteristics of messages affect their preparation and processing by sender and receiver. These charac-teristics include load, timing, format, speed, and familiarity. While transmitting a message, too many factors can affect it. These include distortion, lag and lead times, and influence of the channel or medium.

However, other factors are often overlooked that can add barriers to communicating by filtering or "massaging" the messages. These factors include culture, perceptions, trust, organizational climate, history, role expectations, ethnicity, psychological motivations, and power of people in responsible positions.

Not surprisingly, therefore, the intent and meaning of a message can get modified or lost. Fortunately, feedback plays an important role. Sender and receiver alike can exchange signals verifying whether a message has or has not been properly received and acted on as intended.

Communication can also occur on different planes. It can occur formally or informally. For example, it can occur via documentation, e.g., reports or memorandums, or by casual one-on-one discussions with stakeholders without any recordkeeping. Communication can occur verbally and nonverbally. An example of a verbal level is a presentation or e-mail. An example of a nonverbal communication is body language. Communication can also be in oral and written form. An example of the former is a presentation; for the latter, a report.

Communication can flow in different directions. It can move in a downward direction, e.g., from management to the rank and file; upward, e.g., from the team to the senior management; and laterally, e.g., among team members.

The ultimate goal is that a sender wants to ensure that a message sent is the one received by the recipient and in the manner intended. In *Human Communication,* Stewart Tubbs and Sylvia Moss write that the success of communication occurs when the intent matches the intended response.[9] Douglas Benton agrees but in a more practical way, noting that successful communication is reflected by whether a message is understood.[10] From a project management perspective, effective communication results when a message is understood as intended and mutually engages both sender and receiver.[11]

## WAYS TO HURT COMMUNICATION

Project managers can hinder their effectiveness as communicators on their projects in many ways.

### Treat Communication as Unidirectional

In other words, the only people who seem to communicate are project managers. A major reason for this situation is that some project managers think that being in charge means not listening to anyone. After all, many project managers occupy their positions because they are good, if not better, than anyone else available. Unfortunately, this success can result in an arrogance that can limit communication, mainly from project managers to team members. Conversation becomes one way. Since 75 percent of oral communication is lost, chances increase that project managers — who mainly use oral communication — find their messages ignored or forgotten.[12]

However, an important requirement of effective communication is that it goes two ways. A "give and take" in the dialog must occur where signals, whatever they may be, flow freely between two people or among group members. This communication should occur at all levels and should be open and fluid throughout an organization, and a leader has the responsibility to remove any roadblocks.

Communication, therefore, does not only flow downhill, so to speak. It flows throughout an organization in many directions. It flows vertically, up and down. It also flows laterally with people communicating with each other on a peer level. Project managers must foster lateral communication as much, if not more so, than its vertical counterpart for no other reason than to help people to complete their work successfully.

## Exercise Poor Emotional Intelligence

Effective communicators, whether in a leadership position or not, exercise good emotional intelligence. They are aware of their own emotions and desires and can control them to have the desired effect. They also have good empathetic ability; they can acquire an understanding of the emotional state of other people.[13] Both self-awareness and empathy give people, therefore, the capability to communicate effectively.

Unfortunately, many project managers lack this emotional intelligence. They are so focused on method and result, they forget that both involve the necessary cooperation of people to make it all happen. They fail to become aware of their own behavior on the emotions of others and vice versa. Consequently, major barriers to communication can arise between project managers and the people with whom they must work.

One barrier is a disconnection between what the project managers say and how they actually behave. This incongruous behavior can create a communication block and can be aggravated if the project manager fails to ascertain nonverbal cues during exchanges. Daniel Goleman notes the importance of using body language to detect and understand other people's feelings.[14] Indeed, this nonverbal mode may be as important, if not more so, than the verbal one as Goleman continues to observe that the incongruity between words and body language can reveal emotional truth about another person.[15]

## Overemphasize Data and Information

Many project managers assume that more is better and the more data released, the better the communication. Nothing could be further than the truth. Too much data or information can worsen circumstances.

A perfect example is the tendency for project managers to generate many reports containing superfluous data. Often, project managers generate way too much data in the wrong format for the wrong people. In addition, they generate much "bad" data. That is, the data are incomplete, inaccurate, cryptic, and perhaps even contradictory. In the end, it causes more harm than good to communication.

I believe project management software is a major contributor to this situation. This software places considerable power in the hands of project managers. The danger is that this software provides too much power. Data get collected for collection sake and many reports are generated. Unfortunately, data and information are often incorrect or incomplete, resulting in miscommunication. Like many things, the perception is the more, the better. Too much of a good "thing" can prove burdensome, especially if incomplete and inaccurate.

## Fail to Perform Audience Analysis

This failure in communication is closely allied to the previous point. Rather than define the audience for their communication, many project managers communicate using a "shotgun" approach in the hope that the right people get their message. This approach, however, can result in people losing a meaning of the message or ignoring it altogether.

The reality is that projects have multiple audiences, each with unique needs. Audiences, called stakeholders, really involve multiple levels of communication. One level of communication is that which applies to all stakeholders, from senior management to individual team members. There is also a level applicable to a selective audience, e.g., steering committee members or team members.

Failure to ascertain the informational needs of audiences can negatively impact communication flow, especially on the performance of a project team. Ignoring the communication needs of a team can hurt team development and performance, causing it to be inefficient and ineffective. Therefore, project managers cannot assume that good communication will occur naturally.

## Rely Too Much on the Technology of Communication

Like data and information spewing forth from them, the number of technologies themselves used in the project environment are immense — beepers, cell phones, fax, e-mail, analog and digital phones, voice mail, and software packages. Whether at work or at home, people are increasingly using multiple tools, not just one. All this technology has caused a flood of information in the form of messages and continues to rise in volume.

What is worrisome is that many project managers construe using such tools as the same as communicating. Just the opposite is the case and the greater the reliance on technology, the greater the potential for miscommunication and poor communication will increase and lead to trouble. In *The Pursuit of Wow!*, Tom Peters says that one of the biggest culprits is overreliance on the technology, such as e-mail. The reason? The vital face-to-face interaction gets ignored, only adding to more problems.[16]

More importantly, I believe, is that such situations interfere with communication in general and a message in particular is the personal touch that makes exchange between two people so meaningful. In other words, it lessens the "human moment" that Edward Hallowell describes as "an authentic psychological encounter" in the same physical space. This space, according to Hallowell, is people's physical presence and their emotional and intellectual attention. According to him, this loss of the human moment can result in "toxic worry."[17] Naturally, people's guards rise and effective communication, no matter the technology, decreases or ceases.

Project managers, therefore, should view using more tools with great suspicion because they can generate a false sense of effective communication. Ray Boedecker observes that using tools and methodologies often creates a false sense of security when communicating information.[18]

## Fail to Listen to Multiple Views

Many project managers exhibit poor communication skills in one big, obvious way — they fail to listen, particularly to alternative viewpoints. Instead, they act like they know the answer to everything. The reality is that they do not know all the answers, resulting in tunnel vision. Part of the problem, I believe, is that many project managers rise to their position because they know a specific subject area very well. As their scope widens, however, their knowledge requirements widen but what they know narrows. They need, therefore, to consult with people who know more than they do in a specific area. Unfortunately, few project managers recognize this circumstance, sending signals that cause barriers to effective communication. Barriers include feeling that they know everything, perceiving that consulting others is a sign of weakness, and subscribing to Theory X. Such barriers result in filtering communication up and down the chain of command, internally and externally to their projects. Examples of situations that can lead to filtering communication include a fear of "shooting the messenger," a concern about embarrassing someone in authority, and a mistrust of colleagues and superiors.

Of course, project managers gain much by expressing a willingness to listen to different viewpoints, e.g., improved morale and better decisions. Unfortunately, few people really exercise good listening skills in general or in managing projects in particular. In *Love 'Em or Lead 'Em,* Beverly Kaye and Sharon Jordan-Evans observe that few people are effective listeners and that skill often remains undeveloped.[19]

Even when many project managers do listen, they do so poorly. They interrupt people or become defensive, increasing a barrier or creating another one. Either way, communication breaks down, especially if it results in a debate rather than a dialog.

## Take a Win-Lose Approach Towards Conflict

Conflict may not necessarily be negative although the common perception is that it is because of the high level of emotional intensity it involves and the difficulty in handling it.

On projects, the opportunity for conflict is quite prevalent, especially if it is defined in a way that Stewart Tubbs and Sylvia Moss describe as a struggle between parties over incompatible goals and resources and the interference of others.[20]

Unfortunately, a negative perception of conflict seems to prevail among many project managers. They react to it in a manner that destroys communication, e.g., trying to avoid, accommodate, or squash it. Avoiding and accommodating conflict affects communication because project managers hope that it will fade away, only to result in a Lose-Win or Lose-Lose outcome. Squashing conflicts affects communication because project managers demonstrate their superiority in the chain of command, resulting only in a Win-Lose outcome. Whether accommodating, avoiding, or squashing conflict, communication will suffer because of fear, mistrust, resentment, or a combination of them.

Project managers must use confrontation to address conflict. They must bring out the real issues and open a dialog on them; otherwise, conflict will not disappear but fester until an explosion occurs. The idea is to open and maintain communication during and after conflict to come to a Win-Win outcome by encouraging everyone to work together and communicating openly and empathetically. To make that happen, project managers need to identify the reasons for disagreements and exercise the necessary degree of empathy to achieve understanding.

Many project managers must also realize that poor handling of conflict affects communication at many different levels, not just interpersonally. It also affects communication within the team and other organizations outside a project, e.g., senior management. Project managers who fail to acknowledge this relationship can find themselves and other team members outside of the communication loop, especially if in an adversarial position.

## Rely Solely on One Approach to Communication

For example, some prefer meeting one-on-one to communicate to a group. Others prefer communicating electronically, e.g., via e-mail. While having a preferred approach is fine, the danger comes when relying on only one way to communicate. When that happens, some project managers find that their messages may get inadequate attention, or worse, overlooked. To be really effective communicators, therefore, project managers should employ multiple means of communication.

One interesting phenomenon that is gaining momentum is to communicate project information visually. Before the advent of microcomputers, short of a histogram and a bar chart, visual communication was not commonplace. With visuals, many project managers have found it much easier to overcome communication barriers. They must employ them discretely, however. Format and content can have an impact on how a message is perceived and reviewed. More often than not, it is a visual one.

Once again, project managers need to define the audience for whom they are communicating. Many project managers fail to do so and employ an inappropriate approach that causes or yields to communication barriers.

An interesting observation that I have found over the years is that some project managers who do not communicate well in person have no problem doing so through e-mail. While e-mail can prove very helpful to overcome communication barriers, it should not be used as an alternative to more effective approaches to communication. Unfortunately, some project managers rely exclusively on e-mail, failing to interact with stakeholders and sacrificing rapport, or the "human moment," so essential to engender meaningful communication on projects.

## Stress the Negative

Nothing can be more demoralizing to a team than a leader who is constantly negative in thought and action. Negative leaders are "downers."[21]

Project managers can exhibit negativity in many ways that impact the quality of communication. They can "shoot down" ideas from team members, or they can rescind the actions of others just because an idea was not their own.

Project managers, through their thoughts and actions, therefore, set the stage to determine how communication will occur. If they take a positive, proactive approach, communication will likely be effective. If they take a negative, re-active approach, communication will likely be inefficient and ineffective.

A very common indicator of how well project managers handle communication is their handling of "bad" news. They must do so carefully or their action will negatively impact their relationships with stakeholders.

One case, for example, is how project managers respond to negative information. Do they blame someone when something goes wrong? Do they get hostile towards people? If yes, the barriers to communication will arise and affect the relationships with stakeholders.

Another example is how well project managers communicate negative information. Do they do so with a lack of understanding or empathy? Because project managers must continually address issues dealing with corrective actions and replanning, they must be especially sensitive to this issue if they hope to develop and sustain trust with stakeholders.

The real issue is that project managers must be sensitive about how they come across when dealing with negative information. If negative, they will increase barriers to effective communication. If positive, the barriers will decline, perhaps even disappear. It is more of a question of how it is handled rather than what it is.

## Treat Communication as an Ad Hoc, Even Passive Function

Of course, communication will happen whether project managers do anything or not. However, the quality of communication will be key, and project managers can do much to influence that quality.

Many project managers do little to influence the quality of communication on their projects and that is reflected in the results: rework, meaningless meetings, lost information, and much more. All this contributes to schedule slides, budget overruns, and poor quality of work.

The reality is that the quality of communication directly reflects the overall personality of the project manager and that of the entire team. Sloppy communication increases the chance, therefore, that the overall quality of managing projects will be the same and reflect back on the work of the project manager.

All too often unfortunately, communication is treated in a matter of fact manner. What project managers should do is take the initiative and provide the infrastructure that sets the stage for effective communication. They need to create that sense of community that John Gardner discusses in *On Leadership,* whereby people willingly communicate and offer to initiate it.[22]

Project managers must do more, however, than provide common meeting grounds. They need to receive the necessary feedback on overall progress. Many project managers fail here, too, by not giving feedback on personal or group levels. It is an important aspect of communication on projects that project managers keep everyone informed of ideas, issues, and progress as well as see and give feedback on overall performance. It is not enough to give people feedback on their own performance.

## Lack Self-Awareness of Thoughts and Actions on Others

Self-awareness, so important for emotional intelligence as Daniel Goleman discusses, can influence the quality of communication. A lack of self-awareness manifests itself through the actions of project managers, either on an individual or group level. What follows are a few common ones.

Criticizing someone before a group can lead to a huge barrier to communication. Thinking perhaps to demonstrate their dominance, some project managers will criticize someone before peers or superiors. Nothing can squash future dialog between a project manager and team members faster; no one will take the chance to be humiliated.

Threatening people, either on an individual basis or before a group, can erect another big barrier. After making a threat, typical of an experienced project manager subscribing to Theory X, communication wanes or stops. Fear of encouraging additional threats may or may not be realized. People start filtering their words, resulting in measured or no communication.

Excessive questioning can inhibit communication, especially if impugning an individual's character. After hearing an idea start, some project managers shoot questions like an aggressive prosecutor on a caffeine addiction. Although reflecting great analysis of an idea, such an approach can wreak havoc on the person proposing the idea. Small wonder he or she then behaves and communicates defensively to avoid another attack from the project manager.

Jumping to a solution before defining a problem or considering alternatives is another way that project managers can negatively affect communication. When a problem arises, some project managers develop a solution on the spot; often it is their own solution. When addressing a problem with others, they work desperately to convince and ratify an already preconceived solution. Often, the listeners simply say it is a good idea and shake their heads, wondering why they were even asked in the first place.

In *People Skills*, Robert Bolton identifies twelve common communication "spoilers" that he groups into three categories: judging, which consists of criticizing, name-calling, diagnosing, and praising; sending solutions, which consists of ordering, threatening, moralizing, excessive/inappropriate questioning, and advising; and avoiding other's concerns, which consists of diverting, logical argument, and reassuring.[23]

## Treat Communication as Simple; In Reality, It Is Not

Achieving high-quality communication is tough and the more project managers invest into it, the greater the returns. It is extremely complex. Yet, many project managers think it is nothing more than saying a few words, issuing an e-mail, or making a telephone call.

The complexity of communication is due to many subjective factors, some observable and many subtle, that affect — positively and negatively — a message when sent and the way it is received.

For example, a sender crafts a message that reflects his or her perceptions. The receiver, in turn, gets the message and interprets it according to his or her perceptions. Many times a mismatch occurs and, if feedback is not transmitted, the message is either ignored or interpreted in a way never intended by the sender.

These different perceptions add complexity to the communication process of which project managers must always be cognizant. In many regards, these perceptions reflect paradigms to consider when communicating a message and, if not, can lead to a serious communication barrier, making it difficult to come to agreement or consensus.

Communication can get complicated additionally when considering the variety of barriers. For example, distance can add to the complexity of different perceptions, on a global level. Another example is the political barriers that exist within a large organization of stakeholders. Each stakeholder has not only a different perception of a message but may also have varying, subtle interests in an outcome not shared by others.

Then there is the added complexity of communication on a more intrapersonal level that goes beyond a paradigm. It is the listening skills of the people, their education, their interests, their psychological motivations, and thinking styles.

Project managers, therefore, must understand that achieving good communication is not a simple task. It is hard work and failure to acknowledge that fact can have considerable consequences — as Dale Emery notes in *STQE Magazine,* writing that people often take communication for granted because it occurs often without event. When communication does go awry, even on a small scale, it can grow to a big, unintended scale, resulting in poor performance.[24]

## WAYS TO OVERCOME CHALLENGES

So what can a project manager do to overcome the challenges discussed above? Plenty.

## Establish an Integrated Communication Infrastructure Early

As emphasized repeatedly, good communication does not just happen. Project managers must orchestrate it via a communication infrastructure. A communication infrastructure consists of concepts, tools, and techniques for ensuring that information is transferred both efficiently and effectively.

Project managers, if they expect efficient and effective communication to occur throughout a project life cycle, must establish a communication infrastructure as early as possible. A good approach to do that is to develop a communication plan.

A communication plan identifies the essential elements to establish and maintain communication. At a minimum, it should address the senders and receivers of messages, the desired level and format of the contents, when to generate messages, where to deliver the messages, why the need to develop messages, and how to deliver the messages.

Under no circumstances, of course, should project managers develop a communication plan in a void. They should meet with stakeholders to identify the requirements. They should not think that developing the plan is one-time affair; they need to constantly refine and update the plan to adapt to changing circumstances.

The communication plan is, however, only one aspect of establishing a communication infrastructure. The other side is establishing appropriate measures to ensure implementation of the plan.

Identifying the right communication network is an important act. There are basically a handful of network patterns. These include the circle, "Y," wheel, chain, and star. Adopting the design depends on how project managers hope to manage the flow of communication on their projects. Increasingly, the trend appears to have a project manager be more of a broker and facilitator, e.g., in the star network, and less of a controller in a chain network.

Also, project managers should consider how to handle the direction of communication. For example, how should they handle upward communication? Downward communication? Lateral communication? Formally or informally?

Project managers need to establish ground rules for employing different means of communication. These rules may or may not be included in the communication plan but are typically developed as procedures that support and implement it. The ground rules might include conducting meetings, preparing e-mail, decision-making approaches, and resolving conflict. The key is to address the ground rules early to limit problems that may appear later in the project life cycle.

Another important tool is the project repository. This repository, essentially a database, allows people access to information, ideally at the right place, time, and format. It does that by providing a convenient location to collect and disseminate information among all stakeholders.

Using automated tools, when compatible, allows the establishment of such a repository. This repository, of course, must be well planned from design and update perspectives. Once in place, of course, it must be continuously populated to ensure people can access what they need.

In addition to the repository is the development and implementation of a project web site. The web site can provide many advantages, e.g., accessing and disseminating information, giving considerable visibility to projects, allowing for ongoing update. Contents of a project web site can include schedules, action items, statistics, minutes, and forms.

The project site must be updated continuously. Failure to do so lessens its usefulness to stakeholders. It is important, therefore, to have someone on projects to serve as the web master for design and content.

A very important caveat: Neither the repository nor the web site should be developed alone. Project managers should involve stakeholders, ensuring ownership and enabling projects to provide a useful tool.

Finally, project managers need to look at the flow of information to all the stakeholders throughout the project life cycle. Indeed, the flow of information will have a very important influence on determining and designing the communication network, repository, and web site. Because information is the lifeblood of most projects, project managers need to determine its flow. They must consider the dependencies of information as it flows throughout their projects. By doing so, people will know what critical information feeds which subsequent tasks and so on.[25]

## Understand an Audience's Information Requirements and Tailor Accordingly

While developing and implementing a communication infrastructure, project managers should address this issue. However, some important insights are necessary.

One major insight is to recognize that a good communicator has two main goals: to make positive contact with an audience and to be effective. Positive contact is influencing the recipient of the message. Hersey and Blanchard define communication as conveying a message that is easily understandable and acceptable.[26] Being effective is getting the desired response from a message. The best way to achieve both is to ensure that what is sent to the audience is aligned with the needs of the sender and recipient.

Knowing the requirements of an audience allows greater alignment because it helps to overcome some barriers that can easily interfere with communication.

A major barrier is a person's paradigm. By knowing that paradigm, senders can couch their messages to achieve the desired level affect and effect.

To best serve an audience, project managers can identify needs across many levels. One level consists of needs common across all stakeholders. Another level has needs unique to a particular group, e.g., management or team members. Project managers need to identify specific needs and tailor their messages to each one.

Regardless of level, however, project managers must ask the fundamental questions and receive answers from the appropriate stakeholders. These questions include: What information does the stakeholder need? At what level of detail? In what format? How frequent? Over what medium? How should the information be protected e.g., confidential or proprietary? Does the stakeholder wish advance notification if there is bad news to communicate? These and other questions apply to reports and presentations.

There is, however, another point. Defining requirements is not just for hard copy documents. There are also specific audience needs at meetings. At certain types of meetings, some stakeholders will have different needs from others. For example, team members will likely have different needs than senior management at status collection meetings. Project managers must identify those needs and adapt accordingly.

Getting to know the audience's requirements makes very good sense although it is rarely done. People think it is a matter of just pumping out reports from project management software; such an approach can result in lead times, lags in information delivery, and useless detail. Defining the requirements early, however, reduces the chance of such problems and leads to less conflict throughout a project's life cycle.

Conflict resulting from poor audience analysis can be especially difficult for projects spanning different cultures. The opportunities for barriers can grow. Most of the challenges result from cultural and language barriers. For example, some messages may be more appropriate to send to some stakeholders than others. Even the use of words and body language can influence receptivity of a message. A major important step to preventing such barriers is to define audience requirements, laying the groundwork for effective communication.

## Adopt a Communication Approach That Is Appropriate to a Situation

Communication requires exercising sound judgment when applying an approach or tool and sending the message. Making a sound judgment is, of course, a prime responsibility of project managers. Yet, few project managers exercise sound judgment when communicating to stakeholders. For example, many project managers broadcast messages when it might be wiser to do so in a more discreet manner. Project managers might use technology, e.g., e-mail, when a more effective approach to build rapport would be one-on-one meetings to discuss critical issues.

The medium is the message, to quote Marshall McLuhan; however, in the project environment so is the content. Project managers must constantly determine which tool, technique, and message is most appropriate.

Project managers must consider many factors: the sensitivity of the content, need to control it, people who need to know, criticality of contents, and appearance. In some cases, words are more appropriate than graphics and vice versa.

The approach towards communication depends, to some extent, on the recipient. In *Successful Meetings* magazine, Merna Skinner identifies four communicator types. The Director, according to Skinner, is someone who processes information rapidly and likes to get to the point. The Free Spirit is the person who has to see the picture and likes to identify various alternatives. The Humanist is someone who is a social animal who strives to satisfy everyone's needs. The Historian is detail oriented, preferring structure and precision. Each one seeks to present and process information in a certain way.[27]

Project managers must also make a decision about communicating in regards to time and place. In *PM Network,* Carl Singer identifies four communication modes based on time and place. For the same time and place, face-to-face meetings will likely work best. For a different time and place, e-mail and repositories may be better. For a different time and same place, a control, or war, room might be the best way to communicate. For the same time but different place, communication via e-mail might work.[28]

Project managers often judge whether to use formal or informal communication. Formal communication works best when task-related issues need to be communicated in one direction, e.g., from project manager to team member or from project manager to senior management. Informal communication works best when dealing with social issues, e.g., conflict among team members, and tends to be multidirectional, e.g., laterally and up and down the chain of command.[29]

Project managers should use judgment when communicating. The goal is not to retreat to a method to avoid feeling uncomfortable. Instead, project managers should take a flexible approach even if it feels uncomfortable. Despite the increasing role of technology in communication, the personal touch still seems to have great influence, particularly at the beginning of a project. In *PM Network,* Larraine Segil says that what she calls "enhanced communication" can help a team to maintain focus on what is important while at the same time maintain commitment. Enhanced communication can augment the effectiveness of other means of communication, e.g., teleconferencing and e-mail.[30]

## Aggressively Remove Barriers to Communication

Much has already been said about these barriers. Plenty exist and few project managers can remove or overcome them. It is important, however, that project managers make a concerted effort to do so when communicating information is the lifeblood of projects. Tarnish the communication and the results are often tarnished as well.

Project managers need to be vigilant about ensuring that communication flows unimpeded among stakeholders. If a barrier exists, they should remove it quickly to ensure messages are received and have the desired affect and effect.

After removing barriers, the work of project managers is not over. It only begins. They must also remain attuned to how well communication occurs. The secret is to be aware of the signals from stakeholders.

There are many indicators that barriers to communication exist. Not only may the messages and information contained be dated, for example, but they may also possess incomplete or inaccurate contents. Also, the message and the contents may be unclear, lengthy, convoluted, and lack meaning.

The tragedy is that some project managers make very little effort to remove or overcome such barriers to communication. Instead, they continually think and behave in a way that inevitably leads to negative conflict, building walls rather than bridges among people. The presence of negative conflict, if mishandled, can create many barriers. This conflict can occur on an interpersonal, intragroup, and intergroup level.

Project managers can take one of four approaches towards resolving negative conflict that results from poor communication. They can avoid doing anything about it; however, that approach does nothing to remove the conflict; communication barriers remain. They can take a competitive Win-Lose approach; again, that does nothing to remove conflict and may actually augment it. They can seek compromise, finding a middle ground. While compromise may reduce or eliminate negative conflict, it can easily arise once again if one party perceives the other as breaching it or gaining an advantage. They accommodate the other party but, like compromise, may only temporarily soften the conflict; it has the potential to resurface, causing even bigger barriers to communication later. Finally, and most effectively, they can deal with conflict in a collaborative manner, meaning both parties address an issue that results in a Win-Win situation. Communication often improves immediately and lasts.

Just the opposite of conflict can occur that can inhibit meaningful communication — Groupthink, which is intense peer pressure that does not allow for dissent. Consequences are severe, including an unrealistic appraisal of situations as well as limited alternatives to driving decision making. In an effort to maintain open communication, project managers must ensure that Groupthink does not inhibit communication. They can do that by conducting brainstorming, having one-on-one sessions, and encouraging the free exchange of ideas.

Although communicating is a responsibility of all stakeholders, the reality is that project managers have the bigger share of it. They are the ones who will be ultimately responsible for achieving results. They have the onus and responsibility, therefore, to engender and sustain open communication with other people.

## Take a Nonlinear Approach to Communication

Typically, many project managers think that communication flows down to the team and up to stakeholders like senior management. In a highly technological environment, the communication is more like a network with channels of communication flowing in all directions. This complex array of channels is due to the advent of digital technologies, which allows stakeholders to communicate in all directions. It is not uncommon, for example, for a team member to communicate directly with a senior manager about an issue or request information. In yesteryear, such communication was rare, not today.

The key is for project managers to understand and accept this reality, but few do so. Instead, many try to control the content and destination of messages. However, technology weakens such an endeavor. Instead, they should concentrate on setting guidelines on what to communicate under specific conditions using certain technologies. The point is that the content and delivery mode of messages can have a major impact.

An effective way to ensure that team members will follow guidelines is to have them participate in setting them and then the project manager gives visibility to inculcate ownership and accountability for all messages sent.

## Listen More and Talk Less

Just about all the thinkers on communication make this point. And just about all thinkers on leadership agree. Unfortunately, few people follow this advice, reflected in the fact that it is one of the top five leadership failures.[31] This failure to listen is rampant among all levels of the chain of command, from team members up to the highest positions in the corporate hierarchy, including projects.

By listening more, project managers become better communicators for several reasons. Listening enables them to learn more about issues and problems. If done correctly, they can suspend judgment, thereby providing the ability and capability to acquire an objective viewpoint. It also allows them to identify and focus on the main issues of conversations. The mere act of listening, not hearing, helps them to build closer, meaningful relationships. Finally, with a more objective viewpoint and focus on main issues, they can deal with conflict, particularly negative conflict, more appropriately.

Listening, of course, deals with more than hearing. It also requires involving the person speaking, both in what and how something is said. What is being said pertains to content, e.g., the choice of words and phraseology. How something is said relates to the physiological behavior of a speaker, e.g., body language and inflection. Project managers must attune themselves to both to ensure knowledge of content and meaning.

To have a worthwhile listening experience, project managers should be aware of and practice different types of listening.

Active listening is doing so eagerly and consists of two parts. Part one is empathic listening, doing so with the purpose of understanding from a speaker's perspective, such as asking probing questions. Part two is reflective listening, exhibited behavior that reflects understanding of what was said, such as paraphrasing and expressing similar feelings. The opposite of active listening, of course, is passive listening, that is, not providing any feedback to the speaker.

When performing active listening, good practices for project managers include: be patient and do not interrupt, be attentive to the speaker, be nonjudgmental about what is said, focus on the speaker and the main issues, be attuned to verbal and nonverbal cues, and be considerate of both content and feelings of a speaker.

## Add Passion to Communication

A major challenge in business in general and project management in particular is the overemphasis on "facts and data" and "logic." The basic premise is that by emphasizing the two, action is inevitable. The reality is that facts and data, along with logic, are justifications for action; they do not necessarily encourage people to act. What gets people to act is an emotional involvement in the outcome depicted through facts, data, and logic.

To be effective, therefore, communication must involve the emotional side of people. "How" as well as "What" is being communicated is as important for a message. As William Cohen notes in *The Art of the Leader,* the way a message is conveyed is as important as its contents. He encourages communicating a message in a manner that enlivens people.[32]

Quantity may not be important. Just a few words or messages that touch the emotional side can have more of an impact than messages filled with pages of facts and data that most people will not bother to absorb. The degree of passion put into the communication, of course, depends on many variables including culture, mores, history, distance, delivery mode, personal style, interpersonal relationships, audience, and overall context. All of these variables require judgment by project managers to determine the degree of passion to include in their communication.

Many project managers associate passion with giving a speech. Yet, they can also employ passion to get people to act on an issue, solve a problem, or complete their tasks. The bottom line is action, not compiling facts and data and doing long exercises of logical gymnastics.

An interesting way to generate passion in messages, particularly oral ones, is for leaders to apply storytelling to give meaning behind facts, data, and logic. Peter Giuliano stresses the need to bring "life" to presentations. The way to do so is through storytelling, which puts the content into context. He recommends that stories should be simple, have some mystique, be memorable, and pointed."[33]

Another great way to generate emotion is to give a "positive spin" to facts and data. While important to even acknowledge and communicate that facts and data may paint a negative picture, project managers will find it better to use a positive context to avoid discouraging people. For example, a schedule slide is often viewed as negative; however, it can also be postured as being positive for several reasons, e.g., an opportunity to improve performance on some tasks. It is how project managers present such facts and data that will determine emotional acceptance and the actions taken.

## Keep Communication Ongoing

Good communication is something that project managers must continually nurture throughout the life cycle of projects. Without active involvement by the project managers, communication channels can quickly clog and filter or stop message flow. Communication entropy can easily arise.

Project managers, therefore, must continuously apply the principles and practices of good communication, as described above, they must also endeavor to ensure that continuous feedback occurs and that it contains positive and negative messages. More often than not, project managers will have to take the initiative to obtain that feedback. Feedback can be formal or informal, written or oral. It can also have a regular or ad hoc frequency or both. Whatever the form or frequency, feedback must contain the necessary information to satisfy its purpose.

Project managers can obtain feedback through all the typical avenues of communication, e.g., meetings, reports, one-on-one sessions. Naturally, they also must be aware of the barriers to communication by maintaining awareness of their existence and taking a proactive approach to overcome or eliminate them.

A major problem that hinders the communication effectiveness of many project managers is the tendency to use selective hearing, that is, hearing only what they want to hear. Often, this sends clear signals to messengers that can only result in bias in interpreting the content of messages. Selective hearing can result in project managers making poor decisions due to filtering data or ignoring it entirely. A good approach to overcome this selective hearing is to seek feedback from multiple sources and "play back" the messages to verify what was heard. Both approaches are excellent ways to avoid the negative impacts of selective hearing. Project managers should hear what they need to hear and not what they want to hear.

## Emphasize Quality Over Quantity of Information

A major theme of this chapter is that more is not necessarily better when communicating. Too much can lead to overload for the recipient and cause oversight of important contents within a message. However, the amount of information is just one characteristic. There are also the qualitative characteristics to consider.

Timeliness is an important characteristic. Information delivered to stakeholders must be delivered in the right format at the right level of detail at the right moment to make the right decisions. Information that arrives too late is as much use as not receiving any information.

The integrity of the information is also important. Are the data contained in the message accurate? Is it "dirty," that is, is the validity of the data tarnished in some way, e.g., mixture of correct and incorrect data? Are the data cryptic, that is, not very understandable to the people receiving the message? Are they ambiguous in any way? Bad data in messages may result in making bad decisions that, in turn, means taking the wrong action to deal with a situation.

The key for project managers is to ensure that the content of the data satisfies qualitative requirements by establishing a process to collect data up front, turn it into information, and distribute it to the right audiences. At the end of the process is a product: communication. The quality of the result reflects the quality of the process producing it.[34]

It would be erroneous to think, however, that the quality of information is simply putting it in a message. To be of value, data must be correct at the point of origin. A process should emphasize accuracy, precision, timeliness, completeness, and consistency if content is to be of value to an audience. Too frequently, "bad data" are mixed with "good data," creating a fruit salad of "apples and oranges." This circumstance can lead to confusion, frustration, and loss of credibility by the recipient, with the message and its creator. Project managers, therefore, must establish a reliable process to have effective communication.

A process should go beyond defining the who, what, when, where, why, and how of a communication plan. It should also ensure that the scrubbing of data occurs at the point of origin. Project managers must, therefore, recognize early some of the challenges for collecting and processing data, e.g., receiving data from multiple sources with different values or introducing bias during the data collection. It is only through dealing with data at the point of origin that project managers can avoid the challenges of data scrubbing; converting data into information; and incorporating it in a message, e.g., a report.

## Apply Good Communication Skills and Techniques

This application happens not just at the beginning of a project but throughout its life cycle. It also applies whether or not application occurs on an interpersonal level, during presentations at meetings.

Project managers need, therefore, to be cognizant of basic communication skills and techniques, to include defining the goal of a message, determining the audience, providing a logical and emotional aspect to it, selecting the most appropriate medium, and conducting follow-up to determine if the desired response occurred. Above all, project managers must recognize that the responsibility for establishing and maintaining an effective communication process rests with them.

# NEVER FORGET!

Project managers must always consider the importance of communication in just about every activity of a project, e.g., managing conflict, working collaboratively, negotiating, conducting meetings, or interviewing. They should also be mindful that how they communicate will influence the quality of the communication. If they exude negativity or indifference in their communication, then they can expect barriers to arise. So it behooves project managers to apply good written and oral communication skills on individual and group levels.

A good way to remember what is important in all communication is that it consists of four basic elements: needs, logic, emotion, and integrity. Project managers must define the requirement (need), organize the contents (logic), present it in a manner that "grabs" the attention of the recipient (emotion), and do not mislead in any way (integrity). More often than not, recipients, regardless of whether or not they object to a message, will then at least be willing to listen.

Above all, project managers must recognize that communication is a two-way process that requires them to take the initiative to ensure that the relationship is free of barriers and filters both for their own and the project's sake. The ultimate test, remember, is to achieve results and the first action is for project managers to initiate a communication exchange among themselves and stakeholders.

## CASE STUDY: COMMUNICATE

The project manager knew that communication was key to the success of any project. Therefore, an effective communication infrastructure was quickly established and sustained throughout the project. A number of actions were performed to establish the infrastructure.

The first was to design and deploy a web site. This site was used to profile all activities of the project from planning to execution. It also contained procedures on managing the project and relevant templates and guidelines on the new and proposed policies and procedures infrastructure. The site was constantly updated to ensure that everyone had the latest information.

The next action was to set up a series of ongoing meetings for the project team. A procedure was prepared and published on the web site. The document provided details for the meetings, e.g., purpose, location, attendees, schedule. At the meeting, the project manager documented and distributed results among team members.

A set of reports was also developed for all the stakeholders. However, a careful audience analysis was done to ensure that the category of stakeholders received the appropriate information to help them succeed. For example, the project manager met with different categories of stakeholders to determine their reporting needs and then tailored reports to meet their requirements. The goals were to provide meaningful information and to avoid confusion and frustration. All reports, of course, were posted to the web site.

Throughout the project, the project manager was responsive, not reactive, when communicating. Concerted actions were taken to ensure that communication was ongoing, especially when difficult issues arose. An issues management process was deployed that addressed concerns and problems not captured in the work breakdown structure. These issues were discussed during meetings to ensure that an ongoing dialog occurred on their resolution and provided visibility to them.

The project manager did not restrict himself to one method of communication. In addition to meetings and the web site, the use of e-mails to communicate issues relevant to stakeholders was encouraged. He avoided, however, the all too frequent shotgun approach to e-mails and carefully constructed distribution lists for e-mails covering certain issues.

## REFERENCES

1. John W. Gardner, *On Leadership,* The Free Press, New York, 1990, p. 26.
2. Robert Bolton, *People Skills,* Touchstone, New York, 1986, p. 6.

3. Paul Hersey and Kenneth H. Blanchard, *Management of Organizational Behavior,* 6th ed., Prentice Hall, Englewood Cliffs, NJ, 1993, p. 327.
4. 2002 Research Report from Canadian Manufacturers and Exporters, *PM Network,* p. 10, March 2003.
5. Joel Schettler, Leadership in corporate America, *Training,* p. 70, September 2002.
6. Top ten, *Training and Development,* p. 10, February 1999.
7. Harold Kerzner, *Project Management,* Van Nostrand Reinhold, New York, 1995, p. 275.
8. Joan Knutson, You owe your project players a common infrastructure – Part 1, *PM Network,* p. 21, November 1999.
9. Stewart L. Tubbs and Sylvia Moss, *Human Communication,* 8th ed., McGraw-Hill, Boston, 2000, p. 20.
10. Douglas A. Benton, *Applied Human Relations,* 6th ed., Prentice Hall, Englewood Cliffs, NJ, 1998, p. 194.
11. Michelle Keiserman, Project team communications: the grease, the glue and the...gum? *PM Network,* p. 17, May 1999.
12. Robert Bolton, *People Skills,* Touchstone, New York, 1986, p. 30.
13. Daniel Goleman, What makes a leader? *Harvard Business Review,* pp. 93–102, November–December 1998.
14. Daniel Goleman, *Emotional Intelligence,* Bantam Books, New York, 1995, p. 96.
15. Ibid., p. 97.
16. Tom Peters, *The Pursuit of Wow!,* Vintage Books, New York, 1994, p. 257.
17. Edward M. Hallowell, The human moment at work, *Harvard Business Review,* pp. 59–62, January–February 1999.
18. Ray Boedecker, Communications: the project manager's essential tool, *PM Network,* p. 20, December 1997.
19. Beverly Kaye and Sharon Jordan-Evans, *Love 'Em or Lose 'Em,* Berrett-Koehler, San Francisco, 1999, p. 175.
20. Stewart L. Tubbs and Sylvia Moss, *Human Communication,* 8th ed., McGraw-Hill, Boston, 2000, p. 199.
21. James M. Kouzes and Barry Z. Posner, *The Leadership Challenge,* Jossey-Bass, San Francisco, 1987, p. 121.
22. John W. Gardner, *On Leadership,* The Free Press, New York, 1990, p. 116.
23. Robert Bolton, *People Skills,* Touchstone, New York, 1986, p. 17.
24. Dale H. Emery, Untangling communication, *STQE Magazine,* p. 18, July/August 2001.
25. Stephen Denker, Hugh McLaughlin, Donald Steward, and Tyson Browning, Information-driven project management, *PM Network,* p. 50, September 2001.
26. Paul Hersey and Kenneth H. Blanchard, *Management of Organizational Behavior,* 6th ed., Prentice Hall, Englewood Cliffs, NJ, 1993, p. 325.
27. Merna L. Skinner, So, talk to me, *Successful Meetings,* pp. 87–88, November 2000.
28. Carl A. Singer, Leveraging a worldwide project team, *PM Network,* p. 37, April 2001.
29. Nancy Mercurio, Effective communication: getting your message across in simple terms, *Federal Training Network* (presentation), 2000.

30. Larraine Segil, Global work teams: a cultural perspective, *PM Network,* p. 29, March 1999.
31. Why leaders fail, *Industry Week,* p. 15, March 2002.
32. William A. Cohen, *The Art of the Leader,* Prentice Hall, Englewood Cliffs, NJ, 1990, p. 160.
33. Peter Giuliano, Successful methods, *Successful Meetings,* pp. 64–65, July 2000.
34. Yair Wang and Richard Y. Wang, Anchoring data quality dimensions in ontological foundations, *Communications of the ACM,* p. 87, November 1996.

# 12

# RESPOND

While appearing obvious, a major characteristic of a project is that change occurs in many ways, internally and externally to it. In fact, a project is really a manifestation of change. The very reason for a project is to implement change; otherwise, a project is nothing more than an ongoing service.

## COMMON PERSPECTIVES

Because a project is a change, project managers must understand change and exhibit the appropriate leadership behaviors, just as all leaders must do and, like all leaders, they must share perspectives on change when leading.

### Transformative Rather than Transactional

Much has been already been written in this book about the differences between transformative and transactional actions of leaders. Nothing manifests the differences between the two actions more than how project managers perceive and deal with change.

Managers strive to protect the status quo; leaders do the opposite, seeking changes that improve efficiency and, perhaps more importantly, effectiveness. As Warren Bennis says in *On Becoming a Leader,* the distinguishing characteristic between a manager and a leader is whether he or she accepts or challenges the status quo.[1]

Leaders take the initiative when dealing with change. They do not wait for something to happen to them; rather, they make change happen. They identify ways to change the status quo in a radical, revolutionary way, as Kouzes and Posner observe in *The Leadership Challenge.*[2]

If change comes to them, they do not shrink from it. Instead, they respond rather than react to it. They view leadership as being dynamic, not dependent on someone or something else to dictate an agenda. Leadership, not surprisingly, is active and not passive.[3]

Of course, leaders who adopt a transformative approach can experience some high drama, a distinguishing difference between transformative and transactional leadership. Consequently, the most memorable leaders are those who helped lead us through very difficult times, whereas managers are remembered during stable periods.[4]

John Kotter agrees. He makes a distinction between leadership and management as they relate to change. Management — more specifically, transactional management — strives for predictability and order almost to the point of wanting to create an architectonic framework for an organization. These actions focus on short-term results and are incremental. Leadership seeks more dramatic results, creating long-term, lasting changes. Kotter also notes, however, that leadership still requires management, as it is not mutually exclusive.[5]

Project managers, as leaders, therefore, must act like change agents. They cannot remain passive and wait for events to happen. They must take the initiative to create change and, if change happens, respond to it.

The role of a change agent is not limited inside the confines of a project. Instead, project managers must see their projects in the context of an overall environment in which their projects reside. Their role as a change agent, therefore, goes into the organization at large once their projects are executed.

## Have an Important Set of Roles and Responsibilities for Dealing with the Turbulence of Change

Due to their position within the chain of command in a project, project managers play a large role and exercise responsibilities for managing change. While most stakeholders often have a narrow focus or have other responsibilities unrelated to a project, project managers are often the ones filling a position that can deal with something as ubiquitous as change on a large, integrated scale.

One of those roles and responsibilities is to cope with change. Coping is not just for themselves but for other stakeholders, too. Two parts exist to these roles and responsibilities.

The first part is to instill the confidence in people that change can be harnessed in a way that does not result in defeatism, while at the same time acknowledging the risks. Leadership, then, is about how certain individuals direct us through the unknown.[6]

Leaders do that by setting the example. They exhibit courage to advance into the fog of change. Kouzes and Posner liken leaders to pioneers who guide people through the unfamiliar.[7]

Of course, risk taking is not everyone's cup of tea. However, true leaders must take the necessary risks or little progress will occur. William Cohen says that taking risks is similar to a turtle popping its head out to move forward. A leader does the same and that translates into success.[8]

It is incumbent on the leader to face risks even in the midst of displeasure by other stakeholders. There is a good reason. Many people avoid risk; leaders, by the nature of their position alone, must take them on to succeed.[9]

The other part is that leaders must maintain a "stiff upper lip" when facing change and adopt innovative ways to respond. Often, change cannot be managed simply by following routine practices; by their very nature, such practices involve something unanticipated and different, which incurs a high level of risk. Risk and innovation go together and put not just the innovator at risk, but others too.[10] Consequently, the application of innovative responses to change creates considerable uncertainty. That very uncertainty, however, helps to distinguish the differences between leaders and managers. Furthermore, leaders must master both change and the uncertainty that accompanies it.[11]

This uncertainty can result in great angst and sometimes even failure, either individually or as a group, providing a defining moment. Warren Bennis and Robert Thomas refer to such circumstances as the crucibles of leadership. How leaders and others respond to such circumstances demonstrates the quality of leadership. A set of skills exists for doing so that distinguishes between mediocre and above-the-norm leadership. According to Bennis and Thomas, hardiness and contextual understanding enable people to survive difficult periods but, perhaps more importantly, it is the ability to learn from the experience that enables a person to gain in strength and commitment.[12]

## Use Persuasion Rather than Coercion to Manage Change

Quite clearly, leaders not only manage change but they also make it happen.

However, leaders do not command change to occur because, quite frankly, those who must implement it will not find it acceptable. And even if a decree to change receives compliance, adherence will likely be short lived once the project manager departs and the opportunity arises to revert to the "old" way of doing business.

Leaders, therefore, must apply persuasion to gain acceptance of the need to change as well as have it implemented. The elements of this persuasion include:

applying interpersonal skills at their disposal, e.g., communicating and listening; being open and equitable in all relationships; developing a learning culture; and encouraging a belief in the future.[13]

## Recognize the Importance of Developing Creative Strategies

Leaders, being transformative by nature, must seek innovative solutions when the need arises. Kouzes and Posner observe that leadership is deeply intertwined with the implementation of new ideas and techniques.[14] The more challenging a change, the greater the need for innovative solutions. Otherwise, leaders can find themselves trapped, applying anachronistic solutions to contemporary problems, only to aggravate circumstances. Leaders, therefore, must avoid limiting their options to develop creative solutions to problems or issues. They must think before they act by developing a new but effective approach.

Developing creative responses does not, however, stop with the leader. Leaders must help themselves and the people who support them to overcome mental and other constraints that impact the quality of innovative thinking. Leaders must experiment by combining the old with the new and vice versa, identifying and removing mental constraints.[15]

## Give Equal Time to the Head and the Heart

Too often, overemphasis is placed on the left side of the brain (e.g., logic, reasoning) while ignoring the right side (e.g., emotions, feelings, intuition). Too much emphasis is often placed on dealing with change in a logical, calculative manner when many, even most, issues and problems deal with emotions. This lopsided approach results, however, in treating change more like a thing or object than a phenomenon.

Dealing with change, therefore, requires a holistic perspective because right and left brain considerations come into play. Leaders who recognize the importance of logic are required to determine the need for change and a plan to implement it. That approach is incomplete. Emotional involvement is also necessary for ownership, commitment, buy-in, and accountability. John Kotter demonstrates the difference as being the "heart of the matter more" versus the "head of the matter less." The former consists more of drama and feelings; the latter more of analysis and thoughts.[16]

This combination of logic and emotion provides an added benefit from a leadership perspective. It can help shift the view of change as a problem to avoid to more of an opportunity to embrace, reflecting a whole-brain perspective. In other words, a leader can use a combination of facts, data, and logic (which are never completely accurate) and his or her inner voice to determine ultimately how to deal with change. Bennis cites Ralph Waldo Emerson's idea of a "blessed impulse," which is a hunch or gut feeling and, according to Bennis, we must learn to trust such impulses from time to time.[17]

## Generate an Environment Conducive for Managing Change

Within the limits of their power, leaders seek to provide an environment that enables them (and others) to manage change. With others, they facilitate by removing the obstacles in the environment that prevent dealing with change efficiently, but, more importantly, effectively. They must engender an environment that fosters risk taking and innovation.

Removing obstacles is very important. However, leaders must institute processes that manage change innovatively. In project management, it appears that the most effective processes are the ones that facilitate innovation and learning.[18]

In addition to providing an environment that allows for the development of innovative solutions, leaders must set the example. Leaders must adapt a transformational style that requires a willingness to take risks. Warren Bennis says that curiosity and daring are perhaps basic elements of leadership and that failure becomes a learning experience over the errors made.[19]

Tolerance for failure and learning from it is not just for leaders, of course, but leaders must set the example because dealing with change can be very challenging, even overwhelming, to people. Yet, the returns of this experience can be great. It is not surprising that failure, change, and risk permeate throughout the list of top reasons for Silicon Valley's "once" secrets of success.[20]

The importance of providing an environment conducive to manage change cannot be overstressed. Leaders must provide an open, collaborative environment that encourages taking chances with change. Often, involvement by stakeholders outside the immediate team is necessary because project managers often lack the power to effectuate environmental changes. The overall organizational environment tends to affect the innovation of project teams by limiting the options for project managers to develop a culture of innovation.[21]

Project managers must be able to deal with change, therefore, if they hope to conclude their projects successfully. If not, their projects will only marginally achieve or fail to achieve any success for many reasons, e.g., the inability to adapt to changing circumstances, the tendency of scope creep to overwhelm people. The bottom line is that it affects performance to cost, schedule, quality, and people, positively or negatively.

The insight here is not that change is bad; quite the contrary. If change was bad, the entire human race would still be living in caves and using horses for transportation. The key is to respond to change in a manner that capitalizes on its benefits and minimizes its losses.

## SELF-DESTRUCTIVE BEHAVIOR

Unfortunately, many project managers do not respond to change but react to it, adding to its complexity. This reaction acts like feeding oxygen to a fire; the more pumped in, the bigger the flames. Here are some ways that project managers inadvertently feed the flames of change in a way that adds complexity and deteriorates overall performance.

### Pretend That Change Will Go Away

To use a trite analogy, they are like an ostrich sticking its head in the sand in the hope that the hyenas will go away. The reality is that the hyenas will remain and their presence will increase. In other words, doing nothing will not work. Circumstances will require action of some sort.

Many project managers hope that change will be temporary and that circumstances will change. The problem is not change itself per se but their reaction or unresponsiveness to it. For example, a budget cut will not go away; it will require that project managers take some type of response to deal with change. Another example is that a new tool or methodology is introduced during a project that could produce a better product and reduce costs. A project manager may need to take a different approach.

### Add More People

A change occurs, such as an increase in scope, and the tendency is to add more people. There is a belief that more is better, leading to dramatic improvements. While this approach may work sometimes, more often than not it fails. Adding more people may only add to difficulties. More people increase the number of interactions among stakeholders and also learning curves. This circumstance is quite common on technological projects that require the interdisciplinary cooperation among knowledge workers.

People do not want change to go away even if project managers pretend it does not exist. Change is something that cannot be taken lightly because it permeates everything and occurs constantly, especially on projects. As Tom Peters notes in *The Pursuit of Wow!,* you must avoid taking change and the response to it for granted. It is a double-edged sword because people want it, but they also want constancy.[22]

## Purchase a Silver Bullet

Silver bullets can come in many forms, e.g., tool, technique, or even consultant. They often help adapting in the short-term, but fail to address the underlying issues associated with change. Indeed, they can worsen matters due to addressing the symptoms only. Silver bullets are quite prevalent in high-technology industries, but few have really helped in managing change. In many respects, they have added complexity to change because project managers have exercised little forethought about how to leverage the power of the silver bullets.

## Remove Current People/Replace with Different People

Many project managers are fond of saying that people resist change and that the only solution is to seek people who agree with a change. So, they request that certain people be removed, thinking that a change will be more acceptable to a new set of team members. More often than not, the problem does not lie with these people but how the change is introduced to a team. While replacing people may work in the short run, it may prove costly in the long run. Reasons include: creating a "brain drain," slowing the performance of existing players to help new members, and eroding trust with remaining team members.

## Extend the Schedule

One of the first reactions to dealing with change is to alter the schedule. While sometimes a prudent action, it may prove unnecessary and possibly hurt progress. Changes will constantly occur and taking such a "knee-jerk" reaction will likely disrupt processes and may inadvertently extend the schedule even more than desired. Project managers should first try to accommodate the schedule by adjusting the logic as well as time and cost estimates. In other words, they should concentrate first on working smarter.

## Do the Opposite and Doggedly Stick to What Already Exists

Some project managers think that the best way to deal with change is to resist ideas from stakeholders by establishing procedures that discourage any changes from arising in the first place. These and other strong-armed tactics assume that if a change is accepted, it must be a good one. In addition, some project managers feel the need to be in control but that often reflects that they are not and even seem weak willed. Finally, some project managers adhere to the perception that their role is to preserve and protect when, ironically, they should be transformative.

The above perceptions and assumptions are often fallacious at best because they discourage the free flow of ideas that bring innovative solutions that could encourage further progress. They also represent narrow, linear thinking that can result in missed opportunities to augment project performance as well as lead to project failure. Besides, project managers appear passive when in reality they should be very dynamic, which the generally accepted view of leadership in general.

## Move Erratically from Start to Finish to Control Change

Many project managers, perhaps reflecting indecisiveness more than anything else, fail to respond to change. Instead, they react to it, receptive to it at one point and reversing themselves at another. They end up exhibiting inconsistency. However, such behavior may go beyond indecisiveness. It may actually reflect nonexistent or unclear vision and a lack of discipline when evaluating the impact of changes. As project managers zigzag in thought and action, stakeholders grow increasingly impatient and frustrated since they cannot anticipate what to expect next. A fine line exists between being flexible versus fluid. Being flexible is making adjustments according to a vision while providing structure behind decisions. Being fluid is making adjustments without considering a vision and acting merely to avoid or get past a bad situation. Many project managers are often more fluid than flexible; that is a major reason scope creep hovers above them to the very end of their projects.

Scope creep can prove disastrous. Project managers must deal with it successfully by exercising appropriate will power and discipline. Adrian Abramovici adds that scope creep will occur and when it happens project managers must understand the nature of a change rather than concentrate on protecting the baseline.[23] Daniel Kim agrees, since all goals tend to change from original intent, and writes that goals tend to drift based on what is occurring at the time.[24] The culprit, of course, is the lure of the "quick fix" to satisfy the needs of the moment rather than addresses root causes.[25]

## "Sugar Coat" Situations

They try to deny that a need for change exists. They attempt to convince themselves and others that the change is unnecessary for many reasons, such as being unimportant. Unfortunately, these project managers let themselves and others down because they refuse to take the time and effort to determine if a change might be valuable. It is interesting to listen to the rationalizations and excuses frequently used to justify sugarcoating: "We've tried to do this before on another project and it won't work here." "The change is just temporary. The need for it will go away soon." "The change looks important but it really isn't." "It's more trouble to deal with than it's worth."

Such rationalizations and excuses are grounded in merit. The challenge is to avoid coming to any definitive conclusions without first determining whether a change deserves attention. Failure to be open in regards to dealing with a specific or general change results in overlooking solid opportunities to improve project performance and respond to changes. Tom Peters is right: Change and pain go hand in hand.[26] He is, however, only half right. There other part is that without pain there is no gain.

## Force Change

They assume that, by virtue of their position, people will accept a change by decree. Yet, a decree seldom works; it only illustrates one of Newton's laws — for every action there is an equal and opposite reaction. The harder project managers push, the harder the resistance, causing severe consequences. Project managers may find themselves in confrontation with the very people from which they need support to complete their projects.

Schisms among stakeholders can arise because the stance becomes one of either/or; that is, either for or against a change. Divisiveness can intensify to the point that an issue becomes very personal. Mao Tse-Tung once commented that change comes only from the barrel of a gun. That may be true if project managers have a gun. Most project managers have no gun, either literally or figuratively.

The reality is that, from a project management perspective, this view is unrealistic because people resist change by nature. Despite the prevalence of change in our lives, organizations still resist change at all levels.

The best approach, of course, is for project managers to acknowledge, assess, and evaluate change from the perspective of what is best for a project and do so in a way that encourages acceptance, ownership, and accountability. Change then becomes less of a threat and more of a catalyst to further the interests of stakeholders in general and a project in particular.

## View Change as a Technical Issue When It Is a Behavioral Issue

Many project managers think change has only a technical dimension, e.g., adding functionality to a tool or applying a methodology. Such changes have a much more profound and subtle impact on people who decide to adapt or embrace a change than the tool or technique itself. For example, introducing a new project management package for use on a project may improve data analysis but may also alter the processes and behavior associated with collecting data for entry into the software. It may also affect the way that output is used. Behavioral issues may include how people work together, interpret information, and overcome a learning curve. Many project managers fail to appreciate behavioral considerations, possibly because they often obtain their positions due to technical expertise.

## REALITIES OF CHANGE

Project managers must recognize the realities of change to function effectively as leaders.

### People Respond to Change Differently

It is a truism, perhaps even trite, to say that people are different. Not so in a different context. They also respond differently to change. In project management, this reality is quite evident because projects are endeavors that reflect change and involve many stakeholders, depending on the size and scope of a project. Generally, however, the larger the size and scope of a project, the more varied the people. And the more variety, the greater the varieties of ways people respond.

A number of ways are available for classifying people on how they respond to change. A good categorization is Ackoff's four types of people dealing with the future. The four types are: Reactivists, Inactivists, Proactivists, and Interactivists.

Reactivists manage change incrementally. They try to preserve the best of the past while capitalizing on the benefits of a change in the future. Inactivists manage change reluctantly and strive to preserve the present circumstances. Their focus is on the status quo. Proactivists embrace change to further a predetermined future. These people "get on the bandwagon" to further an inevitable change. They do not create the future, per se, but serve as catalysts. Interactivists, rather than furthering a change, make change happen through visioning. That is, they generate a vision of the future of what ought to be and then execute all activities accordingly. In other words, they make the future, thereby becoming initiators of change.[27]

Another good model is the one by Paul S. Stoltz, but it has less to do with change and more to do with adversity. I found this model very useful for anticipating how people will respond to intense periods of change that make projects difficult but exciting.

He develops the idea of an adversity quotient (AQ) that is really a behavior pattern exhibited during periods of great challenge. It is these moments of great adversity, such as a dramatic change, that distinguish our behavior when dealing with such circumstances. He observes that what matters is how people respond to an adverse situation. This response, reflective of one's AQ, manifests itself in thoughts, feelings, and actions.[28] Accordingly, the higher a person's AQ, the better the resilience exhibited during adversity, to include dealing with change.

He identifies three categories of people when dealing with adversity: Quitters, Campers, and Climbers.

Quitters cease altogether, having the lowest AQ; they are often bitter and avoid any change. Campers take an incremental approach; they accept change as long it enhances their comfort zones. Climbers have the highest AQ; they seek change and see it as an opportunity to grow. Climbers view change as a potential opportunity for growth and learning as well as an improvement.[29]

Diana Lilla takes a different approach, looking less at the emotional side of responding to change and more at the overall way project managers respond to change. She identifies four categories: Leader-driven, Process-driven, Team-driven, and Change management.

Leader-driven refers to project managers who make, or drive, change to occur, starting with themselves. Process-driven refers to project managers who implement change based on the advice of process experts. Team-driven refers to project managers who implement change that originates from stakeholders, e.g., team members. Change management refers to project managers who implement change based on the combination of process-driven and team-driven styles while achieving sponsorship and buy-in for it.[30]

Change involves considerable uncertainty. Some people embrace it; others avoid it at all costs. Uncertainty is, of course, the inverse of certainty. Between the two is a continuum. Drivers of this continuum are what is known and unknown, the expectations surrounding the change, and the degree of pain or gain associated with its actual implementation.

In a study of sixteen projects, Arnoud De Meyer, Christoph Loch, and Michael Pich identify four categories of uncertainty from a project perspective. These are Variation, Foreseen Uncertainty, Unforeseen Uncertainty, and Chaos.

Variation involves small changes to projects, resulting in a small continuum. Foreseen Uncertainty involves changes that may occur and have a substantial impact. Unforeseen Uncertainty involves unanticipated changes that seem to occur randomly. Chaos involves changes that are not determinable in anticipation or impact because the goals and plan of a project are not very well developed in the first place.

Naturally, Variation and Foreseen Uncertainty allow project managers to respond with some confidence when change occurs. The situation becomes more complicated and generates more angst for Unforeseen Uncertainty and Chaos. While project managers should exhibit leadership under all four categories of uncertainty, it is especially important to do so during Unforeseen Uncertainty and Chaos.

For Unforeseen Uncertainty, project managers must work on building relationships with stakeholders to respond effectively, e.g., developing alternative approaches and selecting the best one. De Meyer, Loch, and Pich observe that Unforeseen Uncertainty requires considerable investment of time and effort to get stakeholders to accept unplanned changes.

For Chaos, dealing with change becomes more complicated because the baseline to evaluate performance is not very well defined, if at all. Under Chaos, the appropriate response is one that is flexible and has a willingness to experiment.[31]

## Change Can Rarely be Dealt with Top Down

Barriers to change can have many forms. Two common ways to classify barriers are psychological and physical.

Physical barriers are easy to identify. A project may be spread over a dispersed location making change difficult to implement. Or it may involve an inability to upgrade tools, such as software. Both examples are overt.

Psychological barriers are more difficult to ascertain. However, sometimes they can be overt, e.g., anger or expressions of noncompliance. Subtle barriers include a lack of desire to implement a change.

As leaders, project managers must exert every effort to deal with both categories; otherwise, they will likely fail. The last thing a leader can do is to isolate himself or herself from change; instead, they must actively destroy barriers to it.[32] The most difficult barriers are often those attributed to an organization, on overt and subtle levels. An overt example is the official policies and procedures of an organization; a subtle one is culture.

Such barriers can be quite pervasive and a powerful influence. In *The Systems Thinker,* Stefan Gueldenberg and Werner Hoffmann observe that people's behaviors are influenced and controlled by organizational frameworks. According to the authors, these barriers function as constraints and occur on two levels: at the strategic management level and management control level. The former establishes the direction and infrastructure; the later ensures consistency according to direction and resource allocation to support an infrastructure.[33]

Change, then, is very difficult due to the "chains" imposed by the organization alone. These chains are often called the laws of organizational change.

Like all human laws, they are very difficult to overcome unless people exert the effort to make change happen.[34]

Change can rarely be dealt with top down; it cannot be simply decreed at any organizational level. Too often, project managers think that they simply need to proclaim "it shall happen" and it will be accepted and implemented.

Sometimes, of course, change will be accepted and implemented quite easily; often, that situation is short lived. People will likely revert to a preferred way once the source of coercion leaves, e.g., when the project manager departs.

To have meaningful, lasting change, project managers need to "pull" rather than "push" people to adopt change. As Kouzes and Posner observe, leaders should encourage people to adopt change according to a "natural diffusion process."[35]

Unfortunately, many project managers push rather than pull, only to add and increase existing barriers to change. Resistance, at least for awhile, can become even more stalwart, especially by stakeholders affected by a decreed change.

The key for overcoming or precluding resistance is to obtain the involvement of the key stakeholders most affected by a change. This involvement will generate a sense of ownership and commitment to a change, causing it to be more meaningful and lasting. Even during real periods of traumatic change, a grassroots approach for dealing with it has more impact.

## Change Requires Creative Responses

By definition, change causes something unique. Sometimes "tried and tested" approaches work to handle change. Sometimes, these approaches fail and do so considerably by adding more problems than the change itself. When that occurs, a creative response is required, that is, respond in a unique way.

Unfortunately, many project managers fail to generate creative responses. Instead, they apply the routine, quick fix. These responses work in the short term with long-term complications. This shortsightedness occurs for many reasons, e.g., jumping to the solution without adequately defining a problem or issue. Others reasons include: allowing poor communications to persist, lack of teaming, an atmosphere of mistrust, and a low tolerance for ambiguity. When one or more of these factors arise, the likelihood of creative responses diminishes.

Project managers, therefore, must actively lay the groundwork to develop creative responses to change. This groundwork removes and deals with barriers discussed earlier and encourages involvement by stakeholders. In turn, this groundwork will generate commitment and accountability to ensure that a creative response is implemented. However, project managers must actively involve themselves in building commitment and challenge in order to introduce innovations.

## Change Is Ever Present in the Form of Scope Creep

Most experienced project managers know that the world of projects occurs in a dynamic, not static, universe. They also realize that change comes from many different directions, internally and externally.

Often, failure to deal with such changes, at least from an external source, is due to an ill-defined scope, which often results from an inadequate understanding of requirements from the very beginning of the project.

Naturally, scope creep can also be due to a desire to satisfy the customer by providing more than required. Known as "gold plating," this excess behavior can result in waste, both from a time and money perspective. Going beyond minimum requirements or scope increases risks.

Scope creep can result from a drifting goals phenomenon, which is trying to achieve multiple, competing objectives as opposed to meeting just one.[36] Gradually, the scope enlarges as do the number of objectives. Sooner or later, the aim is off, causing the project to expand beyond the original vision.

An important leadership action, therefore, is to control scope creep and its ally, drifting goals. The key is to define and maintain the scope and continue to focus on it throughout a project.

Project managers can manage drifting goals much like scope creep by looking at the interdependence of goals and mapping their relationships. Through mapping, project managers can determine which goal to focus on and which ones to de-emphasize at a particular point in time.[37]

## Change Is Nonlinear

It comes in all forms and from all directions. In addition, the response to change is nonlinear. All change is directly connected with the past, present, and future and its management can profoundly impact on a large or small organization, e.g., department or project. For example, change can have "hard" impacts, e.g., policies or procedures, or "soft" impacts, e.g., such as to values and assumptions. Change, therefore, can be very difficult to wrestle with.

The problem with managing change is that many people, including some project managers, handle change in a paint-by-the-numbers approach or with a quick fix. Sometimes, perhaps frequently, the approaches may work and most managers are familiar with them because they treat their organizations as stable systems and not dynamic ones. In *Management of Organizational Behavior,* Paul Hersey and Kenneth Blanchard observe that most managers tend to focus on what they refer to as "continuous or first-order" change involving the maintenance of stable systems.[38]

Not all changes, however, are equal and the more complex a change, the more nonlinear it becomes. Actions performed in the past may no longer work and may actually increase the complexity associated with issues like consensus, responsibility, accountability, and conflict resolution. The more subtle the areas, the greater the difficulty to manage change linearly, e.g., apply a quick fix. This type of change is the hardest to handle because the organization, or system, is changing and requires a considerable sophisticated management. Hersey and Blanchard note that what they call "discontinuous or second-order change" affects the basic states and properties of systems.[39]

This view of change requires leaders to understand the dynamics of change that constantly occurs.[40] A major reason why many people, including project managers, must treat change this way is because our institutions require formalized logic from the perspective of a narrow discipline. It becomes, therefore, very difficult to appreciate how everything is interconnected and affected by change to one degree or another.

As one might expect, changing anything on a project can have multiple impacts, some overt and others subtle. Some impacts may not be immediately apparent to people, processes, and culture. Being nonlinear presents many ambiguities that require the best attributes of leaders.

Change is as much psychological as technological and physical. Sometimes it seems it is easier to overcome the laws of physics than the laws of human nature when managing change. Nothing can be closer to the truth than in a project environment where the pace is often fast and furious. Changes constantly press against tight deadlines, limited budgets, and sometimes less than desirable physical conditions. Project managers also find themselves addressing ambiguous, conflicting demands. As Mary S. Kosh and Harold Kerzner observe, project managers sometimes face conflicting demands from people above and below them, e.g., more or less. Some factors contributing to these circumstances include: reliance on the control of resources to line management, need for other people to accomplish specific objectives, and no authority over resources.[41]

These and other stressful situations also affect team members. They usually face the same conditions relayed by project managers. Then add stress on them and burn out will hit sooner or later. Some common symptoms of burn out include an inability to focus, complacency, and carelessness.

While conditions may add to problems for adapting to change, so do psychological factors. For example, some people feel angst or fear when confronted with change. Or, they are unable to tolerate the ambiguity accompanied by change.

It is very important, therefore, that leaders in general and project managers in particular must consider, and perhaps emphasize, the psychology of change. Project managers often focus too much on the financial and technical at the expense of other issues. It is the other issues, e.g., people considerations, which can mean the difference between success and failure.[42]

## Change Is a Learning Experience

Change is constant, but the experience that comes with it is always changing because each situation is somewhat unique. Rarely can a paint-by-numbers routine work when a change is large and complex. It then requires considerable learning as people respond to it. The best way to go about learning is to modify, even change, their current mindsets or paradigm. Managers must adopt a different paradigm, which involves the recognition that people have an incomplete knowledge base and, therefore, require the need to work collaboratively.[43]

Treating change as a learning experience does not come to leaders or managers very easily because of the "blame game," which looks at others for the cause of a problem when the fault may be internal and not with others at all. Managers often receive erroneous feedback about people who work for them.[44]

Another reason that change is not treated as a learning experience is because many project managers, largely due to the technical expertise, are not used to ambiguity that accompanies experiencing change. In *Project Management,* David Hawk and Karlos Artto note that project managers deal more comfortably with decisions that pertain to narrow topics, even if they are potentially wrong, than ambiguous issues requiring decisions that have a reasonable probability of being right.[45]

Team members also face pressure not to treat change as a learning experience. There is often more patience exhibited for putting out fires with costly rework than exercising creative thinking that takes more time but has a lasting, less-costly effect. The rewards often, therefore, go to the people who take the routine, noncontroversial change during a project, e.g., complying with a rigid methodology or technology no matter how ineffective or costly. Emphasis goes to compliance over developing a creative solution that accommodates a cost-effective change.

This pressure to comply with methodology or technique can restrict adaptability to change. Hawk and Artto note that companies following project management disciplines need to adopt knowledge-based, flexible practices in order to adapt to changing circumstances.[46]

## ACTING ON CHANGE

If one fact touches the realities of change on projects, it is that it will not go away. Change will arrive in unpredictable ways and have unanticipated impacts. Project managers do not have to be at its mercy however. They can do the following.

## Be Responsive Rather than Reactive to Change

They must have a good understanding of the context of their projects and try to develop strategies to deal with unforeseen circumstances rather than wait for them. By doing so, they can anticipate and prepare themselves so "surprises" become the exception rather than the norm. This ability to size up context and respond to change efficiently and effectively reflects good leadership. In *The Fifth Discipline,* Peter Senge says that leadership involves assessing stakeholders and situations and developing appropriate strategies.[47]

Project managers, therefore, must be willing to forego the tendency towards perfection and, instead, use approximations to deal with change.[48] This behavior requires a paradigm shift because many project managers arrive via the technical ranks by learning to emphasize precision over approximation. Heuristics requires applying professional judgment that may mean making mistakes.

## Assess and Evaluate Change from a Big Picture Perspective

During the fog of project management, it is so easy to forget about the big picture when so much occurs. This is especially the case when change comes from all directions and at different levels. Emotions can run so high for stakeholders that people can feel overwhelmed. This situation, in turn, can fuel resistance to change. Ronald Heifetz and Marty Linsky observe that when the status quo is shaken for whatever reason, people experience loss and a sense of being incompetent. As a natural consequence, people then exhibit resistance towards the change and the change agent or both.[49]

It is imperative, therefore, that project managers maintain focus on the overall vision, treating it as a guiding light to devise and adjust strategies for their projects. Heifetz and Linsky also note that despite having a vision to guide actions, leadership requires performance from "moment to moment." Leaders must respond as circumstances arise.[50]

By keeping the focus on the big picture, project managers can find it easier for team members and other stakeholders to "stay the course" when changes pour in from all directions and have varying degrees of impact. They can evaluate changes from the perspective of a vision and the big picture. This will require that everyone, of course, develop a wide-angle perspective of their project as well as exercise their ability to focus on major change issues. Hence, their perspectives must not be only on individual and project levels, but also those at departmental, cross-functional, enterprise, and business environment levels. Everyone can then exercise what Bernard J. Mohr calls "response-ability," which he defines as being able to understand the concerns of people and develop innovative solutions.[51]

## Build Resilience in Yourself and Others

Resilience in the face of change is difficult to maintain if considerable adversity occurs. Yet, adversity can be an effective way to build resolve and to deal with endless changes. In fact, it can turn project managers into project leaders. However, project managers must not only build resilience in themselves, they must also build it in others and can do so by engendering an environment that encourages team members to build equivalent resilience, perhaps a much harder task than building their own.

To build such an environment, project managers must have a good understanding of people's capacities to tolerate change and adversity. Paul Stoltz identifies three capacities that relate to coping with adversity: required, existing, and accessed. Required capacity is what is needed to address the world's needs; existing, the complete set of skills and talents that a person possesses; and accessed, what portion of that capacity is actually employed. All three interplay to give people the opportunity to cope with adversity in some way, thereby reflecting a pattern of how they respond to adversity. In fact, it reflects the response patterns that a person exhibits when confronted with events. These patterns, in turn, affect future performance and behavior.

The keys to building resilience are providing an environment conducive for taking risks, encouraging people to embrace change, and stressing the need to remain positive. These are based on the qualities of people having a high adversity quotient, or AQ.

Building resilience is not just for individuals. According to Stoltz, teams can also have an AQ. The AQ value of a team will have a considerable influence on effectiveness. Stoltz writes that when adversity grows in magnitude, it affects what a team does and how it does it. AQ affects all activities from problem solving to information gathering. A team demonstrates its AQ during uncertain, chaotic circumstances. Obviously, as with individuals, a team with a high AQ exhibits focus and determination.[52] The keys to building resilience are much the same as for individuals.

## Recognize and Deal with the Tolls of Change

Do not ignore or run from them. As leaders, project managers view change as a means to further achieve a vision. They manage change, therefore, rather than being managed by it, putting it into perspective for themselves and others. If circumstances appear to be crumbling, Kouzes and Posner note that it is at that time that leaders must articulate a vision for leading out of a world of uncertainty and chaos.[53]

Project managers, therefore, must turn change into an asset rather than a liability, especially from a human relations perspective, e.g., psychological and sociological. They prepare others to cope with change, e.g., having the capacity to adapt to it and to avoid ravages. Often, a failure to deal with change is not the change itself, however, but the inability to cope with the human impacts. This inability is reflected in communication breakdown, sloppy workmanship, and low morale, which translate into overall poor team performance.

They must, therefore, break down barriers to change on their teams, both formally and informally. Formal barriers are easily definable and changeable, e.g., procedures or schedules. Informal barriers are more challenging, e.g., informal networks, overcoming rigid mental models, preparing people to "step outside their shells."

## Establish an Infrastructure to Deal with Change

This infrastructure goes beyond establishing policies and procedures to manage change, e.g., to determine the priority and assess impacts. It also relates to establishing the "right atmosphere" to manage change that entails encouraging and sustaining an atmosphere of trust and open communication. People should be willing to discuss the who, what, when, where, why, and how of any change. They should also be willing to discuss the overall goal and whether a project can be effectively handled psychologically and sociologically. Trust plays an integral role because people will likely share information. Information sharing is especially important during dramatic change.

Project managers must also make an effort to build and sustain relationships with all the key stakeholders. These relationships often establish the "communication channels" for openly sharing information.

This infrastructure should also include adapting an overall framework to deal with change. It should include phases that encourage as much involvement and interaction as possible among people.

In *Transforming the Way We Work,* Marshall identifies five such phases that can be revised to suit any project management environment:

- Phase 1: Need and Commitment
- Phase 2: Preparing for Change
- Phase 3: Assessment, Alignment, and Plan
- Phase 4: Managing Implementation
- Phase 5: Self-Sufficiency and Renewal

What is interesting about this approach is that it stresses less mechanics and more building trust and relationships that are so important to manage change and lower resistance to it. Emphasis is on collaboration rather than competition.[54]

The infrastructure should address other areas, too, and one of them is giving people a sense of control over change when it arrives. This requires the ability to assess change as well as to develop an effective action plan. Of course, this cannot occur without open communication and relationships. Project managers must develop, even out of necessity, an action plan when project control has deteriorated. This action plan is in response to a need to maintain value, support, and morale and at the core of doing so, establishes and maintains open communication with stakeholders.[55]

## Keep the Focus on the Psychology of Change

In the end, it all matters how people think and feel about change. Regardless of whether or not a change is a good idea, if the key players do not think it is valuable and feel it is too uncomfortable, they will never implement a change.

Project managers should focus on the psychology and sociology of change, therefore, not just the technology. That means maintaining and stressing the need for balanced perspectives, being ever mindful of answering questions like:

- Who will exhibit resistance?
- What's in it for me (WIIFM)?
- Who will lose? Who will gain?
- How does a change fit within the overall vision? For an entire organization?
- What are the best ways to communicate the answers to these questions?[56]

It also means identifying the major roles in any change implementation: change sponsor, agent, target, and advocate. The sponsor is the executive or senior manager who supports a change; from a project management perspective, it is a stakeholder to whom a project manager reports. The target is the recipient of a change; often it is the project team or people in the customer ranks. Advocates are people, e.g., members of a steering committee, who advocate change but cannot or will not do anything to support it; often these people come from higher levels in a cross-functional environment.

Project managers must constantly relate on a change-by-change basis with each member participating in those roles. Not only must project managers manage their relationships with each other, they must also deal with the relationships among the others, e.g., between advocates and sponsors.

All roles are important, however, I believe the most important ones are the agents. They are the people who make change happen (although all four to one degree or another play that role). These people are pathfinders who feel committed enough to make a change happen, even before seemingly insurmountable odds. They are the true believers who take the initiative and exercise the necessary zeal and creativity.

Once change becomes acceptable to some extent by stakeholders, project managers must encourage a sense of urgency. Saying that something is a good idea and getting to it later will not make much progress; sooner or later any change will die due to lack of passionate commitment. Project managers can build a sense of urgency by positioning change to further a key goal, establish and follow up on measurable ways to determine progress, hold people accountable for its implementation, and provide the necessary psychological and physical support.

## Encourage Commitment, Ownership, and Accountability when Responding to Change

What project managers need is more than a tacit expression to implement a change. They need a strong emotional tie between people and the change itself. This emotional involvement can be handled by way of ownership and accountability regarding a change, thereby getting the desired level of commitment.

This tie between ownership and accountability has been stressed in many leadership books. This emphasis on creating a sense of ownership, despite all the diatribes about empowerment and delegation, rarely happens, resulting in a loss of shared purpose. Sadly, current organizations rely on compelling people to behave in a certain way.[57]

How can emotional commitment be generated?

Project managers must first involve people in planning for a change. Through participation comes a sense of ownership and accountability because people become emotionally invested. Kouzes and Posner note that providing choice makes it more difficult to back out because of the physical and psychological investment that will occur.[58] Bennis agrees and notes that change is most successful when those affected are involved in the planning.[59]

Project managers must also encourage collaboration when implementing a change. Through collaboration, people will hold each other accountable for following through on promised contributions. Project managers must structure their projects so that this occurs by emphasizing the need to share information, tie dependencies among tasks, obtain involvement and concurrence of key stakeholders for a particular change, and keep focus on the overall vision. Most importantly, they must concentrate on the communication structure to enhance mutual accountability and ownership. Using an approach to change depends on the communication patterns within a group before implementing a change.[60]

## Demonstrate and Support Risk Taking

If project managers expect people to embrace change, they must exhibit the very same desired qualities, which definitely includes the ability to take risks.

Taking risks is difficult for just about everyone because it involves leaping into the unknown, which can result in loss, rejection, and loss of control. Above all, it involves fear. In *Risking,* David Viscott says that a false sense of security, based on anachronistic beliefs and values, hinders one's desire or ability for risk taking.[61]

Project managers must take the first step to embrace risk, especially if associated with change. In other words, they must model risk taking and then engender a climate that encourages risk taking by others, e.g., eliminating penalties for failure, building resilience, and encouraging an atmosphere of creativity and innovation.

Some ways that project managers can encourage risk taking is to adopt approaches that challenge the modus operandi, ask penetrating questions that challenge core values, reward people who take on change regardless of the possibility of success or failure, and embrace diversity in thinking.

The bottom line is that project managers must be open to risk taking if they expect others to do the same. Otherwise, uncertainty associated with risk taking can be quite paralyzing. So project managers must be open to new ideas, be willing to experiment, and face positive and negative consequences.

## Encourage and Apply Creative, Innovative Solutions

This step ties directly with risk taking. Unfortunately, like risk taking, it is harder to do than to talk about. Often times, like risk taking, people have to be encouraged to be creative because, as Tom Peters notes in *The Circle of Innovation,* creativity jolts people "out of their comfort zones."[62] However, creativity does not just happen, since it involves people listening to their intuition and largely acting spontaneously. That is why project managers must lay the groundwork in the following ways to encourage creativity, such as tolerate experimentation, give visibility to creative people and their solutions, and provide an environment of trust and open communication.

Of course, creativity is not just for individuals. Teams can also be creative, contrary to popular belief. Project managers can play a key role in encouraging creativity much the same way John Kao describes as a jam session in jazz. In

*Jamming,* Kao writes that leaders provide direction, inspiration, and facilitation and behavior similar to game masters.[63]

They orchestrate it in such a way to ensure that there is enough discipline while simultaneously allowing enough freedom so creativity can flow. Kao further notes that managers must identify what he calls the "sweet spot" between systems and analysis in carte blanche creativity.[64]

It also involves giving people sufficient autonomy while simultaneously keeping them ever mindful of being a team member. In *Organizing Genius,* Bennis and Patricia Biederman write that the best atmosphere for creativity is a blend of autonomy and concentration on a focused goal.[65]

Creativity is critical for managing nonroutine change. Individuals and teams must take risks by experimenting in thought and action. Project managers lay the groundwork for that to occur.

That is not an easy task for project managers because they and others also face internal roadblocks to being creative. In *Conceptual Blockbusting,* James Adams calls them "perceptual blocks," which are obstacles that prevent a person from hearing a clear perception of a problem and related information. Some examples of perceptual blocks include emotional, cultural, environmental, intellectual, and expressive blocks.[66]

To overcome the blocks, project managers must apply a wide range of creative tools and techniques to think outside the box in order to deal with change. These tools and techniques include brainstorming, listening to one's own intuition, and applying analogous and visual thinking.

Even more importantly, individuals and teams alike should understand the creative process that flows in five stages: problem identification, information gathering, incubation, insight, insight validation.[67]

## PROJECT MANAGER = RISK TAKER

By the very nature of their career path, project managers must be risk takers who have a high tolerance for applying creative approaches by themselves and through others. Effective managers seek creativity in people and apply it to increasingly challenging circumstances. By doing so, these managers encourage risk taking in themselves and others.

Project managers and change, therefore, are made for each other. The minute they lead a project change happens, from start to finish. When change arrives, project managers need to decide whether to respond or react. If they respond, chances increase dramatically that they and their team members will develop a solution that augments team performance. If they react, the chances increase dramatically that they and their team members will develop short-term fixes that lead to long-term problems that will be costlier to address even beyond a project life cycle.

The key is for project managers to place change in the right perspective for themselves and the people they lead. That means change should be something to capitalize on to move their projects forward, thereby dramatically increasing the odds for project successes.

## CASE STUDY: RESPOND

Scope creep haunts just about every type of project in many different issues. Failure to manage scope creep can result in considerable dysfunctional behavior. The project manager knew that managing change was essential because everything on a project was in flux.

An infrastructure was established, therefore, to manage changes to all baselines related to cost, schedule, and quality. A change board was formed consisting of key stakeholders who met periodically to evaluate change and develop a deployment plan. The project manager also constantly communicated the status of each change on a web site and continuously solicited feedback on the effectiveness of a change on implementation.

Throughout the project, every effort was made to identify and evaluate changes holistically. That was done by encouraging the change board to view changes from the perspective of meeting the vision for the project. Unless absolutely necessary, the project manager avoided the tendency of many project managers to simply look for a silver bullet or add more resources to accommodate a change; more was not always better.

Of course, the project manager realized that not all change would be submitted to the change board. Therefore, through stakeholder participation, criteria were established to determine what went to the change board. The criteria were posted to the web site so everyone could reference them.

The project manager also knew that change had a psychological as well as physical component, e.g., cost impact. By involving people in submitting a change and determining its disposition, their resistance to change was lowered because they felt that they had a "say" on what affected them.

Not all change, of course, comes before a change board. More often, it does not. Instead, one or more individuals frequently handle change. Consequently, the project manager laid the groundwork to enable team members to be more creative by removing obstacles from daily decision making, determining whether or not a change should be submitted to a change board, and supporting those people who took unique approaches to deal with routine issues and problems.

By providing the opportunity for people to deal with issues directly, they were able to gain a sense of ownership and accountability.

## REFERENCES

1. Warren Bennis, *On Becoming a Leader,* Perseus Books, Reading, MA, 1989, p. 45.
2. James M. Kouzes and Barry Z. Posner, *The Leadership Challenge,* Jossey-Bass, San Francisco, 1987, p. 33.
3. Ibid., p. 8.
4. Ibid., p. 32.
5. John Kotter, Leading change, *2002 Linkage Excellence in Management* (seminar), pp. 8–9.
6. James M. Kouzes and Barry Z. Posner, *The Leadership Challenge,* Jossey-Bass, San Francisco, 1987, p. 33.
7. Ibid., p. 32.
8. William Cohen, *The Art of the Leader,* Prentice Hall, Englewood Cliffs, NJ, 1990, p. 26.
9. Warren Bennis and Burt Nanus, *Leaders,* Perennial Library, New York, 1985, p. 67.
10. James M. Kouzes and Barry Z. Posner, *The Leadership Challenge,* Jossey-Bass, San Francisco, 1987, p. 60.
11. Ibid., p. 69.
12. Warren G. Bennis and Robert J. Thomas, Crucibles of leadership, *Harvard Business Review,* p. 45, September 2002.
13. Rodney D. Stroope and Frank G. Jenes, In search of the innovative project manager: the human side, in *Proceedings of the Project Management Institute Seminar/ Symposium,* October 8–10, 1984, Philadelphia, PA, Project Management Institute, Newtown Square, PA, p. 88.
14. James M. Kouzes and Barry Z. Posner, *The Leadership Challenge,* Jossey-Bass, San Francisco, 1987, p. 37.
15. Ibid., p. 71.
16. John Kotter, Leading change, *2002 Linkage Excellence in Management* (seminar), pp. 16–17.
17. Warren Bennis, *On Becoming a Leader,* Perseus Books, Reading, MA, 1989, p. 104.
18. John Kenney, Effective project management for strategic innovation and change in an organizational context, *Project Management Journal,* p. 46, March 2003.
19. Warren Bennis, *On Becoming a Leader,* Perseus Books, Reading, MA, 1989, p. 41.
20. Tom Peters, *The Circle of Innovation,* Vintage Books, New York, 1999, p. 85.
21. John Kenney, Effective project management for strategic innovation and change in an organizational contest, *Project Management Journal,* p. 45, March 2003.
22. Tom Peters, *The Pursuit of Wow!,* Vintage Books, New York, 1994, p. 82.
23. Adrian Abramovici, Controlling scope creep, *PM Network,* p. 48, January 2000.
24. Daniel H. Kim, Drifting goals: the challenge of conflicting priorities, *The Systems Thinker,* p. 7, November 1999.

25. Virginia Anderson, Introducing the system archetypes: the fixes that fail, *The Systems Thinker,* p. 7, March 1999.
26. Tom Peters, *The Pursuit of Wow!,* Vintage Books, New York, 1994, p. 81.
27. David L. Hawk and Karlos Artto, Factors impeding project management learning, *Project Management,* 5(1), 62, 1999.
28. Paul G. Stoltz, *Adversity Quotient @ Work,* William Morrow, New York, 2000, p. 37.
29. Ibid., pp. 1–20.
30. Diana Lilla, Project managers must serve as change agents, *ESI Horizons,* pp. 1–3, February 2002.
31. Arnoud De Meyer, Christoph H. Loch, and Michael T. Pich, Managing project uncertainty: from variation to chaos, *MIT Sloan Management Review,* pp. 60–65, Winter 2002.
32. James M. Kouzes and Barry Z. Posner, *The Leadership Challenge,* Jossey-Bass, San Francisco, 1987, p. 59.
33. Stefan C. Gueldenberg and Werner H. Hoffmann, Evolutionary leadership: a dynamic approach to managing complexity, *The Systems Thinker,* pp. 2–5, November 2001.
34. Peter R. Scholtes, *The Team Handbook,* Joiner Associates, Madison, WI, 1990, pp. 1-20 to 1-21.
35. James M. Kouzes and Barry Z. Posner, *The Leadership Challenge,* Jossey-Bass, San Francisco, 1987, p. 224.
36. Daniel Kim, Drifting goals: the challenge of conflicting priorities, *The Systems Thinker,* p. 7, November 1999.
37. Ibid.
38. Paul Hersey and Kenneth H. Blanchard, *Management of Organizational Behavior,* 6th ed., Prentice Hall, Englewood Cliffs, NJ, 1993, p. 371.
39. Ibid.
40. John W. Gardner, *On Leadership,* The Free Press, New York, 1990, p. 124.
41. Mary S. Kosh and Harold Kerzner, Stress and burnout in project management, in *Proceedings of the Project Management Institute Seminar/Symposium,* October 8–10, 1984, Philadelphia, PA, Project Management Institute, Newtown Square, PA, pp. 125–126.
42. Rick Maurer, Weeding out resistance to change, *PM Network,* p. 47, June 1998.
43. Dori Digneti, Collaborative learning: real-time practice for knowledge generation, *The Systems Thinker,* p. 1, June/July 2000.
44. John Sterman, Superstitious learning, *The Systems Thinker,* p. 4, June/July 1997.
45. David L. Hawk and Karlos Artto, Factors impeding project management learning, *Project Management,* 5(1), 57, 1999.
46. Ibid.
47. Peter M. Senge, *The Fifth Discipline,* Currency Doubleday, New York, 1990, p. 344.
48. Rodney D. Stroope and Frank G. Jenes, In search of the innovative project manager: the human side, in Proceedings of the *Project Management Institute Seminar/Symposium,* October 8–10, 1984, Philadelphia, PA, Project Management Institute, Newtown Square, PA, p. 88.

49. Ronald A. Heifetz and Marty Linsky, A survival guide for leaders, *Harvard Business Review,* p. 66, June 2002.
50. Ibid.
51. Bernard J. Mohr, Appreciative inquiry: igniting transformative action, *The Systems Thinker,* p. 1, February 2001.
52. Ibid., p. 210.
53. James M. Kouzes and Barry Z. Posner, *The Leadership Challenge,* Jossey-Bass, San Francisco, 1987, p. 71.
54. Edward M. Marshall, *Transforming the Way We Work,* Amacom, New York, 1995, pp. 140–164.
55. Richard W. Bailey, Six steps to project recovery, *PM Network,* p. 33, May 2000.
56. John Kotter, Leading change, *2002 Linkage Excellence in Management* (seminar), p. 23.
57. Dee Hock, The nature and creation of chaordic organizations, *The Systems Thinker,* p. 1, April 2000.
58. James M. Kouzes and Barry Z. Posner, *The Leadership Challenge,* Jossey-Bass, San Francisco, 1987, p. 226.
59. Warren Bennis, *Why Leaders Can't Lead,* Jossey-Bass, San Francisco, 1989, pp. 147–151.
60. Paul Hersey and Kenneth H. Blanchard, *Management of Organizational Behavior,* 6th ed., Prentice Hall, Englewood Cliffs, NJ, 1993, p. 378.
61. David Viscott, *Risking,* Pocket Books, New York, 1979, p. 19.
62. Tom Peters, *The Circle of Innovation,* Vintage Books, New York, 1999, p. 385.
63. John Kao, *Jamming,* HarperBusiness, New York, 1997, p. 19.
64. Ibid., p. 41.
65. Warren Bennis and Patricia W. Biederman, *Organizing Genius,* Addison-Wesley, Reading, MA, 1997, p. 20.
66. James L. Adams, *Conceptual Blockbusting,* 2nd ed., W.W. Norton, New York, 1979, pp. 13–37.
67. Philip A. Himmelfarb, *Survival of the Fittest,* Prentice Hall, Englewood Cliffs, NJ, 1992, pp. 172–174.

# 13

# FINAL THOUGHTS

I will say it again. Industry does not need any more project managers. What it needs is more project leaders. Although the tools, techniques, and disciplines of project management are valuable contributors to the success of any project, they are only one part of the story. The other part is getting a group of people to focus their energies to accomplish a common vision. Project leadership is the means to make that happen.

Leadership, however, does not reside in one person. Instead, like creativity, it is within everyone, whether the person is a project sponsor, project manager, or some other stakeholder. Whatever their role, everyone can contribute as a leader by performing the patterns of action identified in this book.

## REASONS

There is a reason why I described each pattern with an active verb. An active verb implies action and results. Action, in turn, implies energy and results imply something purposeful. Leadership is all about action, transformative action as Burns would say, for achieving meaningful results.

I use the word pattern for a reason too. A pattern does not always apply 100 percent of the time, but most of the time. To determine the appropriate pattern requires judgment and experience by the leader; otherwise, he or she is simply performing steps to get something done; one does not have to be a leader to do that; little or no thinking or judgment is required. Leadership, by its very nature, however, requires moving forward into the unknown to achieve certain results. That requires thinking and judgment, distinguishing it from repetitive, unenlightened work. Leaders, you may recall, do the right things; managers do things right.

## THE UNKNOWN

Project managers, consequently, must be leaders because they are constantly looking and moving into the unknown and must influence people to follow them. The very nature of projects demands leadership.

Project managers as leaders, however, must learn to *shift* their view of what is required on a project. They need to take a more balanced perspective by looking at a project, for example, as something that requires more than planning, organizing, and controlling. They also need to view it as a people-intensive endeavor whereby all human energies are focused on achieving a common vision. This shift requires looking at projects more critically and less as something of an opportunity to apply a tool or technique.

They must also learn to *visualize* the direction for the project. They must do so, however, in a way that is meaningful to others as well as to themselves. This visualization cannot happen in a vacuum; it requires involvement by the very people who must make it a reality.

Project managers also *integrate.* They must put all they know into a cohesive whole. This requires them to look at all the key elements, from objects to relationships, and determine their degree of importance to achieve the vision for the project. They must also be able to explain it to others so everyone can see the big picture.

They must *understand* the context of their projects. They need to understand the entire circumstances surrounding their projects, to include major issues and stakeholders, to lead effectively. A solid contextual understanding lays the groundwork for effective decision making throughout the project life cycle.

Project managers must *decide* when the circumstances warrant it. They must be willing to make decisions at key moments even when available information is sparse and contradictory. Failure to make a decision at a key moment can bring the most ambitious project to a halt. The capacity and willingness of a project manager to make a decision at a key moment does not excuse being arbitrary and capricious. Rather, it means weighing circumstances and consulting with others to make an effective decision, e.g., one achieving expected results.

They must *motivate,* themselves and others. Project managers need to constantly remind themselves that in order to complete a project, they must do so through other people. However, they often lack formal, functional power and that limits their ability to command obedience or compliance. They must look for ways, therefore, to blend individual and project needs so that a Win–Win result becomes the norm.

Project managers must *team,* that is, encourage people to work together while pursuing a common goal. They should encourage other people to do so in a way that complements each others' strengths and compensates for each others' weaknesses. The idea is that project managers must create a team that is akin to an alloy, whereby the individual elements are not as strong than when combined.

They must *communicate* with all stakeholders in a way that satisfies needs. Their communication must be ongoing with the contents refreshed continuously. They need to provide more information and less data, the former being meaningful to the recipient. The best way to determine that is to listen more and talk less.

They must *respond.* They must constantly have their pulse on the circumstances surrounding their projects to avoid reacting. The idea is that they must take the initiative or seize the momentum for their projects so that everyone feels, or at least appears to feel, in control. Key ingredients to make that happen are for project managers and others to maintain focus on the vision, have the ability to manage change, and encourage involvement and initiative by everyone.

Project managers must *trust* themselves and others. They should expect everyone, including themselves, to follow the "high road" in dealings, positive and negative. Failure to demonstrate trust in others generates distrust, in turn, from others. It also means that project managers should act ethically and with integrity and expect the same of others. The bottom line is that the credibility of everyone on a project is at stake and, once lost, trust is gone.

## PATTERNS OF LEADERSHIP

The patterns of project leadership are not laws; performing them does not guarantee success. However, they are quite evident — most of the time — on projects that succeed and are often quite clearly lacking on the ones that fail.

In the end, patterns of leadership do not just happen. They need to be demonstrated through application. It is this demonstrative behavior that separates the project leader from the project manager.

# BIBLIOGRAPHY

## BOOKS

Abrashoff, D. Michael, *It's Your Ship,* Warner Books, New York, 2002.

Adams, James L., *Conceptual Blockbusting,* 2nd ed., W.W. Norton, New York, 1979.

Bailey, James, *After Thought,* Basic Books, New York, 1996.

Barker, Joel A., *Paradigms,* HarperBusiness, New York, 1993.

Bennis, Warren, *On Becoming a Leader,* Perseus Books, Reading, MA, 1989.

Bennis, Warren, *Why Leaders Can't Lead,* Jossey-Bass, San Francisco, 1989.

Bennis, Warren and Biederman, Patricia W., *Organizing Genius,* Addison-Wesley, Reading, MA, 1997.

Bennis, Warren and Nanus, Burt, *Leaders,* Perennial Library, New York, 1985.

Benton, Douglas A., *Applied Human Relations,* 6th ed., Prentice Hall, Englewood Cliffs, NJ, 1998.

Berryman-Fink, Cynthia, *The Manager's Desk Reference,* Amacom, New York, 1989.

Blake, Robert R. and McCanse, Anne A., *Leadership Dilemmas — Grid Solutions,* Gulf, Houston, TX, 1991.

Block, Peter, *Stewardship,* Berrett-Koehler, San Francisco, 1993.

Block, Robert, *The Politics of Projects,* Yourdon Press, New York, 1983.

Bolton, Robert, *People Skills,* Touchstone, New York, 1986.

Boyett, Joseph H. and Boyett, Jimmie T., *The Guru Guide,* John Wiley & Sons, New York, 1998.

Bradford, David L. and Cohen, Allan R., *Managing for Excellence,* John Wiley & Sons, New York, 1984.

Bramson, Robert M., *Coping with Difficult People,* Dell, New York, 1981.

Briner, Wendy, Geddes, Michael, and Hastings, Colin, *Project Leadership,* Gower, Aldershot, Hampshire, U.K., 1990.

Burns, James M., *Leadership,* Harper & Row, New York, 1979.

Capra, Fritjof, *The Tao of Physics,* Bantam Books, Toronto, 1984.

Capra, Fritjof, *The Web of Life,* Flamingo, New York, 1997.

Capra, Fritjof, *The Turning Point,* Bantam Books, Toronto, 1988.

Cohen, William A., *The Art of the Leader,* Prentice Hall, Englewood Cliffs, NJ, 1990.

Connor, Daryl R., *Managing at the Speed of Change,* Villard, New York, 1992.

Covey, Stephen R., *Principle-Centered Leadership,* Summit Books, New York, 1991.

Covey, Stephen R., Merrill, A. Roger, and Merrill, Rebecca R., *First Things First,* Simon & Schuster, New York, 1994.

Covey, Stephen R., *The Seven Habits of Highly Effective People,* Simon & Schuster, New York, 1990.

Csikszentmihalyi, Mihaly, *Flow,* HarperPerennial, New York, 1990.

Damasio, Antonio, *Descartes' Errors,* Avon Books, New York, 1994.

De Bono, Edward, *Lateral Thinking,* Perennial Library, New York, 1990.

De Bono, Edward, *Practical Thinking,* Penguin Books, London, 1971.

De Bono, Edward, *Six Thinking Hats,* Little, Brown, Boston, 1985.

De Pree, Max, *Leadership Jazz,* Dell, New York, 1992.

De Pree, Max, *Leadership Is an Art,* Dell, New York, 1989.

Donnelly, James H., Gibson, James L., and Ivancevich, John M., *Fundamentals of Management,* Business Publications, Plano, TX, 1981.

Dorner, Dietrich, *The Logic of Failure,* Perseus Books, Cambridge, MA, 1996.

Fisher, Roger and Ury, William, *Getting to Yes,* Penguin Books, New York, 1988.

Gardner, Howard, *Frames of Mind,* Basic Books, New York, 1993.

Gardner, Howard, *Multiple Intelligences,* Basic Books, New York, 1993.

Gardner, John W., *On Leadership,* The Free Press, New York, 1990.

Gawain, Shakti, *Creative Visualization,* Bantam Books, Toronto, 1985.

George, Jill A. and Wilson, Jeannette M., *Team Members Survival Guide,* McGraw-Hill, New York, 1997.

Goleman, Daniel, Boyatzis, Richard, and McKee, Annie, *Primal Leadership,* Harvard Business School Press, Boston, 2002.

Goleman, Daniel, *Emotional Intelligence,* Bantam Books, New York, 1995.

Gordon, Thomas, *Leader Effectiveness Training (L.E.T.),* Bantam Books, Toronto, 1980.

Handy, Charles B., *Understanding Organizations,* Penguin Books, New York, 1986.

Hartman, Taylor, *The Color Code,* Fireside Books, New York, 1998.

Herrmann, Ned, *The Whole Brain Book,* McGraw-Hill, New York, 1996.

Hersey, Paul and Blanchard, Kenneth H., *Management of Organizational Behavior,* Prentice Hall, Englewood Cliffs, NJ, 1992.

Hersey, Paul and Blanchard, Kenneth H., *Management of Organizational Behavior,* 6th ed., Prentice Hall, Englewood Cliffs, NJ, 1993.

Hesselbein, Frances, Goldsmith, Marshall, and Somerville, Iain, Eds., *Leading Beyond the Walls,* Jossey-Bass, San Francisco, 1999.

Himmelfarb, Philip A., *Survival of the Fittest,* Prentice Hall, Englewood Cliffs, NJ, 1992.

Kao, John, *Jamming,* HarperBusiness, New York, 1997.

Katzenbach, Jon R. and Smith, Douglas K., *The Wisdom of Teams,* Harvard Business School Press, Boston, 1993.

Kaye, Beverly and Jordan-Evans, Sharon, *Love 'Em or Lose 'Em,* Berrett-Koehler, San Francisco, 1999.

Keirsey, David and Bates, Marilyn, *Please Understand Me,* Prometheus Nemesis, Del Mar, CA, 1984.

Kerzner, Harold, *Project Management,* Van Nostrand Reinhold, New York, 1995.

Kliem, Ralph L. and Anderson, Harris B., *The Organizational Engineering Approach to Project Management,* St. Lucie Press, Boca Raton, FL, 2003.

Kliem, Ralph L., *The People Side of Project Management,* Gower, Aldershot, Hampshire, U.K., 1992.

Kliem, Ralph L., *The Project Manager's Emergency Kit,* St. Lucie Press, Boca Raton, FL, 2003.

Kouzes, James M. and Posner, Barry Z., *The Leadership Challenge,* Jossey-Bass, San Francisco, 1987.

Kouzes, James M. and Posner, Barry Z., *Credibility,* Jossey-Bass, San Francisco, 1993.

Kuhn, Thomas, *The Structure of Scientific Revolutions,* University of Chicago Press, Chicago, 1970.

Land, George and Jarman, Beth, *Breakpoint and Beyond,* HarperBusiness, New York, 1993.

Leavitt, Harold J., *Corporate Pathfinders,* Penguin Books, New York, 1987.

Marshall, Edward M., *Transforming the Way We Work,* Amacom, New York, 1995.

Maslow, Abraham H., *Toward a Psychology of Being,* 2nd ed., Van Nostrand, Princeton, NJ, 1968.

Mitroff, Ian, *Smart Thinking for Crazy Times,* Berrett-Koehler, San Francisco, 1998.

Nierenberg, Gerard I., *The Art of Creative Thinking,* Cornerstone Library, New York, 1982.

Nirenberg, Jesse S., *Getting Through to People, Reward Books,* Englewood Cliffs, NJ, 1979.

Nutt, Paul C., *Why Decisions Fail,* Berrett-Koehler, San Francisco, 2002.

Palmer, Helen, *The Enneagram,* HarperSanFrancisco, San Francisco, 1991.

Peters, Tom, *The Circle of Innovation,* Vintage Books, New York, 1999.

Peters, Tom, *The Project 50,* Knopf, New York, 1999.

Peters, Tom, *The Pursuit of Wow!,* Vintage Books, New York, 1994.

Pinto, Jeffrey K. and Trailer, Jeffrey W., *Leadership Skills for Project Managers,* Project Management Institute, Newtown Square, PA, 1998.

Pitcher, Patricia, *The Drama of Leadership,* John Wiley & Sons, New York, 1997.

Project Management Institute, *Proceedings of the PMI Research Conference 2002,* Newtown Square, PA.

Project Management Institute, *Proceedings of the Project Management Institute Seminar/Symposium,* October 8–10, 1984, Philadelphia, PA.

Ritchey, Tom and Axelrod, Alan, *I'm Stuck, You're Stuck,* Berrett-Koehler, San Francisco, 2002.

Roberts, Wess, *Leadership Secrets of Attila the Hun,* Warner Books, New York, 1987.

Russo, J. Edward and Schoemaker, Paul J.H., *Decision Traps,* Fireside Books, New York, 1989.

Sapadin, Linda with Maguire, Jack, *It's About Time!,* Penguin Books, New York, 1997.

Scholtes, Peter R., *The Team Handbook,* Joiner Associates, Madison, WI, 1990.

Schultz, Duane P., *Psychology and Industry Today,* Macmillan, New York, 1978.

Senge, Peter M., *The Fifth Discipline,* Currency Doubleday, New York, 1990.

Stoltz, Paul G., *Adversity Quotient @ Work,* William Morrow, New York, 2000.

Tubbs, Stewart L., *A Systems Approach to Small Group Interaction,* 6th ed., McGraw-Hill, Boston, 1997.

Tubbs, Stewart L. and Moss, Sylvia, *Human Communications,* 8th ed., McGraw-Hill, Boston, 2000.

Vaill, Peter B., *Spirited Learning and Leading,* Jossey-Bass, San Francisco, 1998.

Viscott, David, *Risking,* Pocket Books, New York, 1979.

Waterman, Peter H., *The Renewal Factor,* Bantam Books, Toronto, 1988.

Wheatley, Margaret J., *Leadership and the New Science,* Berrett-Koehler, San Francisco, 1994.

Whyte, David, *The Heart Aroused,* Currency Doubleday, New York, 1994.

Wonder, Jacquelyn and Donovan, Priscilla, *Whole Brain Thinking,* Ballantine Books, New York, 1984.

# ARTICLES, SEMINARS, AND PRESENTATIONS

2002 Research Report from Canadian Manufacturers and Exporters, *PM Network,* March 2003.

Abramovici, Adrian, Controlling scope creep, *PM Network,* January 2000.

Abrashoff, Michael D., Playing to win: ten principles of grassroots leadership, *Seminar for Living Leadership,* 2003.

Ackoff, Russell L., Systems thinking and thinking systems, *System Dynamics Review,* Summer–Fall 1994.

Anderson, Virginia, Introducing the system archetypes: the fixes that fail, *The Systems Thinker,* March 1999.

Anderson, Virginia, Introducing the systems archetypes: escalation, *The Systems Thinker,* August 1999.

Astrong, Diane M., Lee, Yang W., and Wang, Richard Y., 10 Potholes in the road to information quality, *Computer,* August 1997.

Bailey, Richard W., Six steps to project recovery, *PM Network,* May 2000.

Baker, Bud, Communication, commitment, and the management of meaning, *PM Network,* December 1997.

Bartolome, Fernando, Nobody trusts the boss completely — now what?, *Harvard Business Review,* March–April 1989.

Belzer, Kate, http://www.pmforum.org/library/papers/BusinessSuccess.htm

Bemoski, Karen, What makes American teams tick?, *Quality Progress,* January 1995.

Bennis, Warren G. and Thomas, Robert J., Crucibles of leadership, *Harvard Business Review,* September 2002.

Bergmann, Horst, Hurson, Kathleen, and Russ-Eft, Darlene, Introducing a grass-roots model of leadership, *Strategy & Leadership,* October–December 1999.

Boedecker, Ray, Communications: the project manager's essential tool, *PM Network,* December 1997.

Borgiani, Fred, Stakeholder's support: the key to getting your ideas implemented, *PM Network,* February 1998.

Cabanis, Jeannette, Passion beats planning, limiting scope is stupid, women rule..., *PM Network,* September 1998.

Cabanis-Brewin, Jeannette, The human task of a project leader, *PM Network,* November 1999.

Cafasso, Rosemary, Few IS projects come in on time, *Computerworld,* December 1994.

Caudron, Shari, Strategies for managing creative workers, *Personnel Journal,* December 1994.

Caudron, Shari, The hard case for soft skills, *Workforce,* July 1999.

Chalfin, Natalie, Four reasons why projects fail, *PM Network,* June 1998.

Chandler, Robert C., The marks of a leader, *Contingency Planning and Management,* September–October 2001.

Constantine, Larry, Lessons in leadership, *Corporate Developer's Survival Guide,* 1999.

Cooper, Robert K. and Sawaf, Ayman, *Executive EQ, Audio-Tech Book Summaries,* Willowbrook, IL, November, 1997 (Booklet).

Cross, Rob and Prusak, Laurence, The people who make organizations go — or stop, *Harvard Business Review,* June 2002.

Cunningham, Julia, Griffin, Ryan, Martin, Keith, and Violette, David J., Soft skills, hard numbers, *PM Network,* June 2002.

De Meyer, Arnoud, Loch, Christoph H., and Pich, Michael T., Managing project uncertainty: from variation to chaos, *MIT Sloan Management Review,* Winter 2002.

Denker, Stephen, McLaughlin, Hugh, Steward, Donald, and Browning, Tyson, Information-driven project management, *PM Network,* September 2001.

Dewhirst, H. Dudley, Project teams: what have we learned?, *PM Network,* April 1998.

Digneti, Dori, Collaborative learning: real-time practice for knowledge generation, *The Systems Thinker,* June/July 2000.

Do you see what I see?, *Projects at Work,* July–August 2002.

Druskat, Vanessa U. and Wolff, Steven B., Building the emotional intelligence of groups, *Harvard Business Review,* March 2001.

Dutton, Jane E., Frost, Peter J., Worline, Monica C., Lilius, Jacob M., and Kanov, Jason M., Leading in times of trauma, *Harvard Business Review,* January 2002.

Edgemon, Jim, Right stuff: how to recognize it when selecting a project manager, *Application Development Trends,* May 1995.

Emery, Dale H., Untangling communication, *STQE Magazine,* July/August 2001.

Eskerod, Pernille and Ostergren, Katarina, Why do companies standardize project work? *Project Management,* 6(1), 2000.

Fraser, Janice C., Groundwork for project success, *Web Techniques,* January 2002.

Gadeken, Owen C., Third wave project leadership, *PM Network,* February 1999.

Galford, Robert and Drapeau, Anne S., The enemies of trust, *Harvard Business Review,* February 2003.

Giuliano, Peter, Successful methods, *Successful Meetings,* July 2000.

Glass, Robert L., Short-term and long-term remedies for runaway projects, *Communications of the ACM,* July 1998.

Goleman, Daniel, What makes a leader?, *Harvard Business Review,* November–December 1998.

Goleman, Daniel, Leadership that gets results, *Harvard Business Review,* March–April 2000.

Gueldenberg, Stefan C. and Hoffman, Werner H., Evolutionary leadership: a dynamic approach to managing complexity, *The Systems Thinker,* November 2001.

Guynes, Steve, Prybutok, Victor, and Windsor, John, Data quality, *Data Management Review,* July/August 1996.

Hallowell, Edward M., The human moment at work, *Harvard Business Review,* January–February 1999.

Hammond, John S., Keeney, Ralph L., and Raifa, Howard, The hidden traps in decision making, *Harvard Business Review,* September–October 1998.

Harari, Oren, The dream team, *Management Review,* October 1995.

Hartman, Francis and Skulmoski, Greg, Quest for team competence, *Project Management,* 5(1), 1999.

Hartman, Lorne, A psychological analysis of leadership effectiveness, *Strategy & Leadership,* October–December 1999.

Hauschildt, Jurgen, Keim, Gesche, and Medcof, John W., Realistic criteria for project manager selection and development, *Project Management Journal,* September 2000.

Hawk, David L. and Artto, Karlos, Factors impeding project management learning, *Project Management,* 5(1), 1999.

Heifetz, Ronald A. and Linsky, Marty, A survival guide for leaders, *Harvard Business Review,* June 2002.

Hildebrand, Carol, Mapping the invisible workplace, *CIO Enterprise,* July 1998.

Hock, Dee, The nature and creation of chaordic organizations, *The Systems Thinker,* April 2000.

Hoenig, Christopher, Brave hearts, *CIO,* November 2000.

Hoffman, Edward J. and Laufer, Alexander, Emerging research into factors of project success and failure, PMI Research Conference 2002, July 15, Seattle, WA, pp. 1–30.

Hoffman, Edward J. and Laufer, Alexander, Stories of project leaders, PMI Research Conference 2002, July 15, Seattle, WA.

Humphrey, Watts S., Why projects fail, *Computerworld,* May 2002.

Hurwitz, Judith, The movable enterprise, *DBMS,* August 1996.

Jaskiel, Stefan, Checking out of the burnout ward, *STQE Magazine,* July–August 2001.

Johnson, Jim, Turning chaos into success, *Software Magazine,* December 1999.

Jugdev, Kam, Thomas, Janice, and Delisle, Connie L., Rethinking project management: old truths and new insights, *Project Management,* 7(1), 2001.

Keiserman, Michelle, Project team communications: the grease, the glue and the...gum?, *PM Network,* May 1999.

Kenney, John, Effective project management for strategic innovation and change in an organizational context, *Project Management Journal,* March 2003.

Kim, Daniel H., The behavior of tragedy of the commons, *The Systems Thinker*, September 1998.

Kim, Daniel H., Drifting goals: the challenge of conflicting priorities, *The Systems Thinker*, November 1999.

Kirk, Dorothy, Managing expectations, *PM Network*, August 2000.

Klein, Gary and Weick, Karl E., Decisions, *Across the Board*, June 2000.

Knutson, Joan, You owe your project players a communication infrastructure – Part 1, *PM Network*, November 1999.

Kotter, John, Leading change, 2002 Linkage *Excellence in Management* (seminar).

Leave a message, *The Industry Standard*, August 1999.

Lilla, Diana, Project managers must serve as change agents, *ESI Horizons*, February 2002.

Lilla, Diana, Navigating the waterline, Presentation at Puget Sound PMI Chapter, March 11, 2002.

Long, Andre, Negotiating the right decision, *PM Network*, December 1997.

Maurer, Rick, Weeding out resistance to change, *PM Network*, June 1998.

McCarthy, Jim, Better teamwork, *Software Development*, December 1995.

McGibbon, Barry, High performance through team building, *Object Magazine*, November 1997.

Mercurio, Nancy, Effective communication: getting your message across in simple terms, Federal Training Network (seminar presentation), 2000.

Message overload, *Knowledge Management*, November 1999.

Mintzberg, Henry, The manager's job: folklore and fact, *Harvard Business Review*, July–August 1975.

Mohr, Bernard J., Appreciative inquiry: igniting transformative action, *The Systems Thinker*, February 2001.

Morris, Peter W.G., Why project management doesn't always make business sense, *Project Management*, January 1998.

Pitagorsky, George, Building a communications infrastructure. *PM Network*, August 1998.

Pitcher, Patricia, Artists, craftsmen, and technocrats, *Training and Development*, July 1999.

Ramirez, Monica, The perfect trap, *Psychology Today*, May–June 1999.

Richardson, Marvin, Reward performance, *Solutions Integrator*, November 1998.

Schaffer, Robert H., Results improvement is the key to creativity and empowerment, *Journal for Quality and Participation*, September 1991.

Schettler, Joel, Leadership in corporate America, *Training*, September 2002.

Searching for skills, *PM Network,* March 2003.

Segil, Larraine, Global work teams: a cultural perspective, *PM Network,* March 1999.

Settle-Murphy, Nancy and Thornton, Caroline, Facilitating your way to project success, *Information Strategy,* Spring 1999.

Shenhar, A.J., Dvir, D., Lechler, T., and Poli, M., One size does not fit all, Presentation at PMI Research Conference 2002, July 15, Seattle, WA.

Sikes, Don, Using project websites to streamline communications, *PM Network,* June 2000.

Singer, Carl A., Leveraging a worldwide project team, *PM Network,* April 2001.

Sitiriou, Dean and Wittmer, Dennis, Influence methods of project managers: perceptions of team members and project managers, *Project Management Journal,* September 2001.

Skinner, Merna L., So, talk to me, *Successful Meetings,* November 2000.

Skulmoski, Greg, Hartman, Francis, and DeMaere, Roch, Superior and threshold project competencies, *Project Management,* 6(1), 2000.

Slobodnik, Alan and Wile, Kristina, Taking the teeth out of team traps, *The Systems Thinker,* November 1999.

Sterman, John, Superstitious learning, *The Systems Thinker,* June/July 1997.

Survey identifies top 10 project management challenges, *PM Network,* September 2002.

Survey looks at what projects lack, *PM Network,* September 2000.

Top ten, *Training and Development,* February 1999.

Urli, Bruno and Urli, Didier, Project management in North America, stability of the concepts, *Project Management Journal,* September 2000.

Van Slyke, Erik J., Resolving team conflict, *PM Network,* June 2000.

Volckmann, Russ, The fourth constraint: relationships, *PM Network,* May 1997.

Wang, Yair and Wang, Richard Y., Anchoring data quality dimensions in ontological foundations, *Communications of the ACM,* November 1996.

Wanted: leaders who can lead and write, *Workforce,* December 1997.

Why leaders fail, *Industry Week,* March 2002.

Wideman, Max R. and Shenhar, Aaron J., Optimizing project success by matching PM style with project type (http://www.pmforum.org/library/papers/PM_Style&Scss.pdf)

Yeack, William and Sayles, Leonard, Virtual and real organizations: optimal pairing, *PM Network,* August 1996.

# AUTHOR INDEX

# INDEX